P9-DFD-873

Ranma 1/2

VOL. 15
Action Edition

Story and Art by
RUMIKO TAKAHASHI

English Adaptation/Gerard Jones and Toshifumi Yoshida
Touch-Up Art & Lettering/Wayne Truman
Cover and Interior Design & Graphics/Yuki Ameda
Editor (1st Edition)/Trish Ledoux and Julie Davis
Editor (Action Edition)/Avery Gotoh
Supervising Editor (Action Edition)/Michelle Pangilinan

Managing Editor/Annette Roman
Director of Production/Noboru Watanabe
Editorial Director/Alvin Lu
Sr. Director of Acquisitions/Rika Inouye
Vice President of Sales and Marketing/Liza Coppola
Executive Vice President/Hyoe Narita
Publisher/Seiji Horibuchi

Printed in Canada.

Published by VIZ, LLC
P.O. Box 77010
San Francisco, CA 94107

1st Edition Published 2000

Action Edition
10 9 8 7 6 5 4 3 2 1
First Printing, January 2005

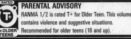

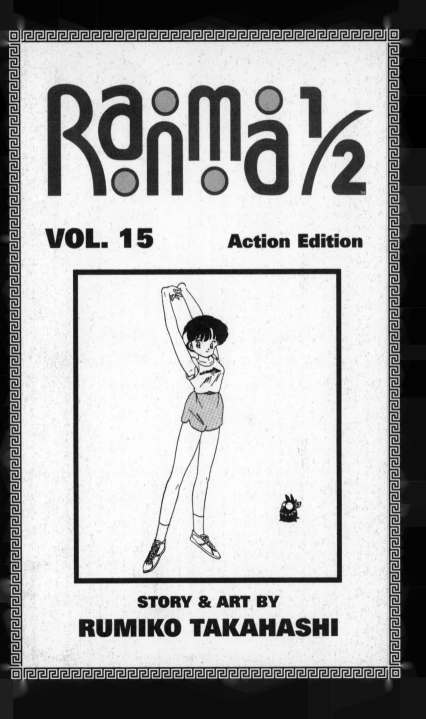

Ranma ½

VOL. 15 Action Edition

STORY & ART BY
RUMIKO TAKAHASHI

STORY THUS FAR

The Tendos are an average, run-of-the-mill Japanese family—on the surface, that is. Soun Tendo is the owner and proprietor of the Tendo Dojo, where "Anything Goes Martial Arts" is practiced. Like the name says, anything goes, and usually does.

When Soun's old friend Genma Saotome comes to visit, Soun's three lovely young daughters—Akane, Nabiki and Kasumi—are told that it's time for one of them to become the fiancée of Genma's teenage son, Ranma, as per an agreement made between the two fathers years ago. Youngest daughter Akane—who says she hates boys—is quickly nominated for bridal duty by her sisters.

Unfortunately, Ranma and his father have suffered a strange accident. While training in China, both plunged into one of many "cursed" springs at the legendary martial arts training ground of Jusenkyo. These springs transform the unlucky dunkee into whoever—or whatever—drowned there hundreds of years ago.

From then on, a splash of cold water turns Ranma's father into a giant panda, and Ranma becomes a beautiful, busty young woman. Hot water reverses the effect...but only until next time. As it turns out, Ranma and Genma aren't the only ones who have taken the Jusenkyo plunge—and it isn't long before they meet several other members of the Jusenkyo "cursed."

Although their parents are still determined to see Ranma and Akane marry and assume ownership of the training hall, Ranma seems to have a strange talent for accumulating surplus fiancées...and Akane has a few stubbornly determined suitors of her own. Will the two ever work out their differences, get rid of all these "extra" people, or will they just call the whole thing off? What's a half-boy, half-girl (not to mention all-girl, *angry* girl) to do...?

CAST OF CHARACTERS

RANMA SAOTOME
Martial artist with far too many fiancées and an ego that won't let him take defeat. Changes into a girl when splashed with cold water.

GENMA SAOTOME
Ranma's lazy father who left his wife and home years ago with his young son (Ranma) to train in the martial arts. Changes into a panda.

AKANE TENDO
Martial artist, tomboy and Ranma's reluctant fiancée. Has no clue how much Ryoga likes her, or what relation he might have to her pet black pig, P-chan.

SOUN TENDO
Head of the Tendo household and owner of the Tendo Dojo.

NABIKI TENDO
Always eager to "make a buck" off the suffering of others, Nabiki is the middle Tendo daughter.

KASUMI TENDO
Gentle and well mannered, eldest daughter Kasumi acts as the family's surrogate mother.

TATEWAKI KUNO
The so-called "Blue Thunder of Furinkan High," Kuno has unrequited crushes on both Akane, and the mysterious "pig-tailed girl."

HAPPOSAI
Martial arts master who trained both Genma and Soun. Also a world-class pervert.

SHAMPOO, UKYO KUONJI, and KODACHI KUNO
Three self-appointed fiancées of Ranma...and all holders of serious grudges against Akane.

CONTENTS

Part 1
KUNG FU STEW

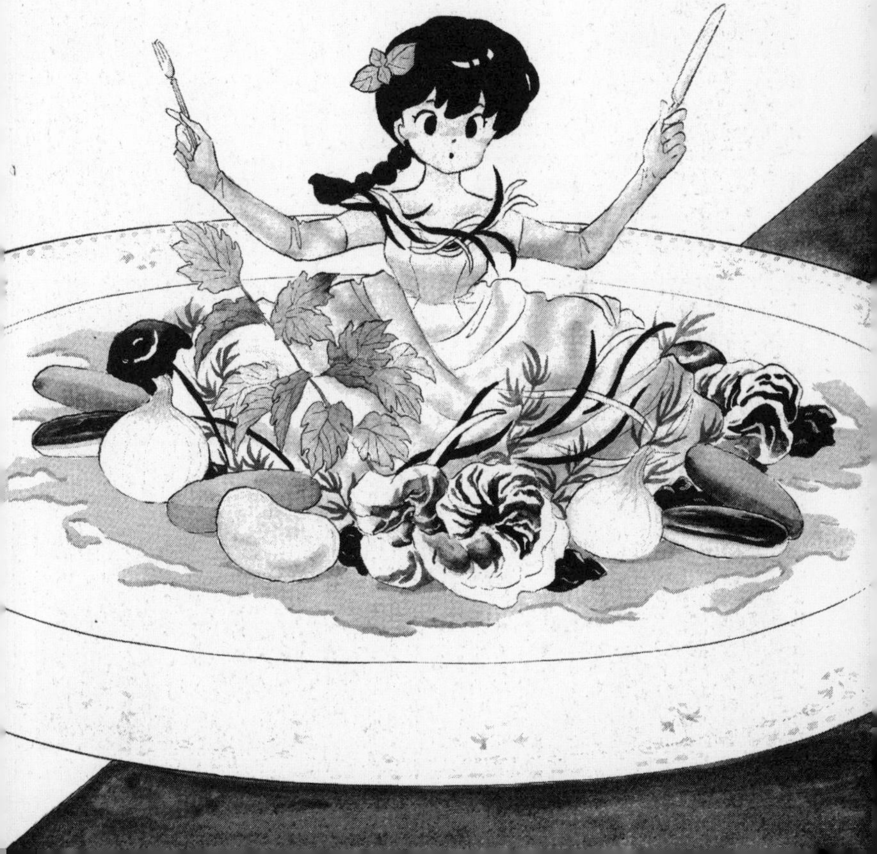

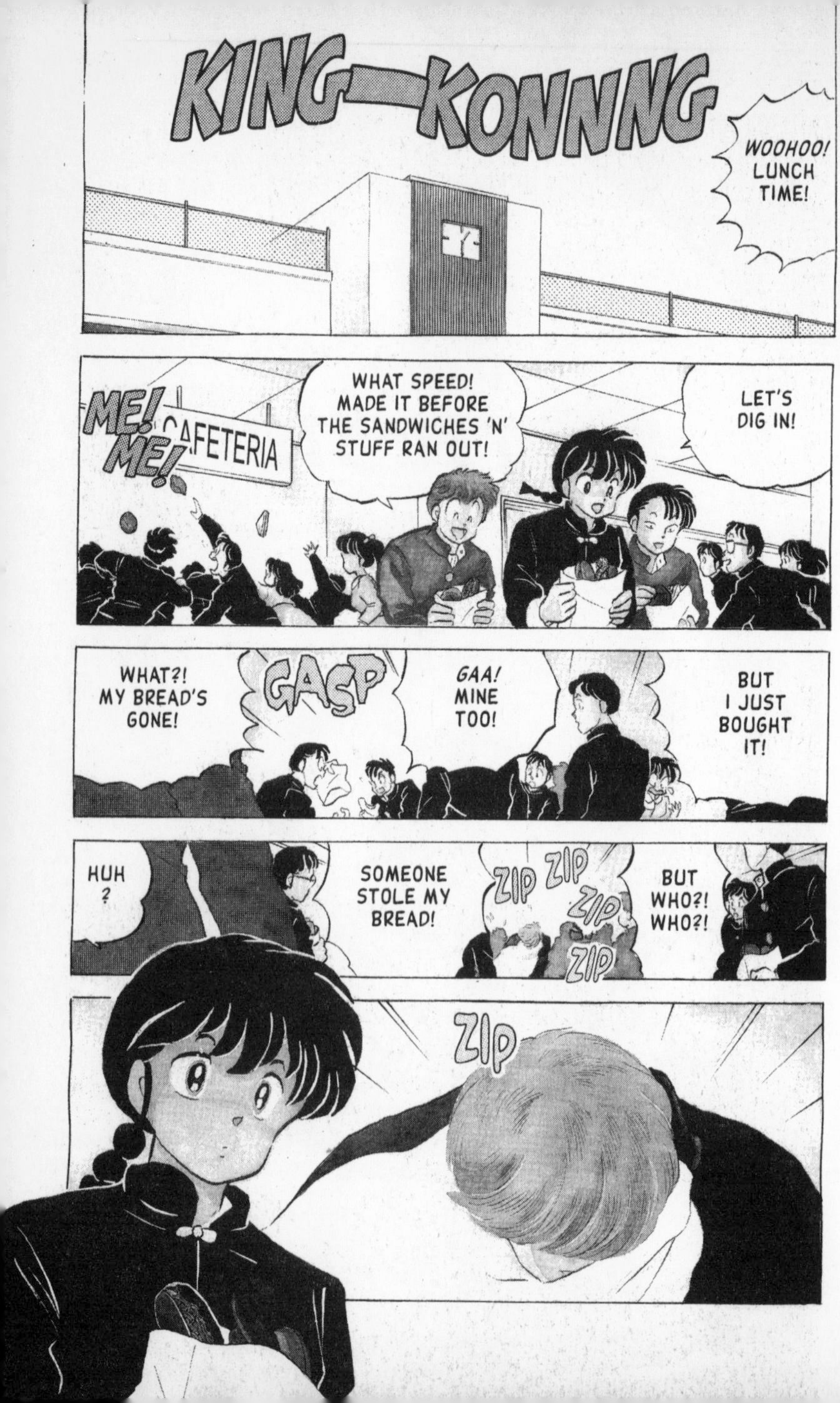
KING—KONNNG
WOOHOO! LUNCH TIME!
ME! ME!
CAFETERIA
WHAT SPEED! MADE IT BEFORE THE SANDWICHES 'N' STUFF RAN OUT!
LET'S DIG IN!
WHAT?! MY BREAD'S GONE!
GASP
GAA! MINE TOO!
BUT I JUST BOUGHT IT!
HUH?
SOMEONE STOLE MY BREAD!
ZIP ZIP
ZIP
ZIP
BUT WHO?! WHO?!
ZIP

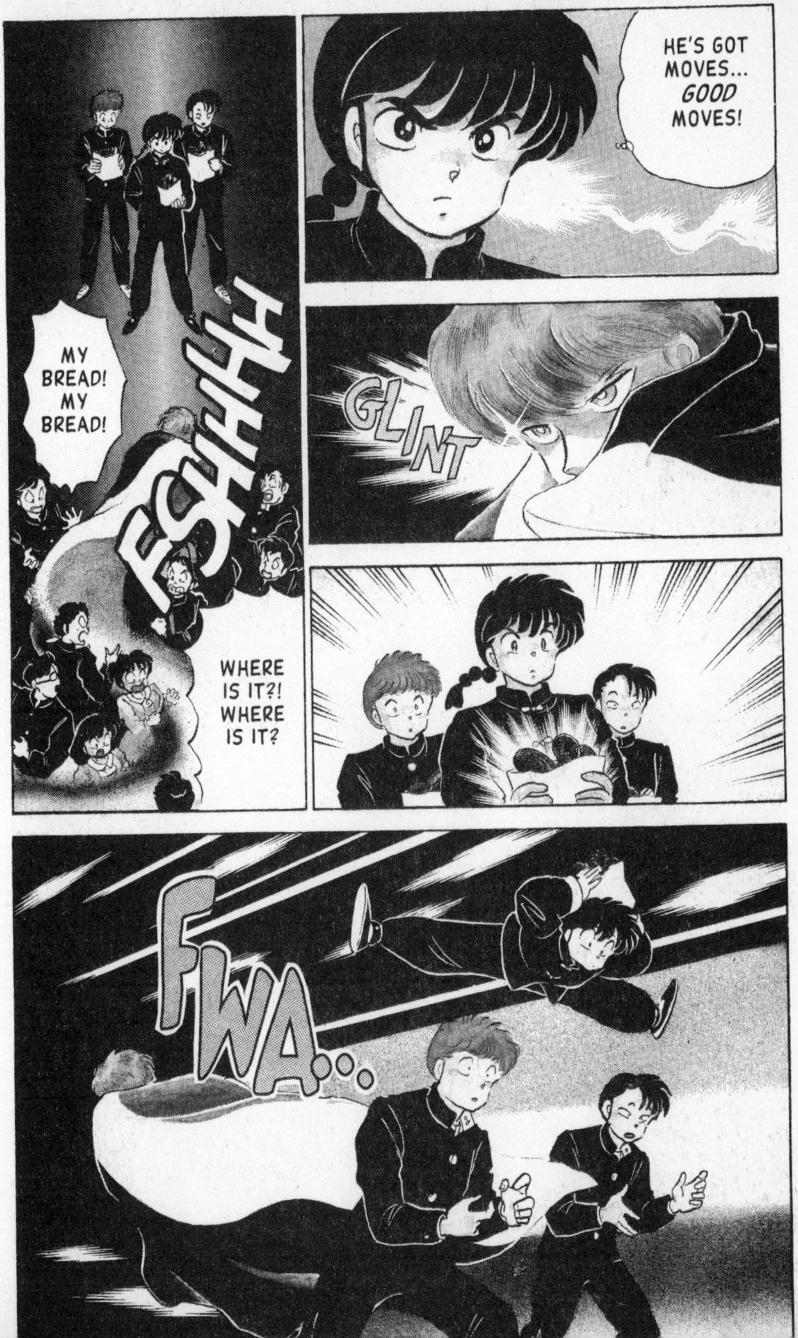
MY BREAD! MY BREAD!
FSHHHH
WHERE IS IT?! WHERE IS IT?
HE'S GOT MOVES... GOOD MOVES!
GLINT
FWA...

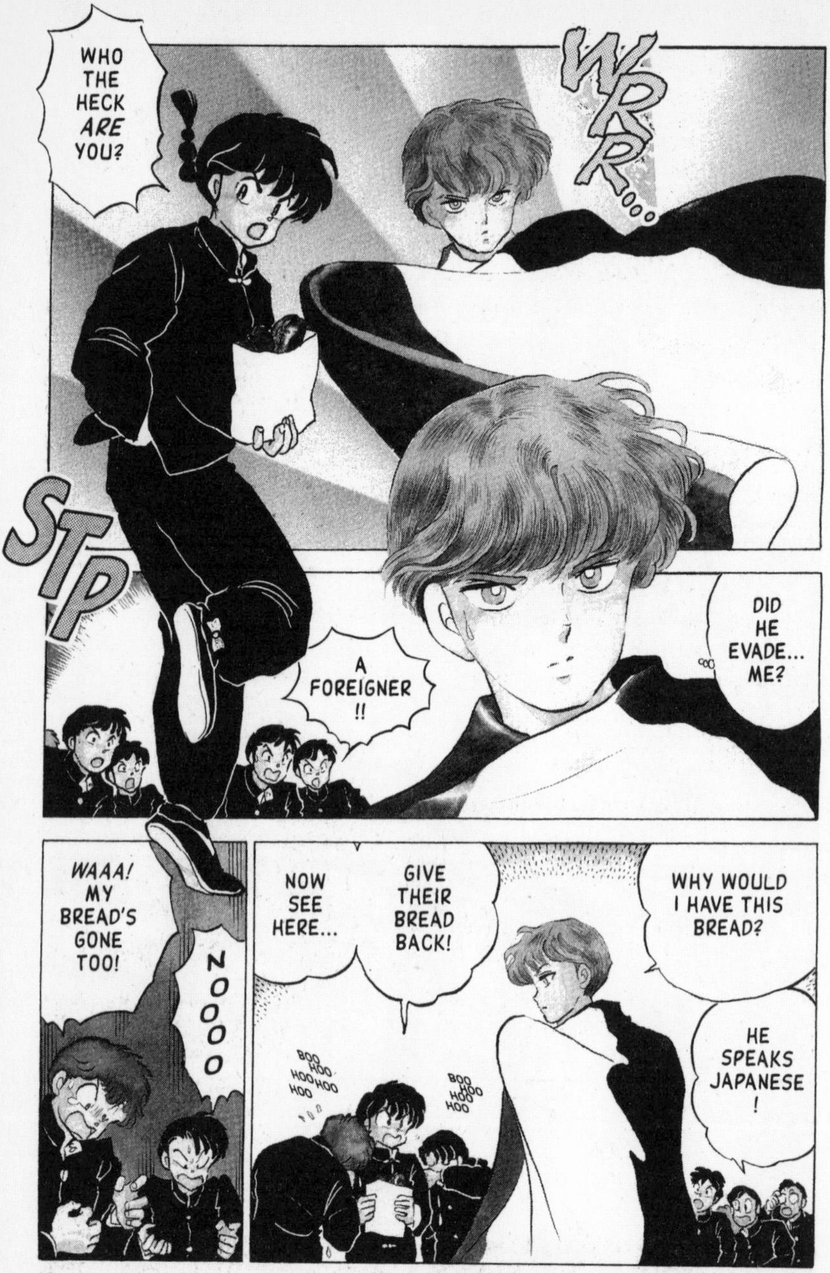
WHO THE HECK ARE YOU?
WRR...
STP
A FOREIGNER!!
DID HE EVADE... ME?
WAAA! MY BREAD'S GONE TOO!
NOOOO
NOW SEE HERE...
GIVE THEIR BREAD BACK!
BOO HOO HOO HOO HOO
BOO HOO HOO HOO
WHY WOULD I HAVE THIS BREAD?
HE SPEAKS JAPANESE!

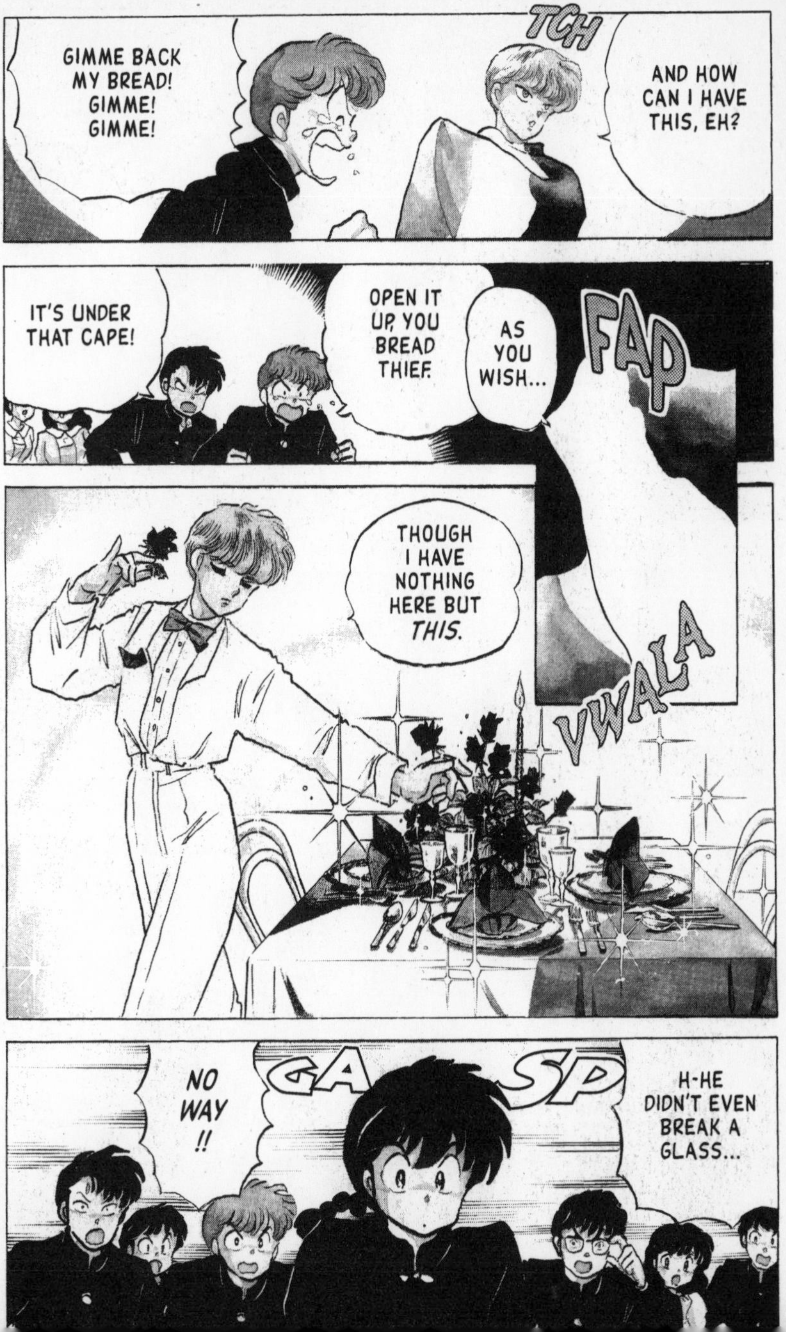
GIMME BACK MY BREAD! GIMME! GIMME!
TCH
AND HOW CAN I HAVE THIS, EH?
IT'S UNDER THAT CAPE!
OPEN IT UP, YOU BREAD THIEF.
AS YOU WISH...
FAP
THOUGH I HAVE NOTHING HERE BUT THIS.
VWALA
NO WAY !!
GASP
H-HE DIDN'T EVEN BREAK A GLASS...

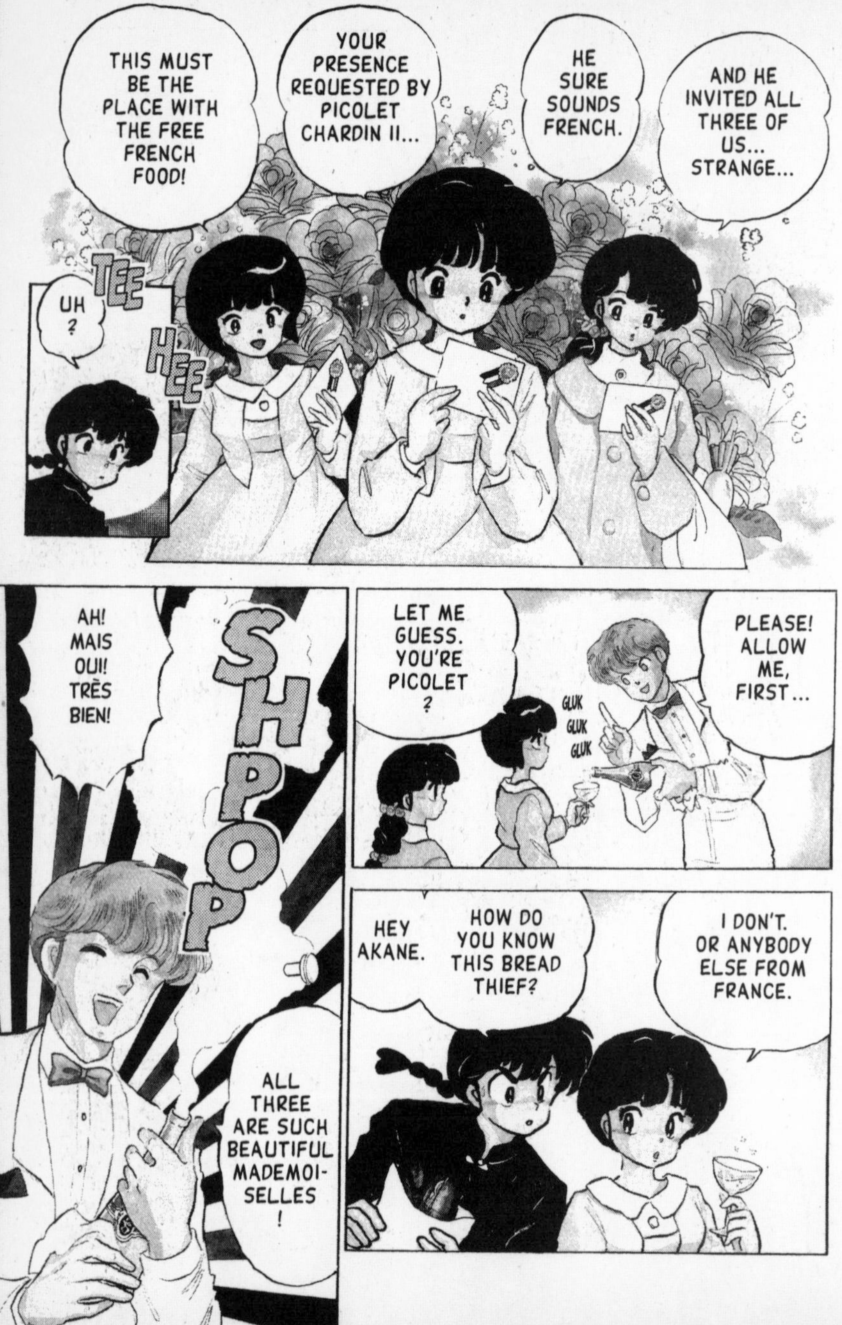
THIS MUST BE THE PLACE WITH THE FREE FRENCH FOOD!
YOUR PRESENCE REQUESTED BY PICOLET CHARDIN II...
HE SURE SOUNDS FRENCH.
AND HE INVITED ALL THREE OF US... STRANGE...
UH?
TEE HEE
AH! MAIS OUI! TRÈS BIEN!
SHPOP
ALL THREE ARE SUCH BEAUTIFUL MADEMOI-SELLES!
LET ME GUESS. YOU'RE PICOLET?
GLUK GLUK GLUK
PLEASE! ALLOW ME, FIRST...
HEY AKANE.
HOW DO YOU KNOW THIS BREAD THIEF?
I DON'T. OR ANYBODY ELSE FROM FRANCE.

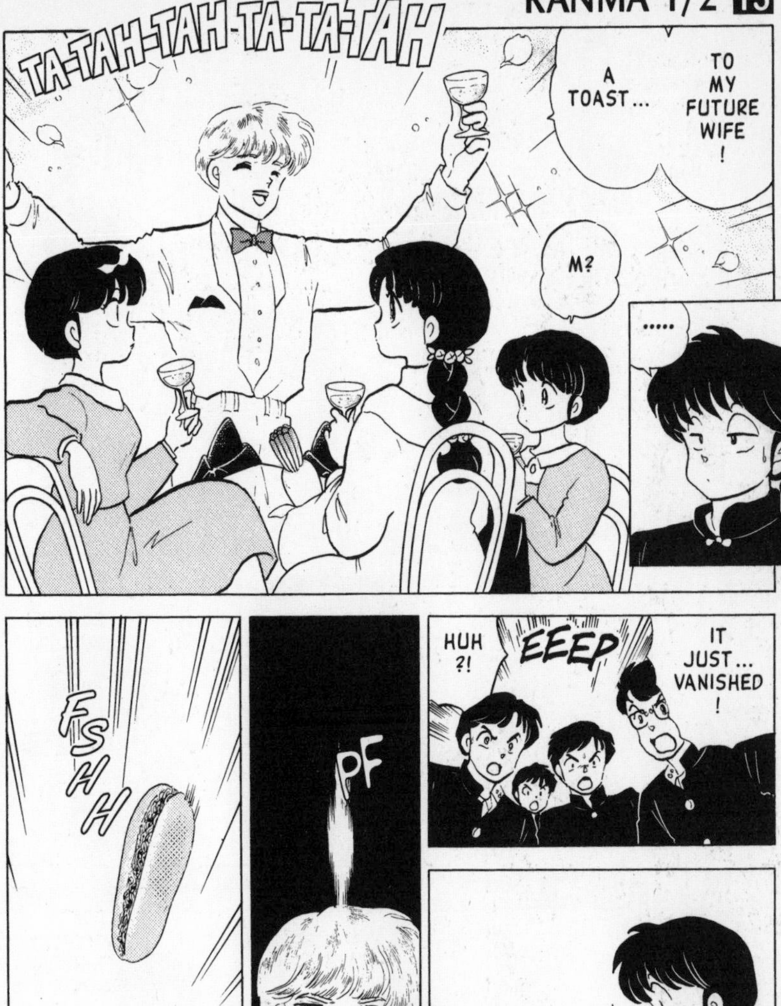
TA-TAH-TAH-TA-TA-TAH
A TOAST...
TO MY FUTURE WIFE!
M?
......
FSHH
PF
HUH ?!
EEEP
IT JUST... VANISHED!

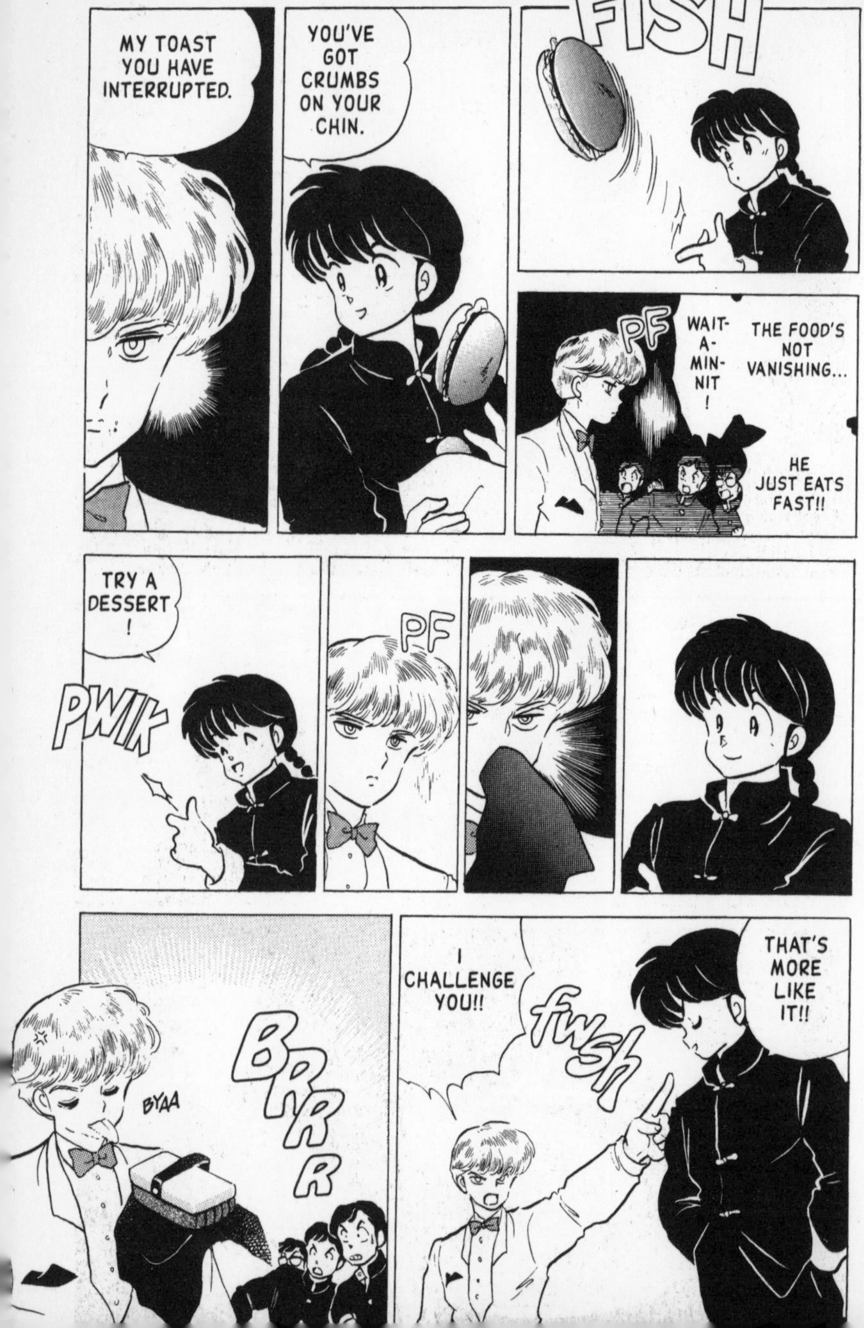

MY TOAST YOU HAVE INTERRUPTED.
YOU'VE GOT CRUMBS ON YOUR CHIN.
FISH
PF
WAIT-A-MIN-NIT!
THE FOOD'S NOT VANISHING...
HE JUST EATS FAST!!
TRY A DESSERT!
PWIK
PF
BYAA
BRRRR
I CHALLENGE YOU!!
fwsh
THAT'S MORE LIKE IT!!

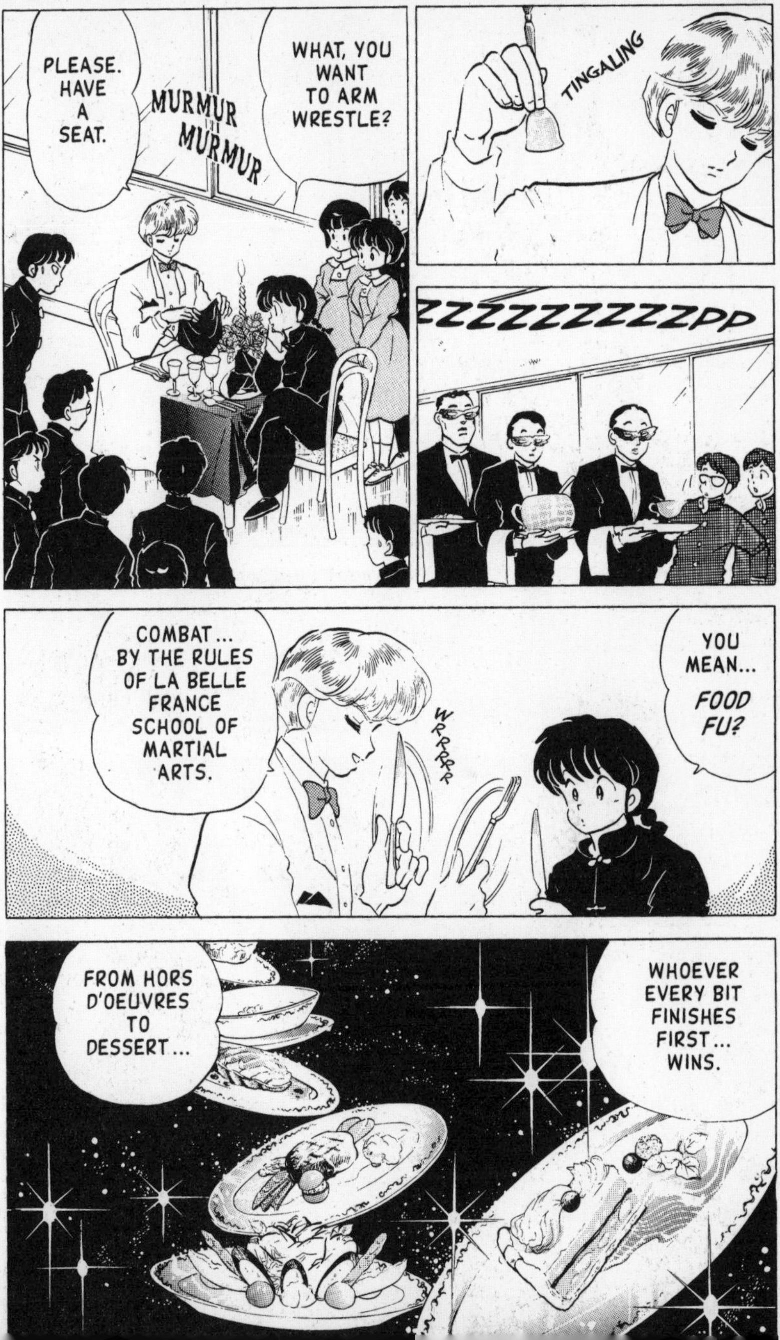
PLEASE. HAVE A SEAT.
MURMUR MURMUR
WHAT, YOU WANT TO ARM WRESTLE?
TINGALING
ZZZZZZZZZZZPP
COMBAT... BY THE RULES OF LA BELLE FRANCE SCHOOL OF MARTIAL ARTS.
WRRRRR
YOU MEAN... *FOOD FU?*
FROM HORS D'OEUVRES TO DESSERT...
WHOEVER EVERY BIT FINISHES FIRST... WINS.

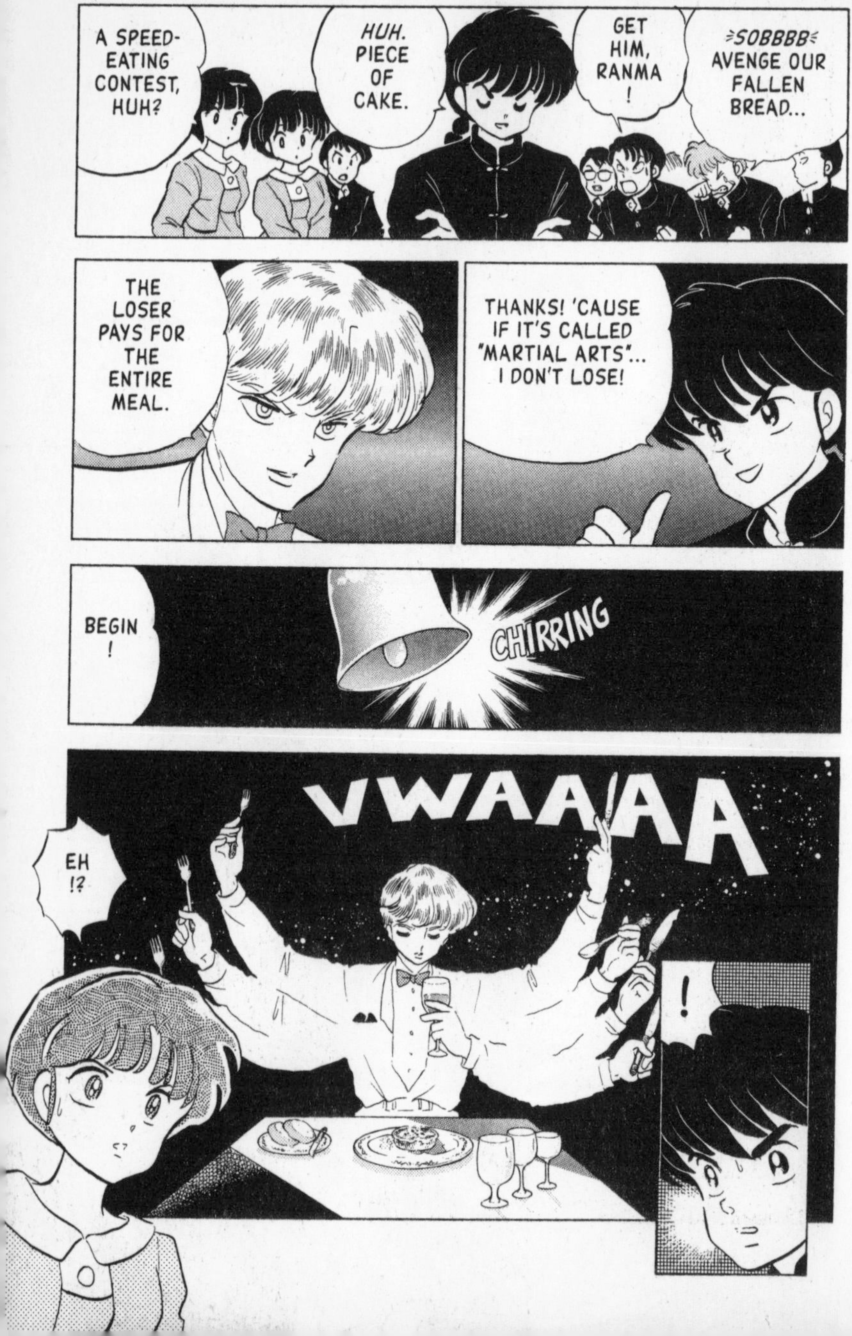
A SPEED-EATING CONTEST, HUH?
HUH. PIECE OF CAKE.
GET HIM, RANMA!
SOBBBB AVENGE OUR FALLEN BREAD...
THE LOSER PAYS FOR THE ENTIRE MEAL.
THANKS! 'CAUSE IF IT'S CALLED "MARTIAL ARTS"... I DON'T LOSE!
BEGIN!
CHIRRING
VWAAAAA
EH!?
!

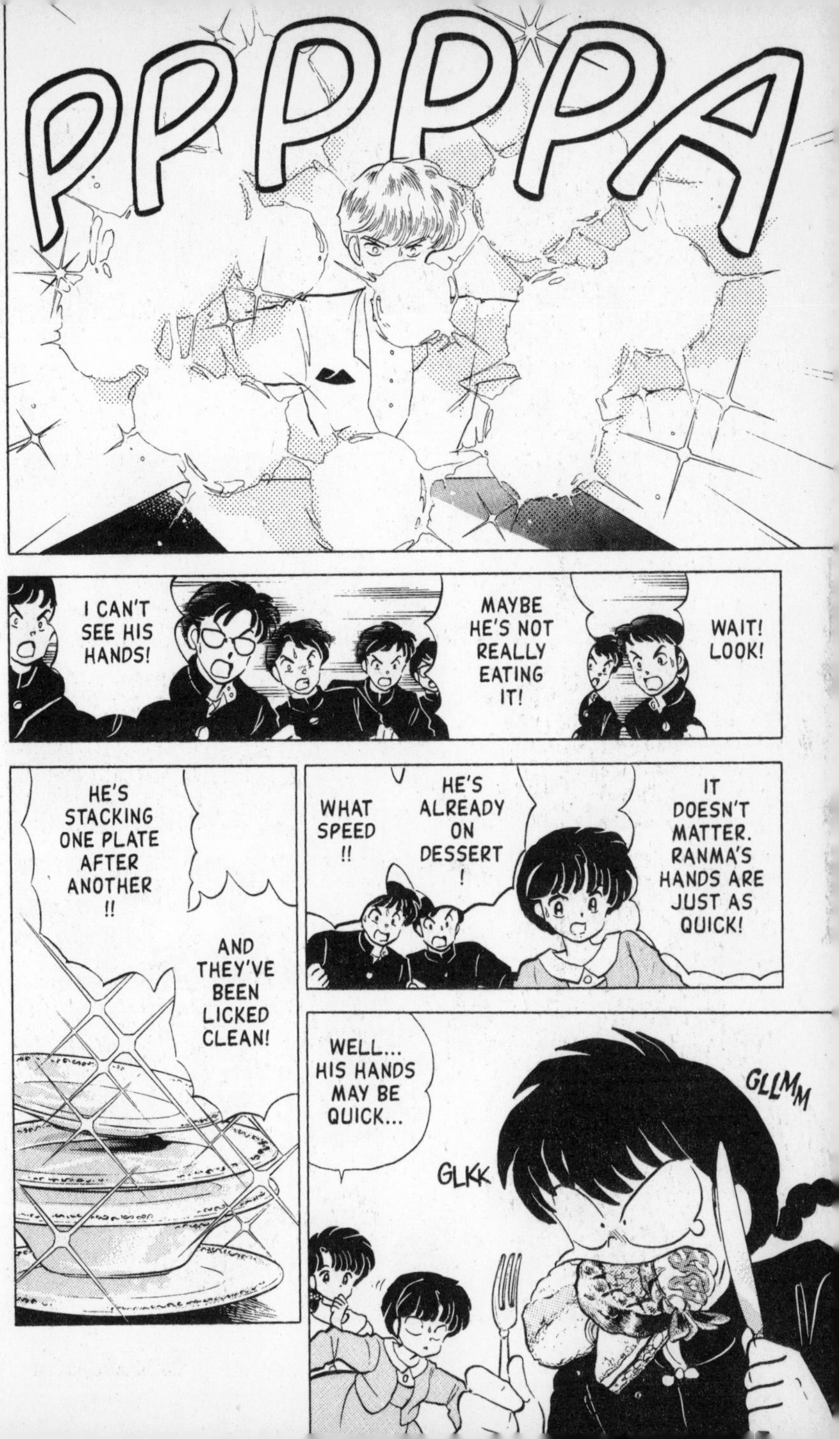
PPPPPA
I CAN'T SEE HIS HANDS!
MAYBE HE'S NOT REALLY EATING IT!
WAIT! LOOK!
HE'S STACKING ONE PLATE AFTER ANOTHER !!
AND THEY'VE BEEN LICKED CLEAN!
WHAT SPEED !!
HE'S ALREADY ON DESSERT !
IT DOESN'T MATTER. RANMA'S HANDS ARE JUST AS QUICK!
WELL... HIS HANDS MAY BE QUICK...
GLKK
GLLMM

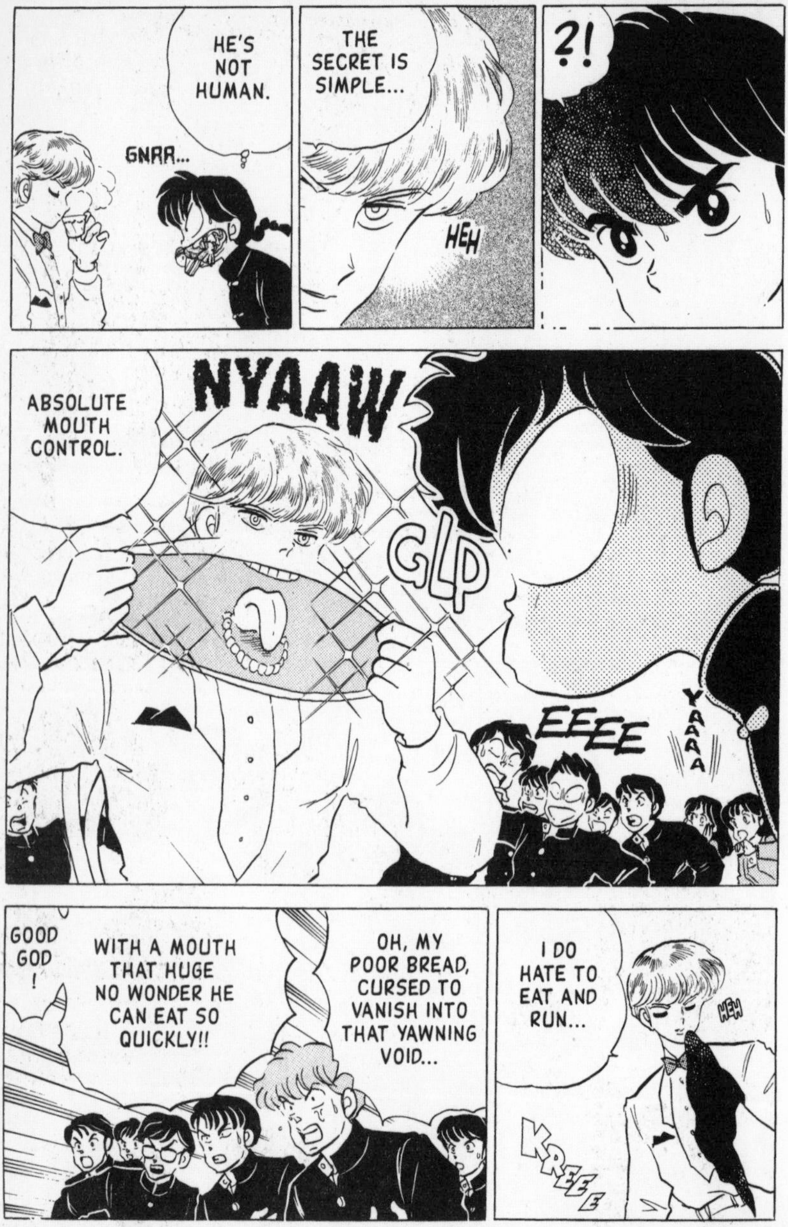

HE'S NOT HUMAN.
GNRR...
THE SECRET IS SIMPLE...
HEH
?!
ABSOLUTE MOUTH CONTROL.
NYAAW
GLP
EEEEE
YAAAA
GOOD GOD!
WITH A MOUTH THAT HUGE NO WONDER HE CAN EAT SO QUICKLY!!
OH, MY POOR BREAD, CURSED TO VANISH INTO THAT YAWNING VOID...
I DO HATE TO EAT AND RUN...
HEH
KREEE

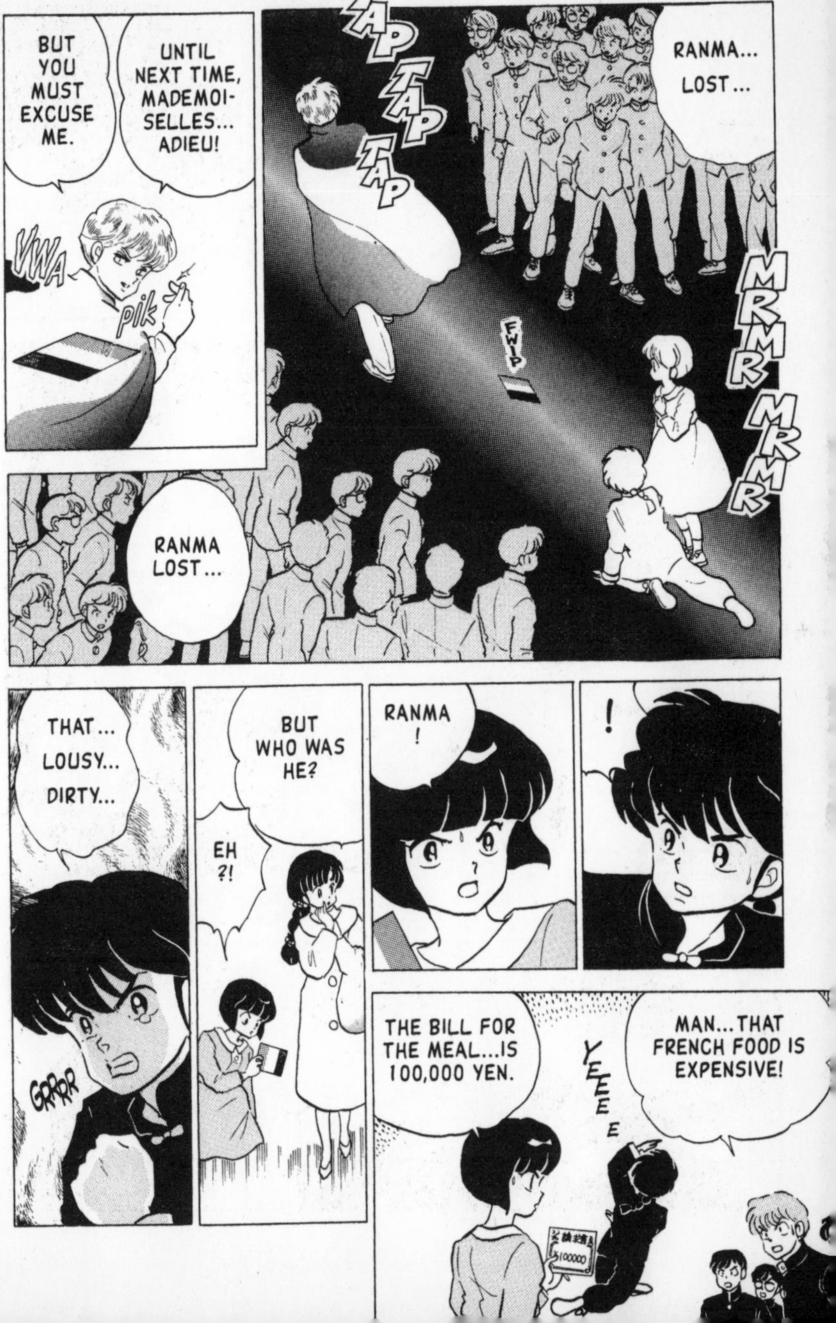
BUT YOU MUST EXCUSE ME.
UNTIL NEXT TIME, MADEMOISELLES... ADIEU!
VWA
pik
TAP TAP TAP
RANMA... LOST...
FWIP
MRMMR MRMMR
RANMA LOST...
THAT... LOUSY... DIRTY...
GRRRR
BUT WHO WAS HE?
EH ?!
RANMA !
!
THE BILL FOR THE MEAL...IS 100,000 YEN.
YEEEE
MAN...THAT FRENCH FOOD IS EXPENSIVE!

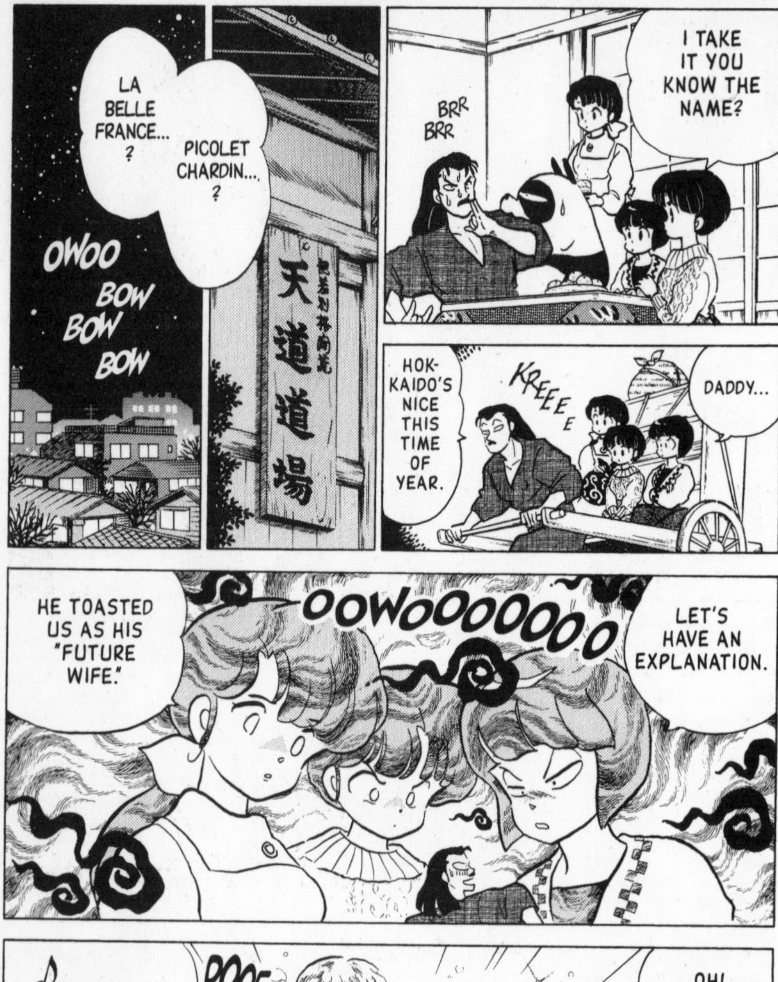
LA BELLE FRANCE... ?
PICOLET CHARDIN... ?
OWOO BOW BOW BOW
天道道場
BRR BRR
I TAKE IT YOU KNOW THE NAME?
HOK-KAIDO'S NICE THIS TIME OF YEAR.
KREEEEE
DADDY...
HE TOASTED US AS HIS "FUTURE WIFE."
OOWOOOOOOOO
LET'S HAVE AN EXPLANATION.
♪ 'TIS A TALE EVEN OLDER THAN I, WHO TELL IT~
POOF
OH! MONSIEUR PICOLET !!

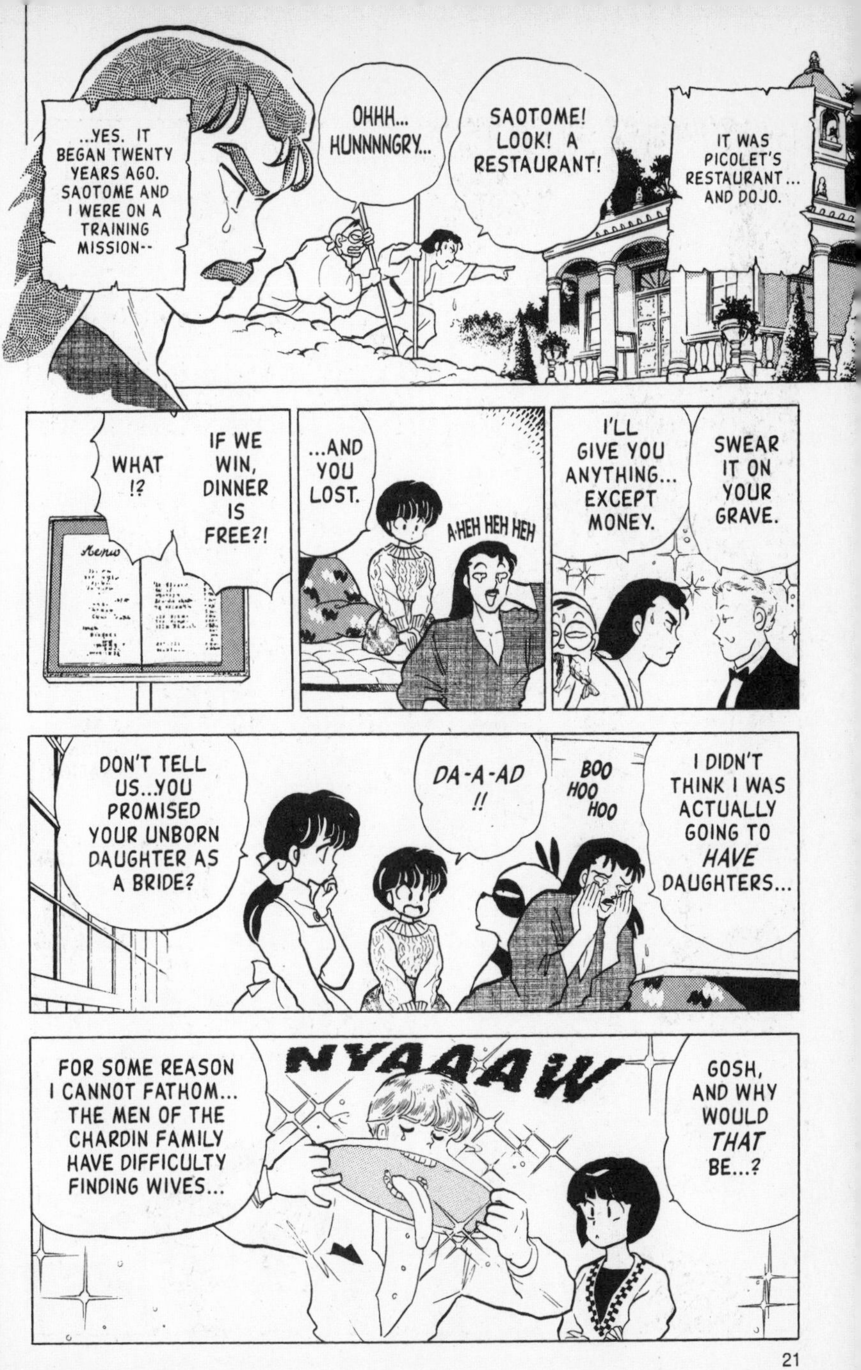

...YES. IT BEGAN TWENTY YEARS AGO. SAOTOME AND I WERE ON A TRAINING MISSION--
OHHH... HUNNNNGRY...
SAOTOME! LOOK! A RESTAURANT!
IT WAS PICOLET'S RESTAURANT... AND DOJO.
WHAT !?
IF WE WIN, DINNER IS FREE?!
Menu
...AND YOU LOST.
A-HEH HEH HEH
I'LL GIVE YOU ANYTHING... EXCEPT MONEY.
SWEAR IT ON YOUR GRAVE.
DON'T TELL US...YOU PROMISED YOUR UNBORN DAUGHTER AS A BRIDE?
DA-A-AD !!
BOO HOO HOO
I DIDN'T THINK I WAS ACTUALLY GOING TO *HAVE* DAUGHTERS...
FOR SOME REASON I CANNOT FATHOM... THE MEN OF THE CHARDIN FAMILY HAVE DIFFICULTY FINDING WIVES...
NYAAAAW
GOSH, AND WHY WOULD *THAT* BE...?

BUT IT MATTERS NOT NOW, EH?

WHICHEVER MADEMOISELLE WOULD BE MY WIFE...SHALL COME TO THE CHARDIN ESTATE TO LEARN THE ART OF MARTIAL DINING!

WHAT SHALL WE DO...?

SNIFFLE

YEAH, DADDY. WHAT SHALL *YOU* DO?

DON'T FORGET THAT YOU HAVE ANOTHER DAUGHTER!

THIS MARTIAL ARTS DINING...

I COULD USE THE LESSONS.

BUT YOU ARE NOT "ANOTHER DAUGHTER"...

YOU ARE THE FINEST OF ALL!

SHPOP

TEE-HEE-HEE. I CAN'T WAIT.

DO YOU THINK RANMA'S HOLDING A GRUDGE...

OH, HEAVENS NO.

AND SO WERE THE GATES OF HELL OPENED.

22

Part 2
BAD MANORS

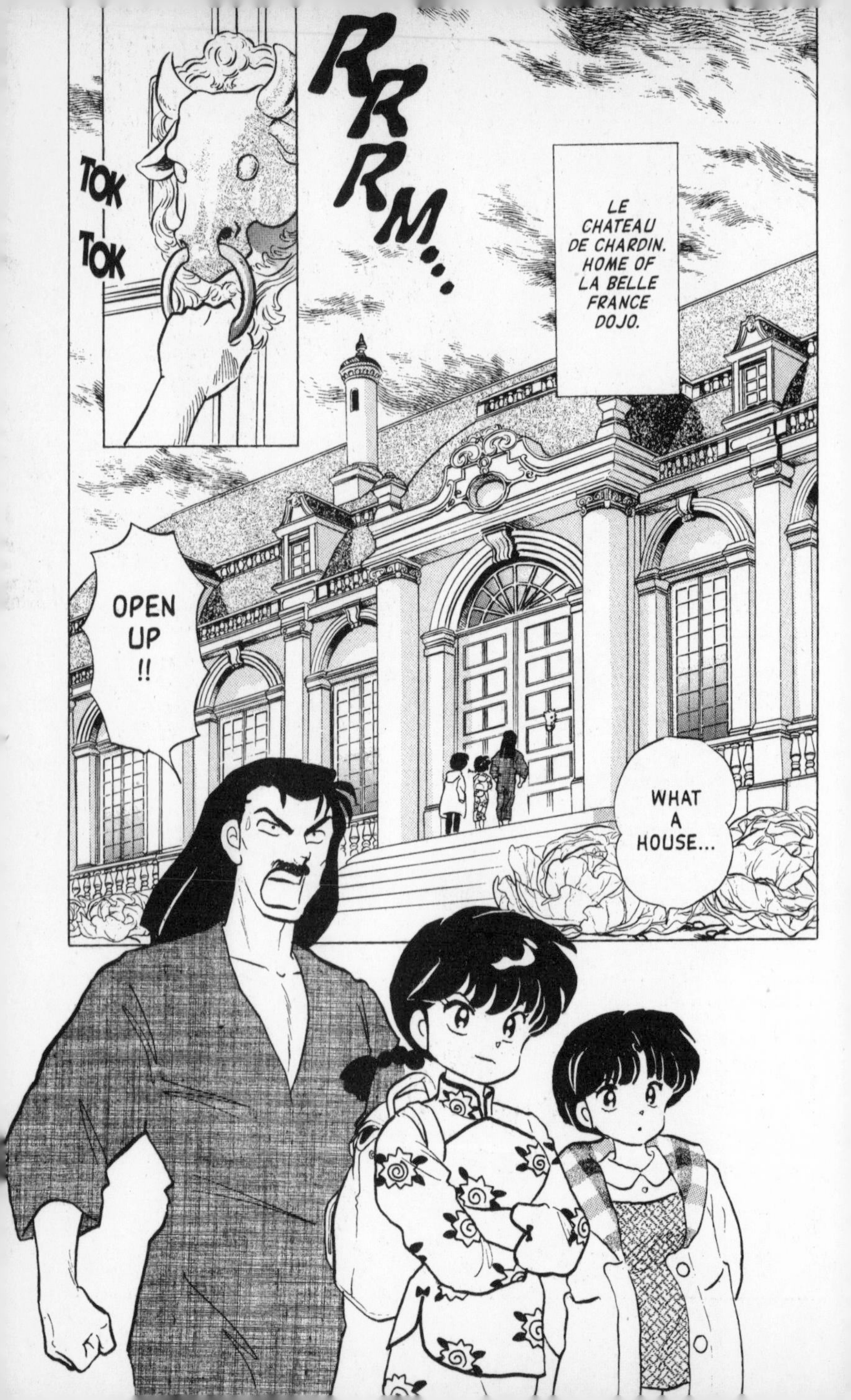

TOK TOK
RRRM...
LE CHATEAU DE CHARDIN. HOME OF LA BELLE FRANCE DOJO.
OPEN UP !!
WHAT A HOUSE...

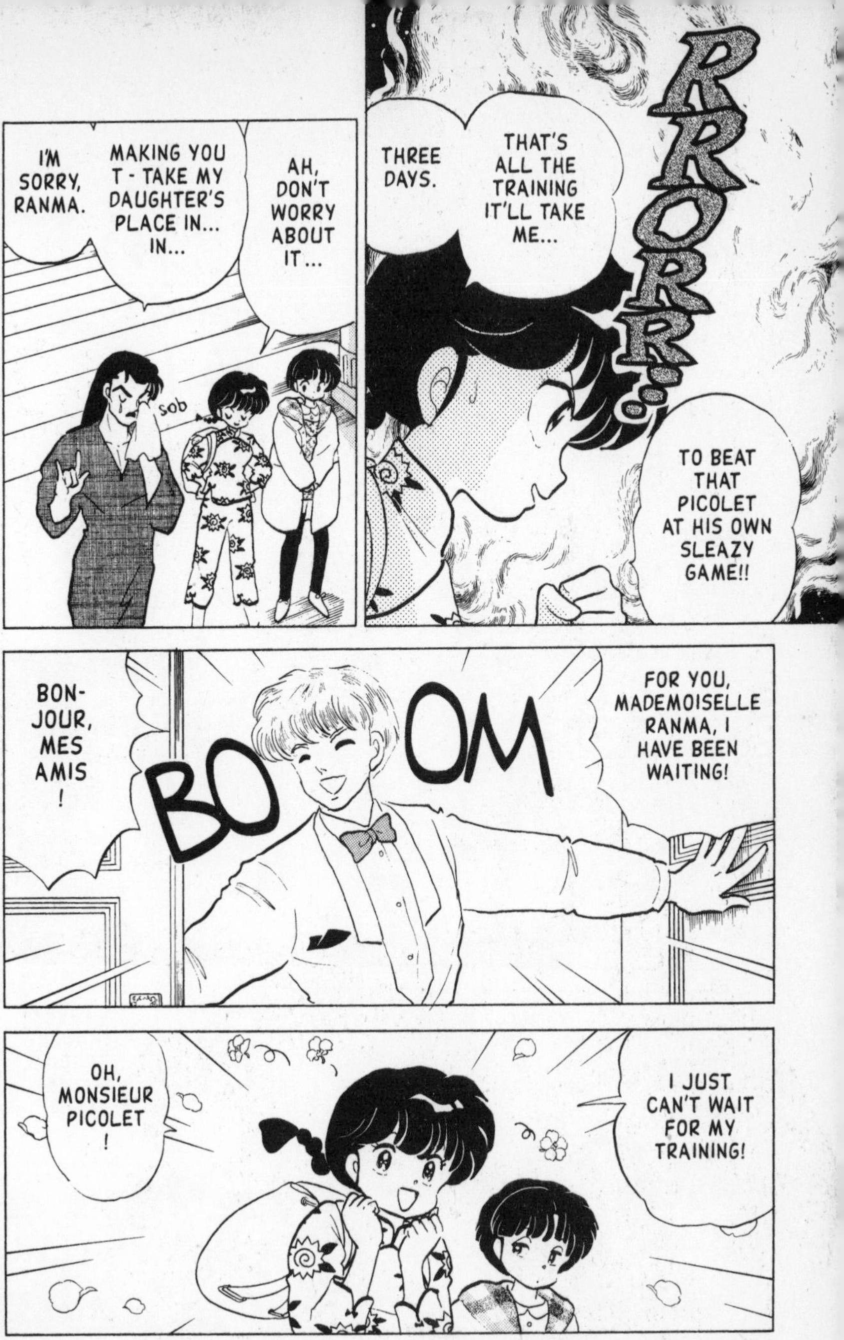
I'M SORRY, RANMA.
MAKING YOU T-TAKE MY DAUGHTER'S PLACE IN... IN...
sob
AH, DON'T WORRY ABOUT IT...
THREE DAYS.
THAT'S ALL THE TRAINING IT'LL TAKE ME...
RRORRR..
TO BEAT THAT PICOLET AT HIS OWN SLEAZY GAME!!
BON-JOUR, MES AMIS!
BOOM
FOR YOU, MADEMOISELLE RANMA, I HAVE BEEN WAITING!
OH, MONSIEUR PICOLET!
I JUST CAN'T WAIT FOR MY TRAINING!

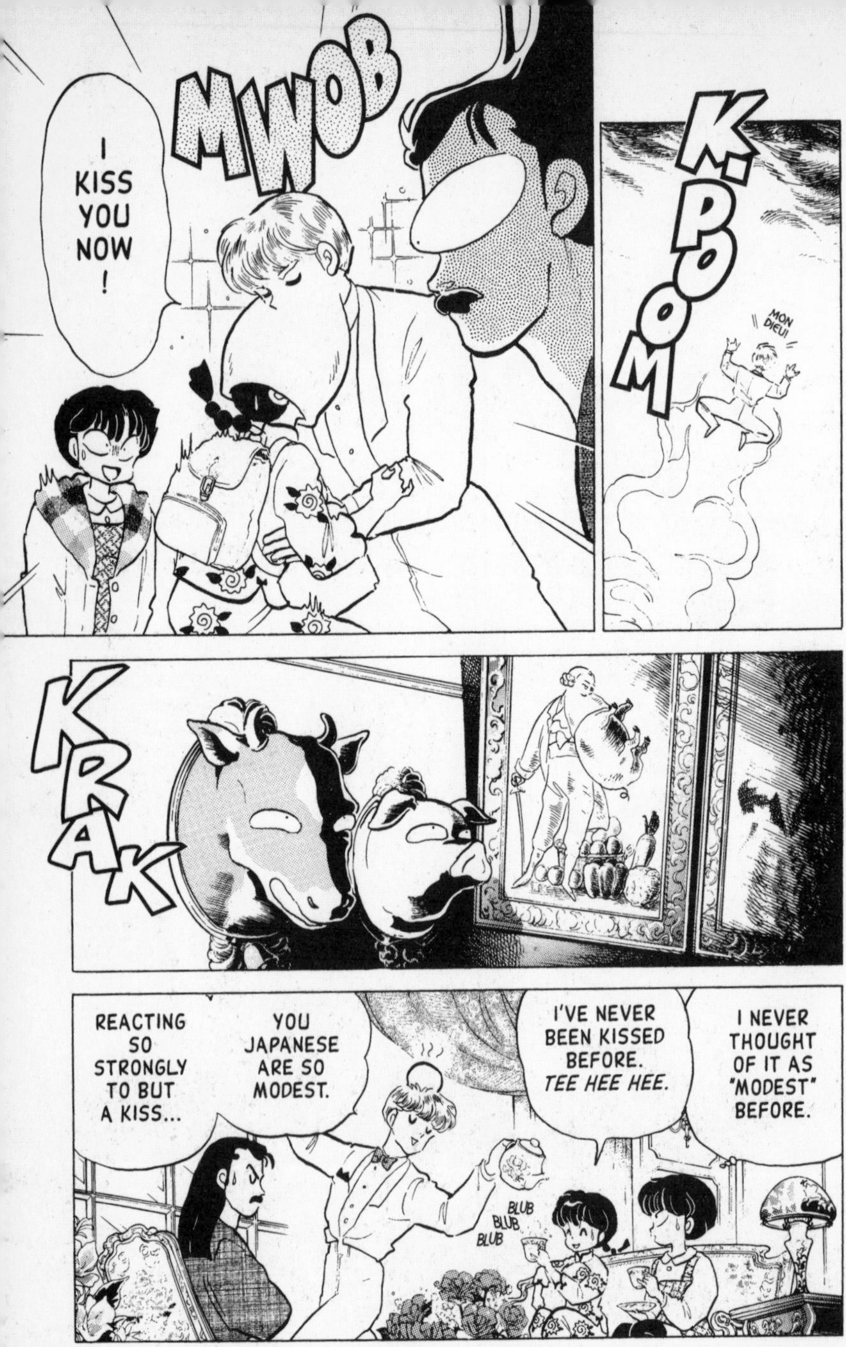
I KISS YOU NOW!
MWOB
K.POOM
MON DIEU!
KRAK
REACTING SO STRONGLY TO BUT A KISS...
YOU JAPANESE ARE SO MODEST.
BLUB BLUB BLUB
I'VE NEVER BEEN KISSED BEFORE. *TEE HEE HEE.*
I NEVER THOUGHT OF IT AS "MODEST" BEFORE.

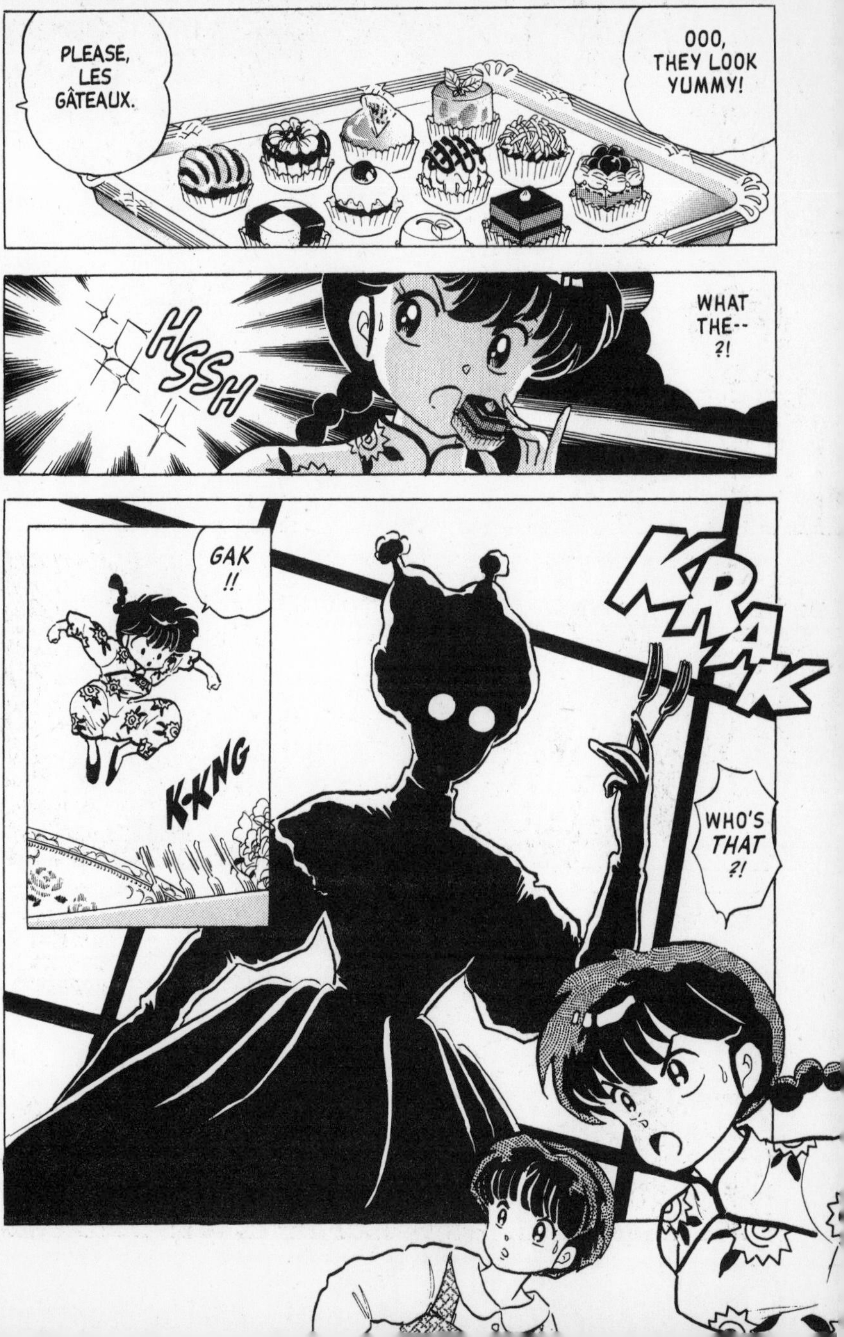
PLEASE, LES GÂTEAUX.
OOO, THEY LOOK YUMMY!
HSSH
WHAT THE-- ?!
GAK !!
K-KNG
KRAK
WHO'S THAT ?!

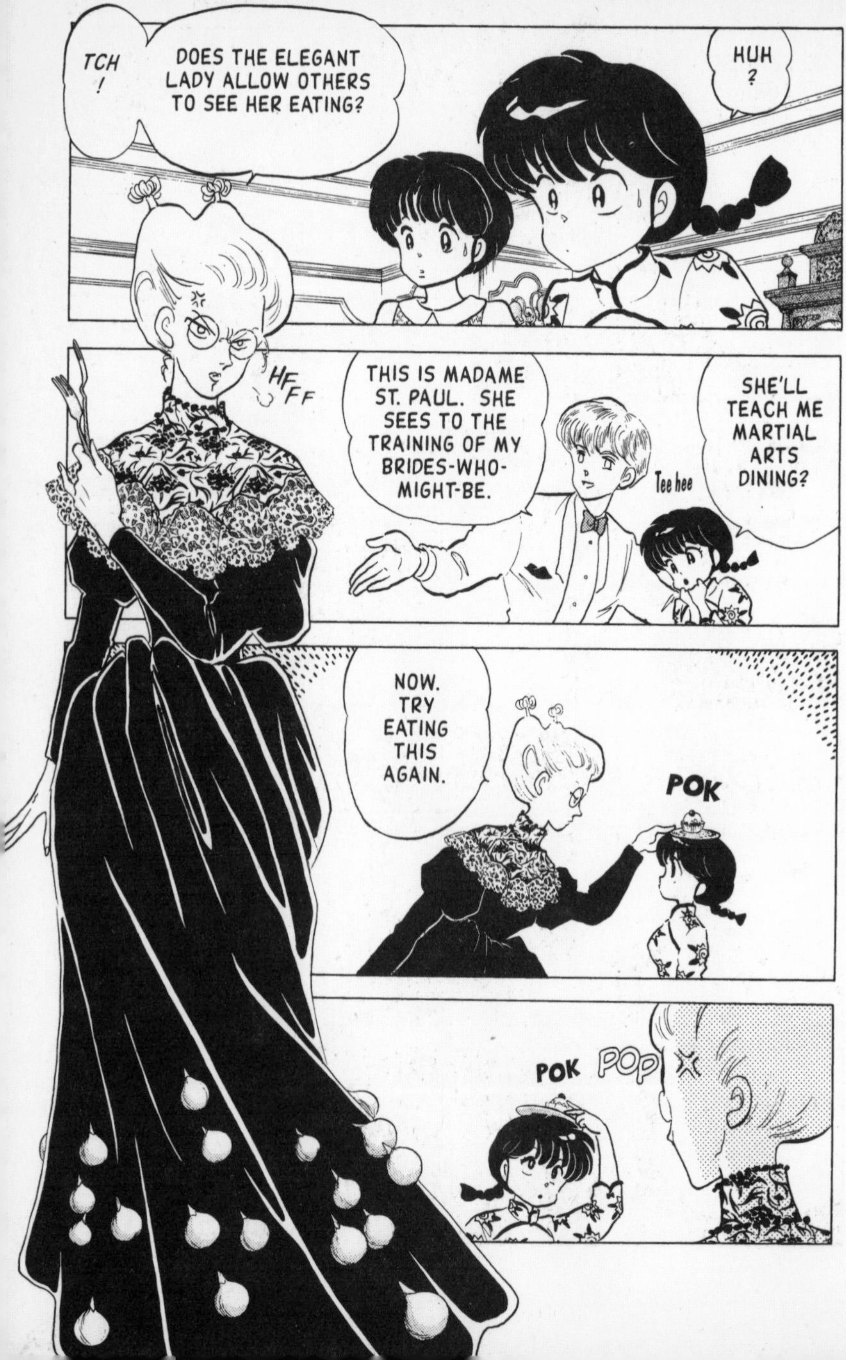
TCH!
DOES THE ELEGANT LADY ALLOW OTHERS TO SEE HER EATING?
HUH?
HFFF
THIS IS MADAME ST. PAUL. SHE SEES TO THE TRAINING OF MY BRIDES-WHO-MIGHT-BE.
Tee hee
SHE'LL TEACH ME MARTIAL ARTS DINING?
NOW. TRY EATING THIS AGAIN.
POK
POK
POP

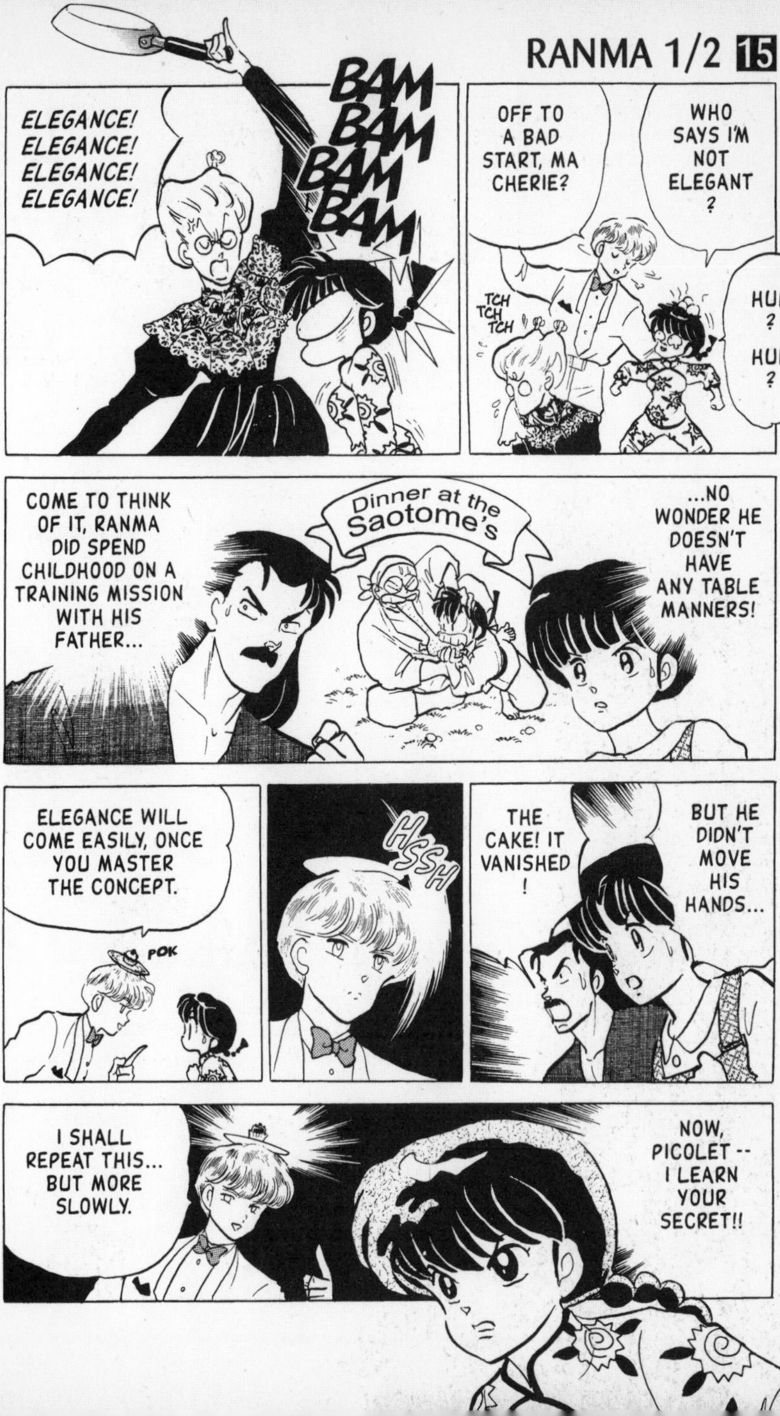
ELEGANCE! ELEGANCE! ELEGANCE! ELEGANCE!
BAM BAM BAM BAM BAM
OFF TO A BAD START, MA CHERIE?
WHO SAYS I'M NOT ELEGANT?
TCH TCH TCH
HUH? HUH?
COME TO THINK OF IT, RANMA DID SPEND CHILDHOOD ON A TRAINING MISSION WITH HIS FATHER...
Dinner at the Saotome's
...NO WONDER HE DOESN'T HAVE ANY TABLE MANNERS!
ELEGANCE WILL COME EASILY, ONCE YOU MASTER THE CONCEPT.
POK
HSSH
THE CAKE! IT VANISHED!
BUT HE DIDN'T MOVE HIS HANDS...
I SHALL REPEAT THIS... BUT MORE SLOWLY.
NOW, PICOLET -- I LEARN YOUR SECRET!!

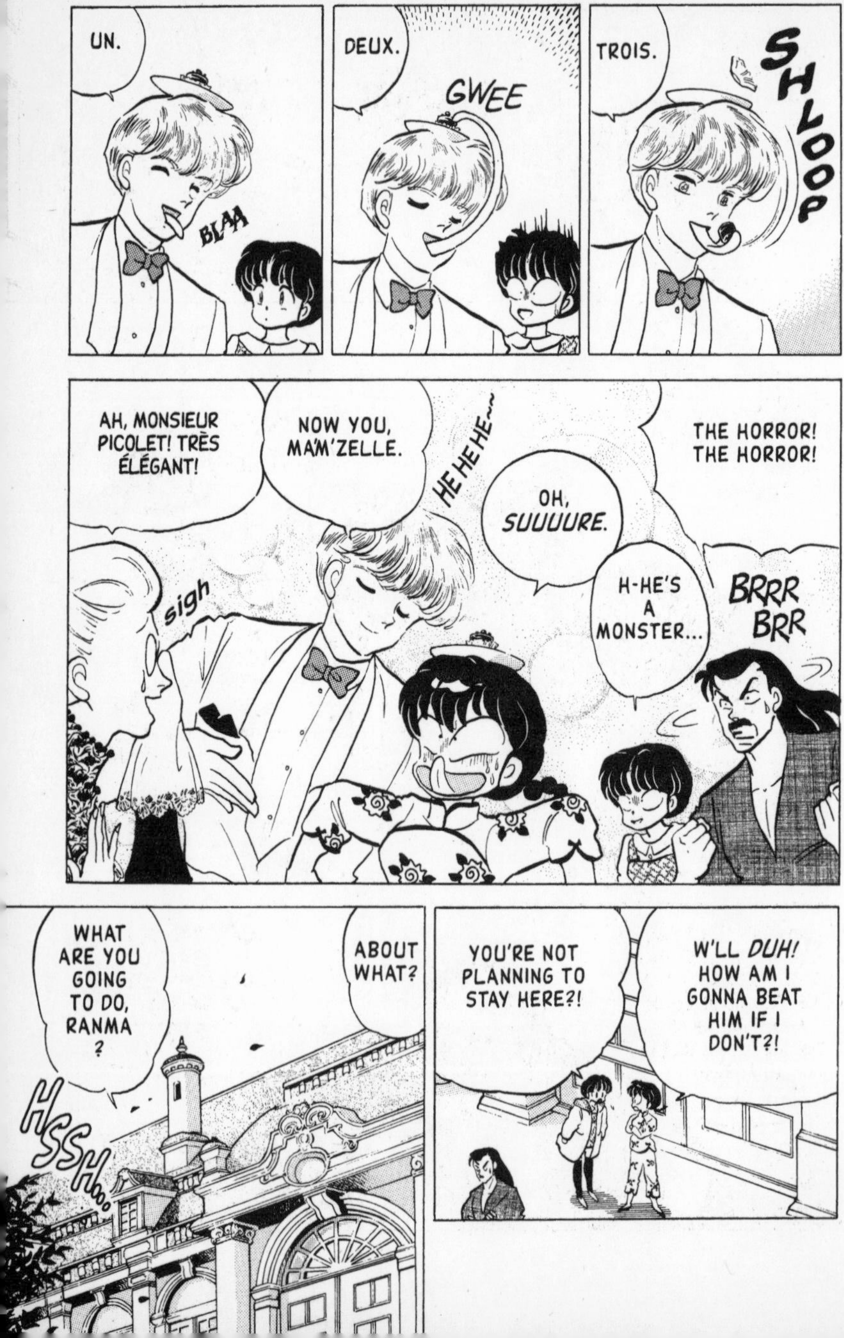
UN.
BLAA
DEUX.
GWEE
TROIS.
SHLOOP
AH, MONSIEUR PICOLET! TRÈS ÉLÉGANT!
NOW YOU, MA'M'ZELLE.
HE HE HE~~
sigh
OH, SUUUURE.
THE HORROR! THE HORROR!
H-HE'S A MONSTER...
BRRR BRR
WHAT ARE YOU GOING TO DO, RANMA?
HSSH...
ABOUT WHAT?
YOU'RE NOT PLANNING TO STAY HERE?!
W'LL DUH! HOW AM I GONNA BEAT HIM IF I DON'T?!

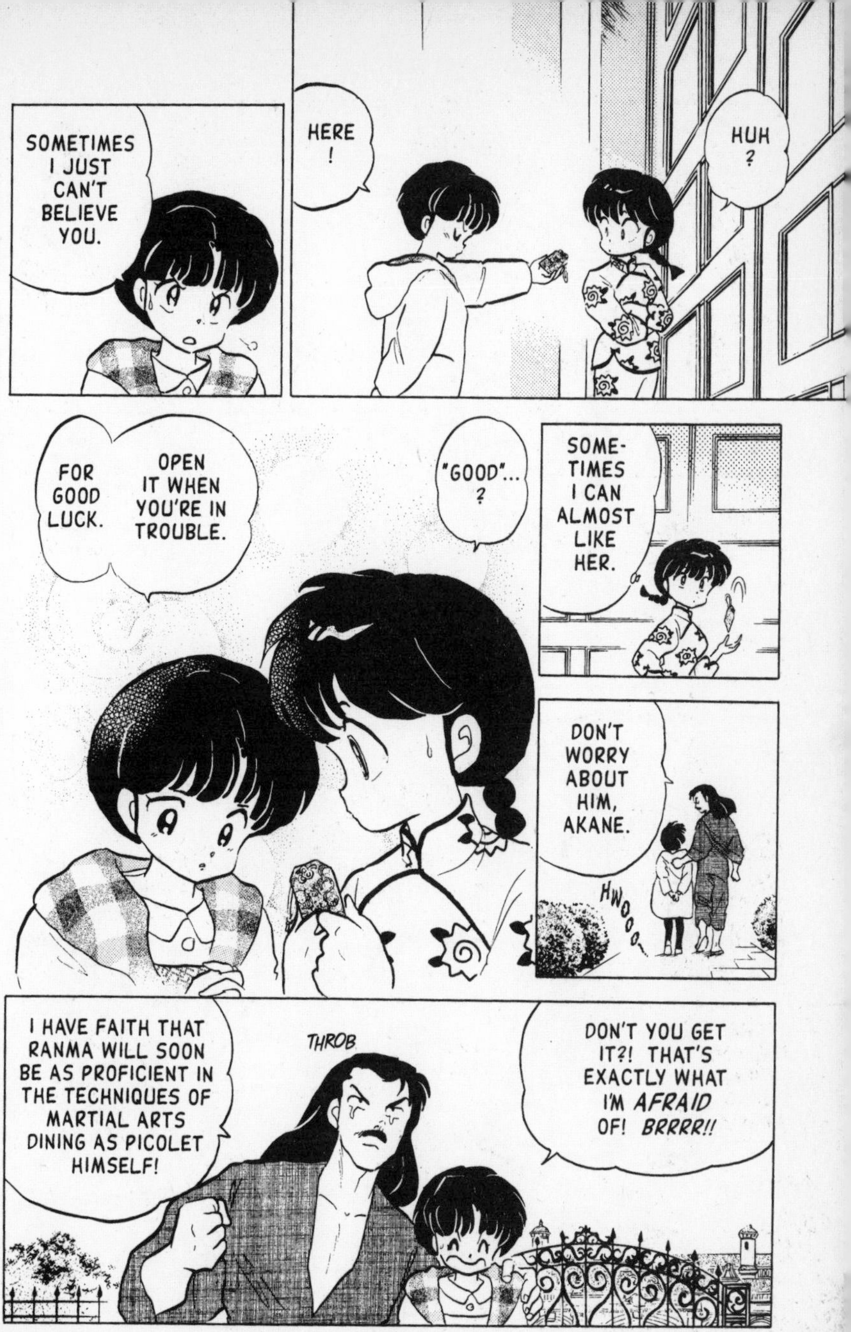
SOMETIMES I JUST CAN'T BELIEVE YOU.
HERE!
HUH?
FOR GOOD LUCK.
OPEN IT WHEN YOU'RE IN TROUBLE.
"GOOD"...?
SOME-TIMES I CAN ALMOST LIKE HER.
DON'T WORRY ABOUT HIM, AKANE.
HWOOOO...
I HAVE FAITH THAT RANMA WILL SOON BE AS PROFICIENT IN THE TECHNIQUES OF MARTIAL ARTS DINING AS PICOLET HIMSELF!
THROB
DON'T YOU GET IT?! THAT'S EXACTLY WHAT I'M *AFRAID* OF! *BRRRR!!*

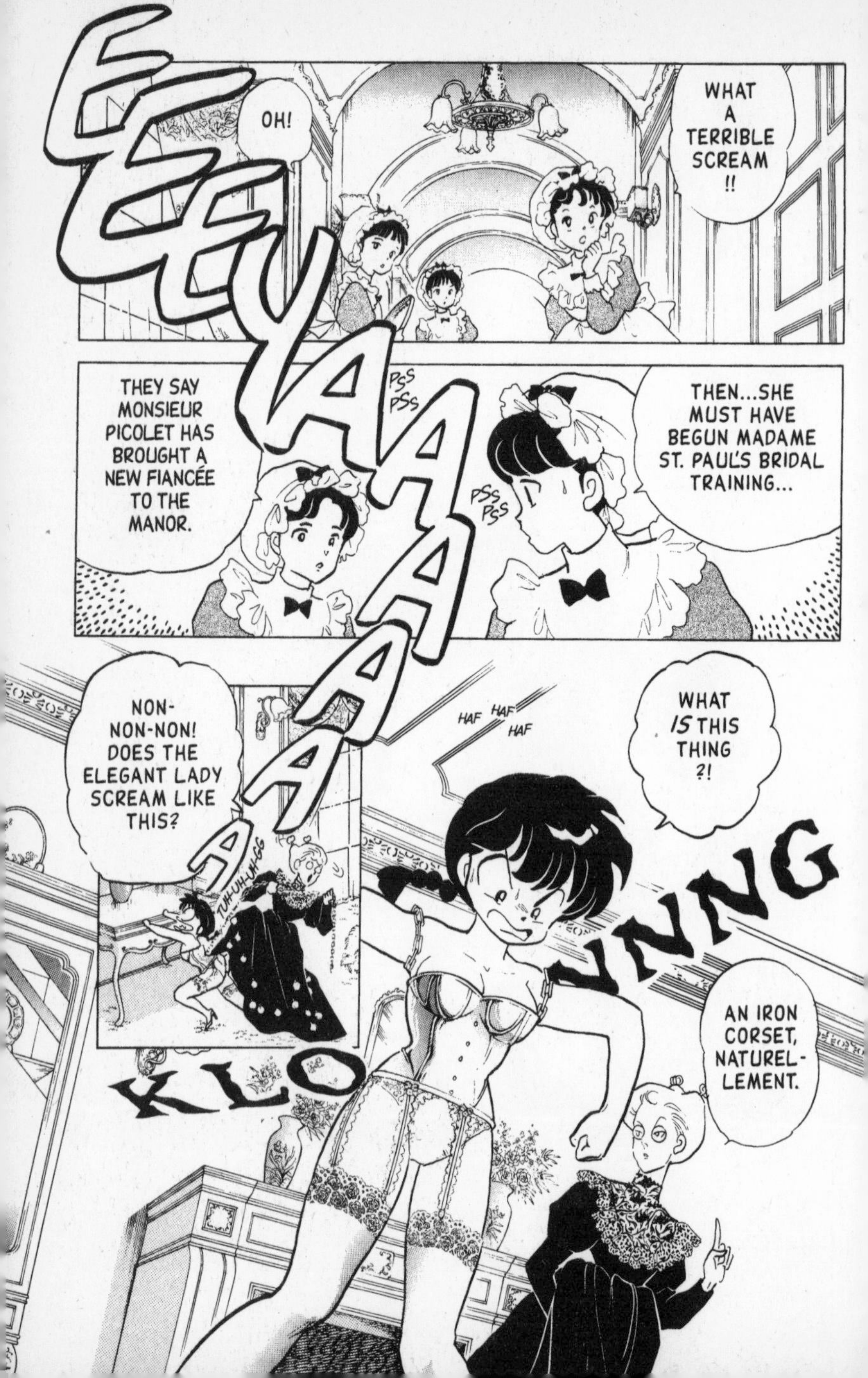
EEEYAAAAAAAA
OH!
WHAT A TERRIBLE SCREAM!!
THEY SAY MONSIEUR PICOLET HAS BROUGHT A NEW FIANCÉE TO THE MANOR.
PSS PSS
PSS PSS
THEN...SHE MUST HAVE BEGUN MADAME ST. PAUL'S BRIDAL TRAINING...
NON-NON-NON! DOES THE ELEGANT LADY SCREAM LIKE THIS?
TUH-UH-UH-GG
HAF HAF HAF
WHAT *IS* THIS THING?!
KLONNNG
AN IRON CORSET, NATUREL-LEMENT.

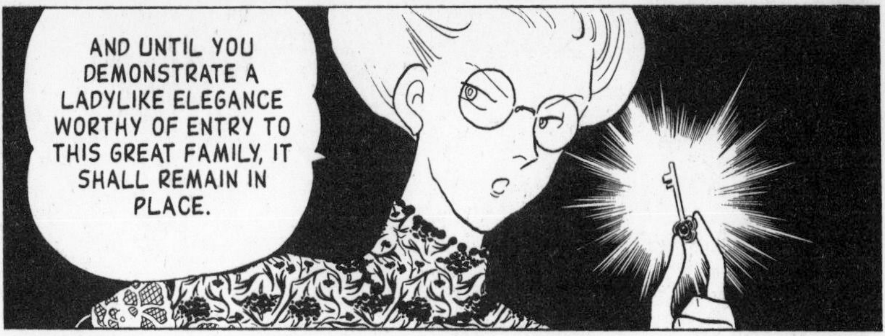
AND UNTIL YOU DEMONSTRATE A LADYLIKE ELEGANCE WORTHY OF ENTRY TO THIS GREAT FAMILY, IT SHALL REMAIN IN PLACE.

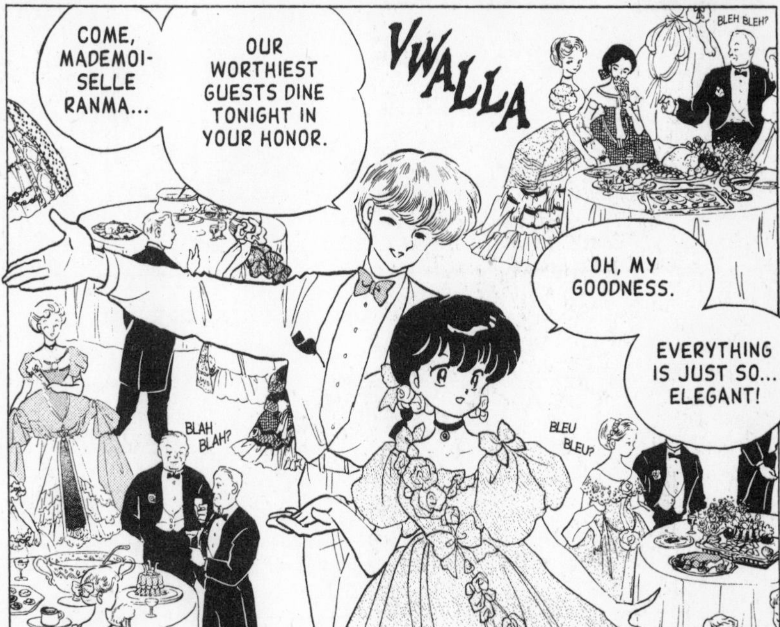
COME, MADEMOI-SELLE RANMA...
OUR WORTHIEST GUESTS DINE TONIGHT IN YOUR HONOR.
VWALLA
BLEH BLEH?
OH, MY GOODNESS.
EVERYTHING IS JUST SO... ELEGANT!
BLAH BLAH?
BLEU BLEU?

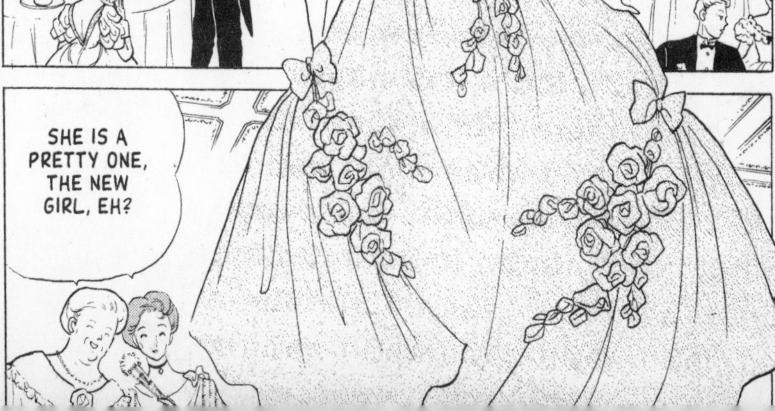
SHE IS A PRETTY ONE, THE NEW GIRL, EH?

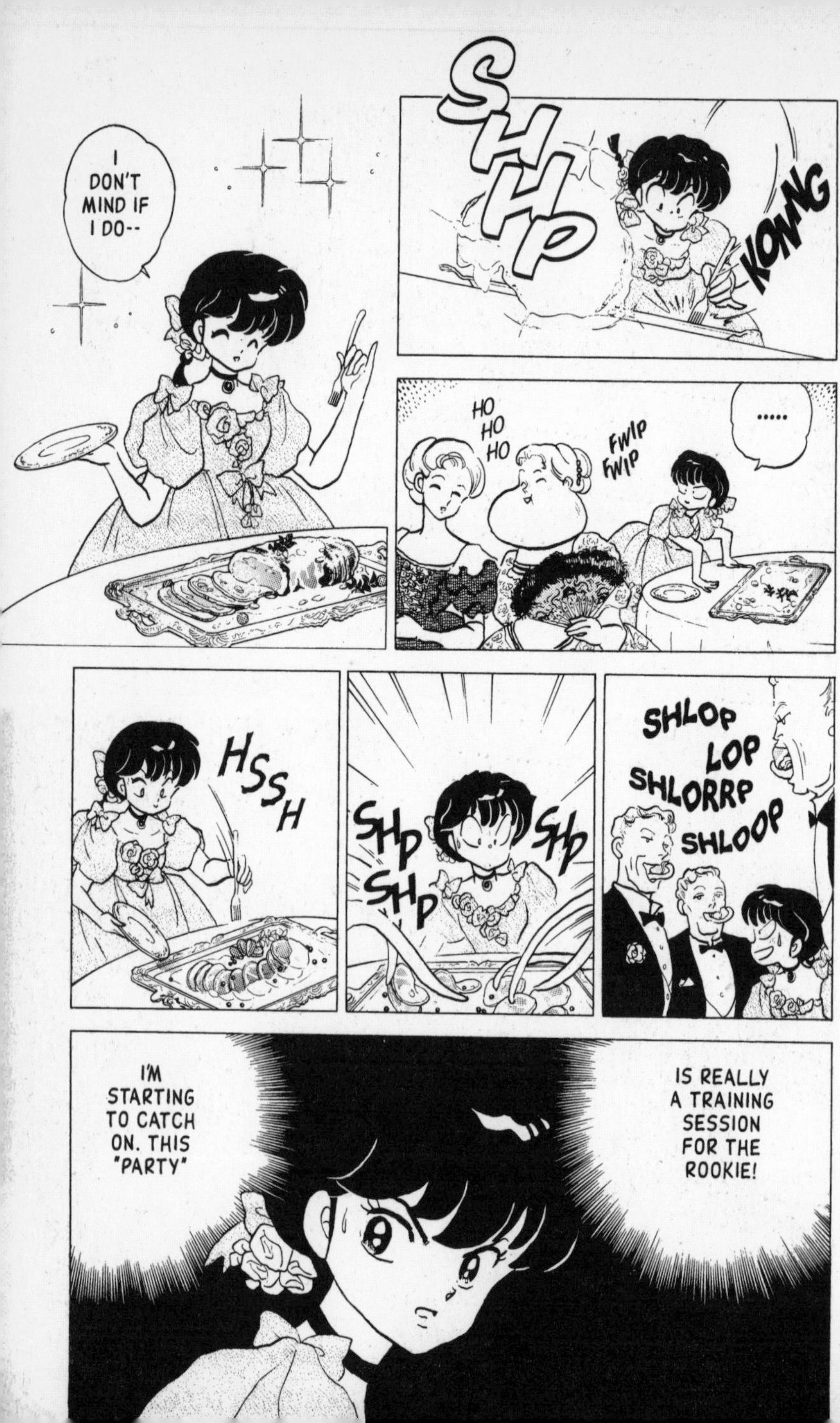
I DON'T MIND IF I DO--
SHHP
KONNG
HO HO HO
FWIP FWIP
.....
HSSH
SHP SHP SHP
SHLOP
LOP
SHLORRP
SHLOOP
I'M STARTING TO CATCH ON. THIS "PARTY"
IS REALLY A TRAINING SESSION FOR THE ROOKIE!

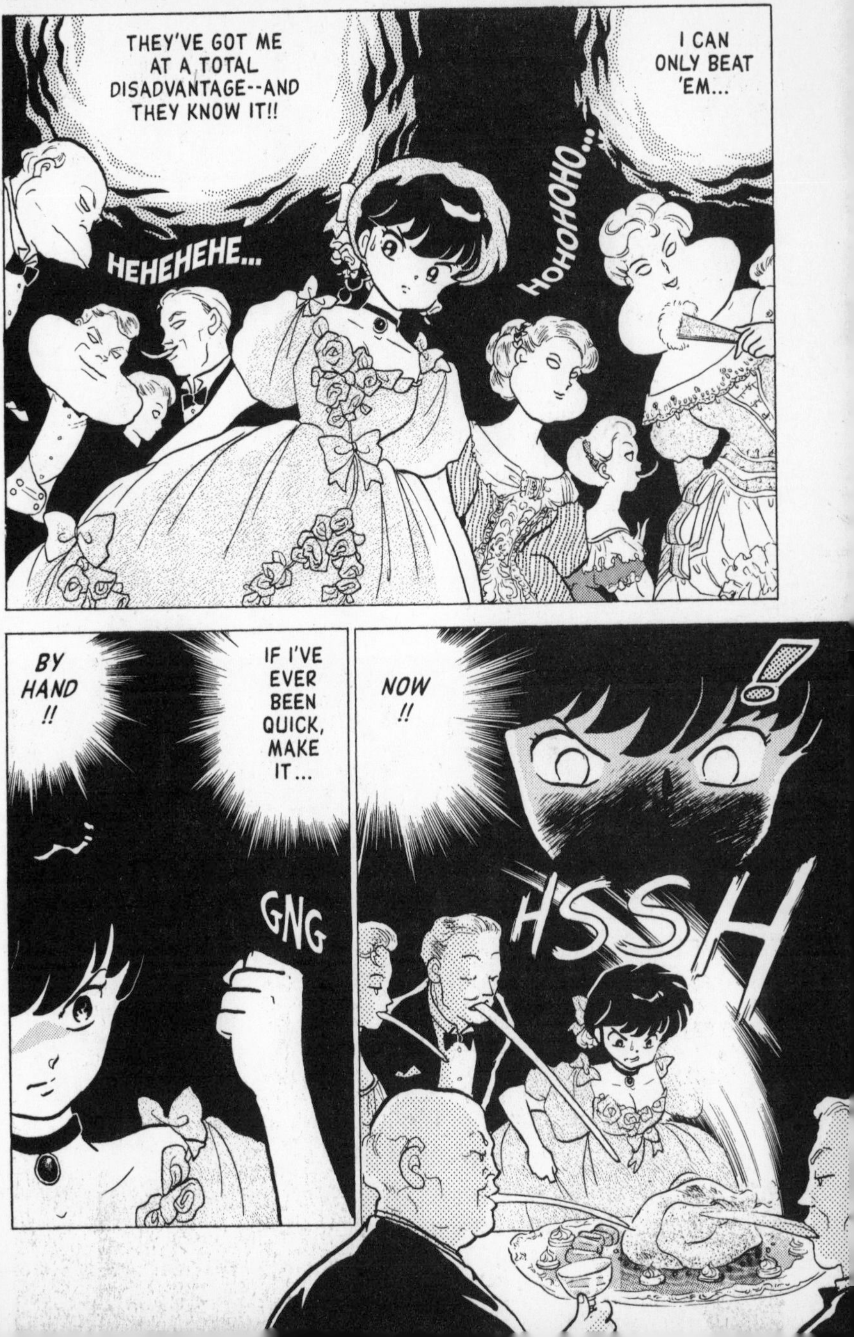
THEY'VE GOT ME AT A TOTAL DISADVANTAGE--AND THEY KNOW IT!!
I CAN ONLY BEAT 'EM...
HEHEHEHE...
HOHOHOHO...
BY HAND !!
IF I'VE EVER BEEN QUICK, MAKE IT...
GNG
NOW !!
!
HSSH

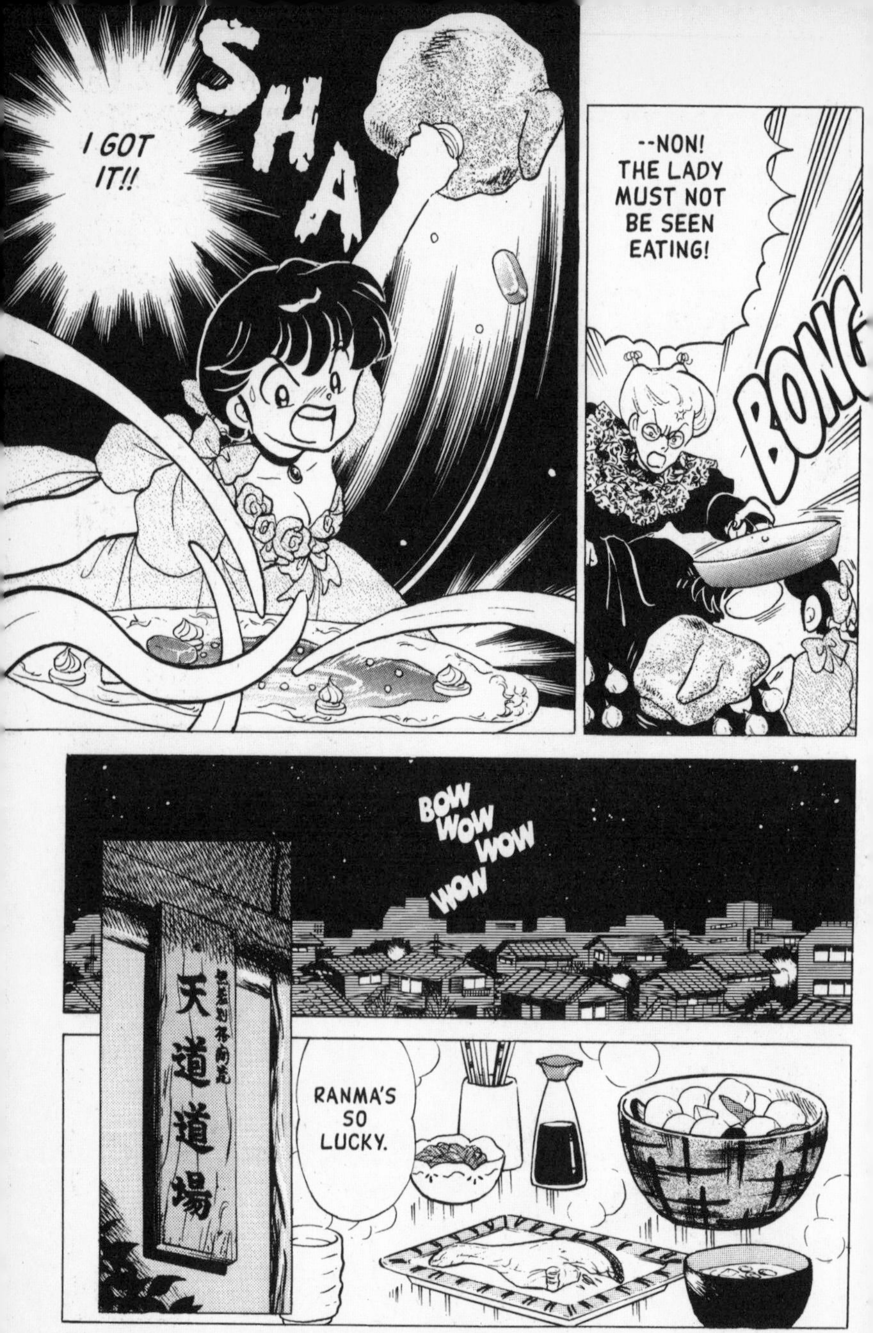

I GOT IT!!
SHA
--NON! THE LADY MUST NOT BE SEEN EATING!
BONG
BOW WOW WOW WOW
天道道場
RANMA'S SO LUCKY.

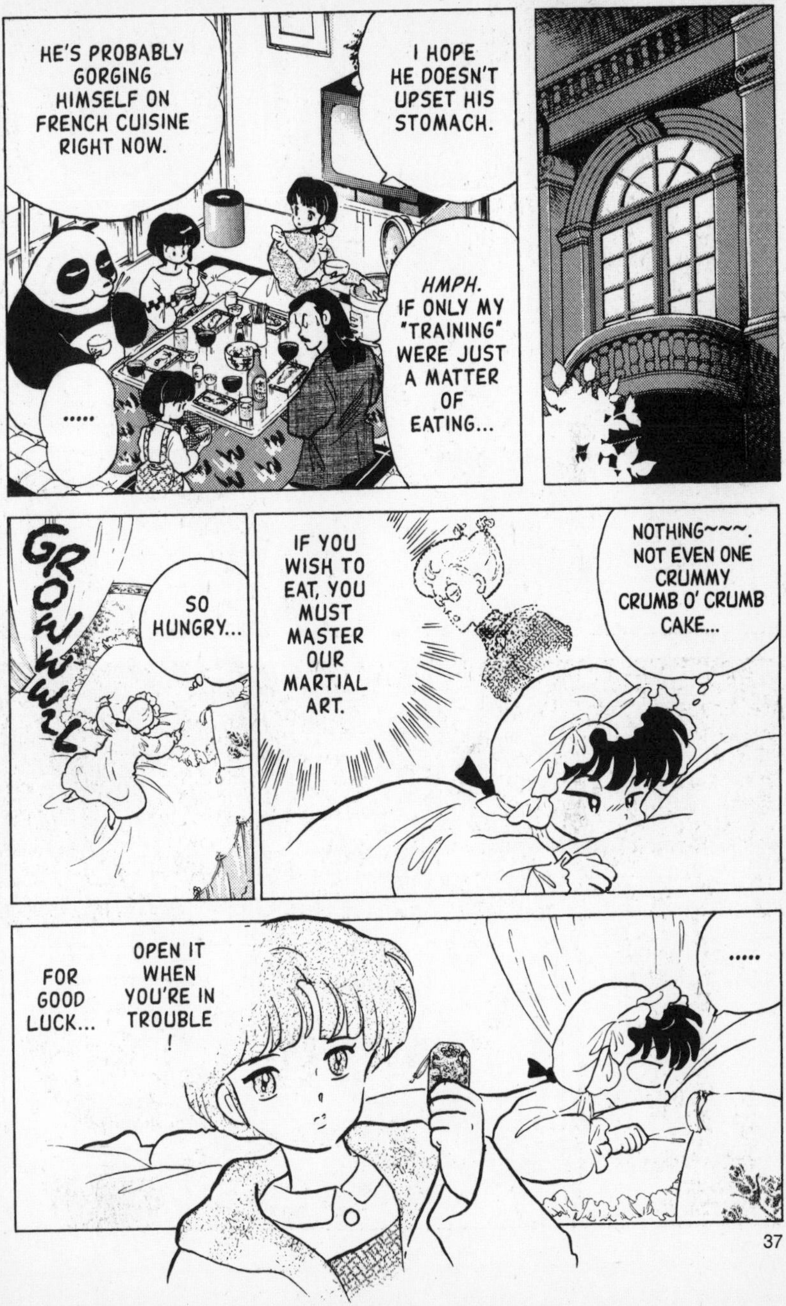
HE'S PROBABLY GORGING HIMSELF ON FRENCH CUISINE RIGHT NOW.
I HOPE HE DOESN'T UPSET HIS STOMACH.
.....
HMPH. IF ONLY MY "TRAINING" WERE JUST A MATTER OF EATING...
GROWWWL
SO HUNGRY...
IF YOU WISH TO EAT, YOU MUST MASTER OUR MARTIAL ART.
NOTHING~~~. NOT EVEN ONE CRUMMY CRUMB O' CRUMB CAKE...
FOR GOOD LUCK...
OPEN IT WHEN YOU'RE IN TROUBLE!
.....

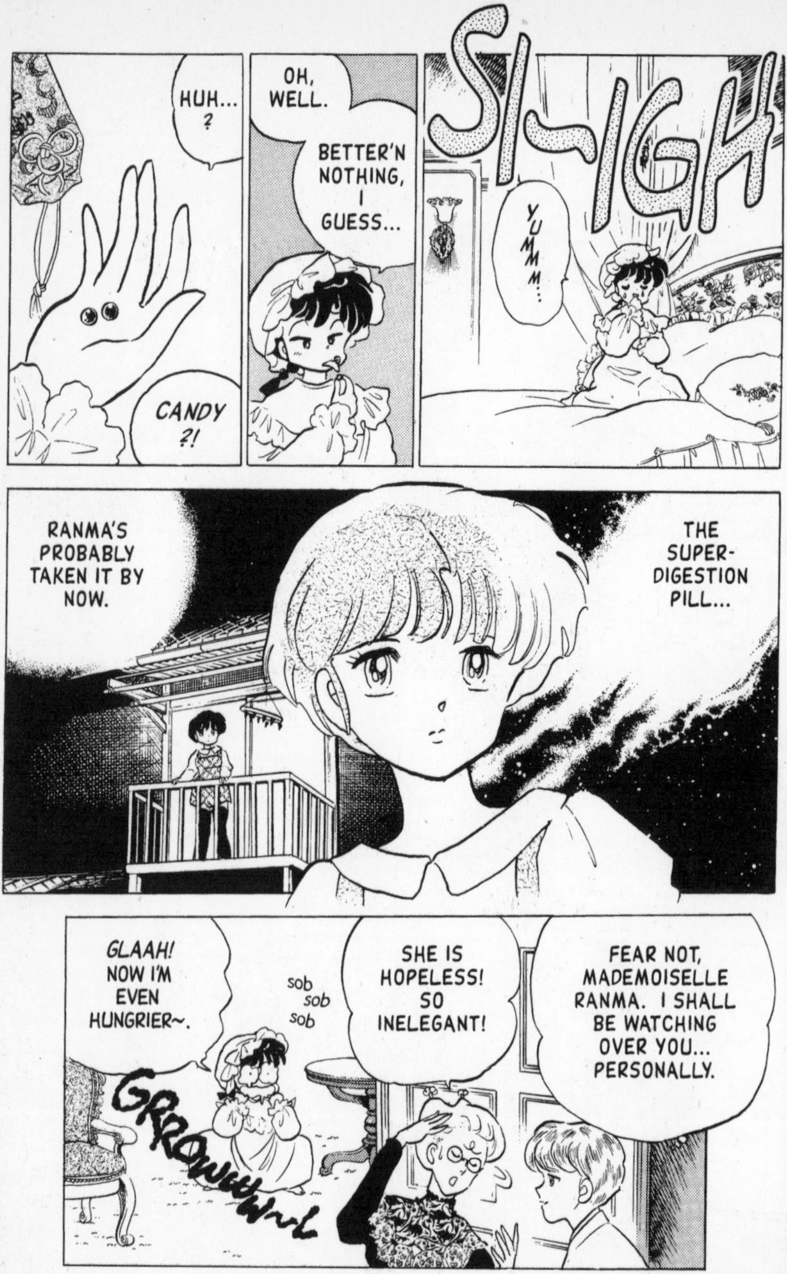
HUH...?
CANDY?!
OH, WELL.
BETTER'N NOTHING, I GUESS...
SI~IGH
YUMMM...
RANMA'S PROBABLY TAKEN IT BY NOW.
THE SUPER-DIGESTION PILL...
GLAAH! NOW I'M EVEN HUNGRIER~.
sob sob sob
GRROWWW~L
SHE IS HOPELESS! SO INELEGANT!
FEAR NOT, MADEMOISELLE RANMA. I SHALL BE WATCHING OVER YOU... PERSONALLY.

Part 3
LA MISERABLE

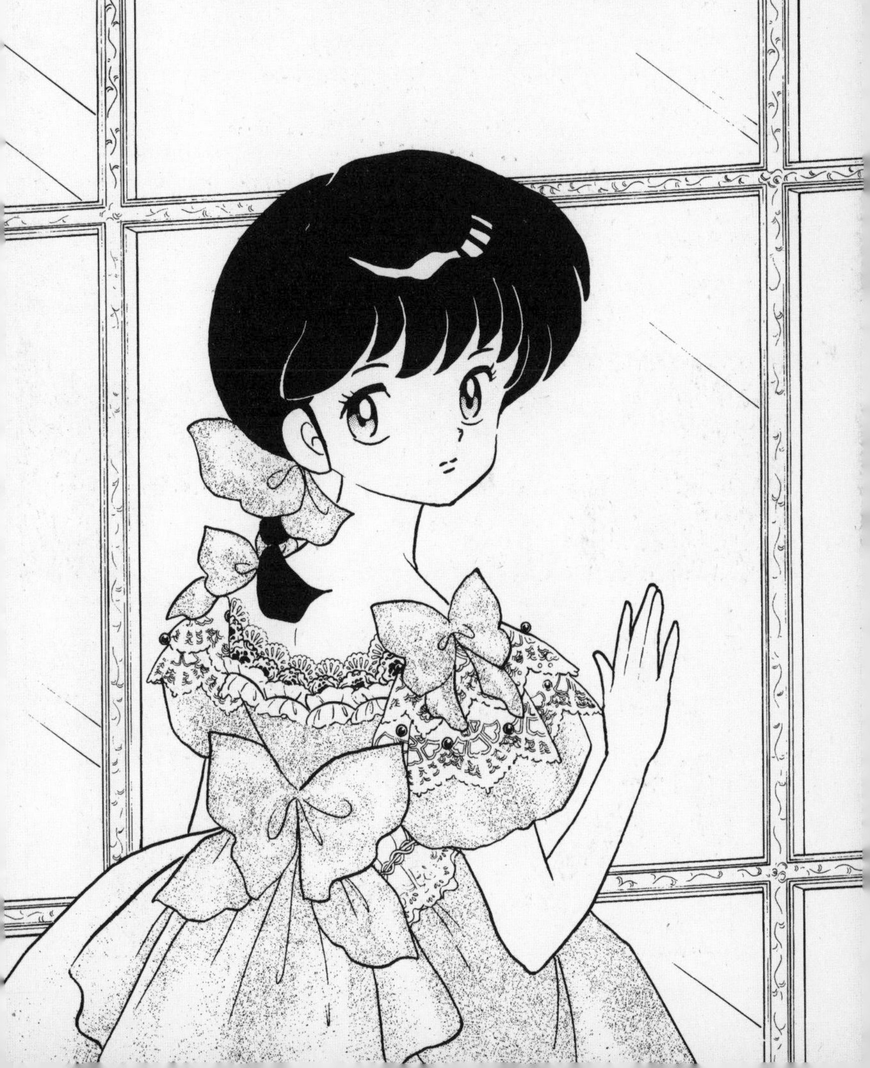

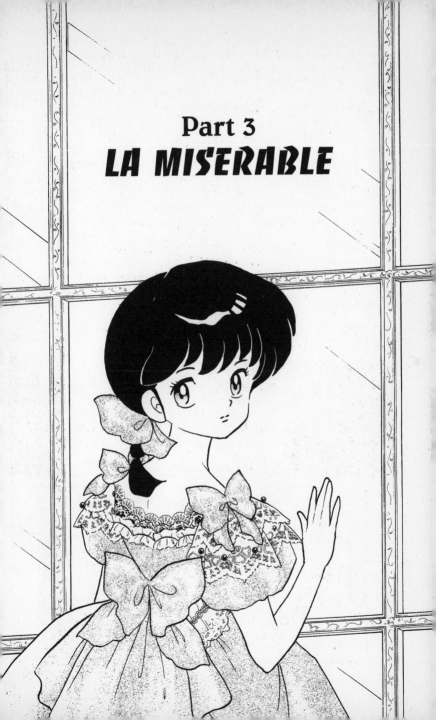

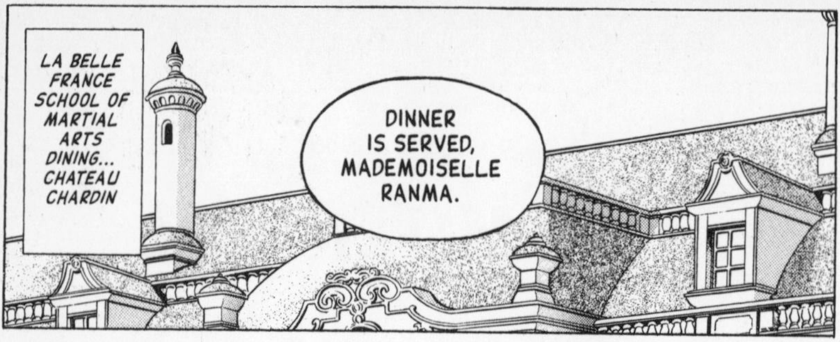
LA BELLE FRANCE SCHOOL OF MARTIAL ARTS DINING... CHATEAU CHARDIN
DINNER IS SERVED, MADEMOISELLE RANMA.

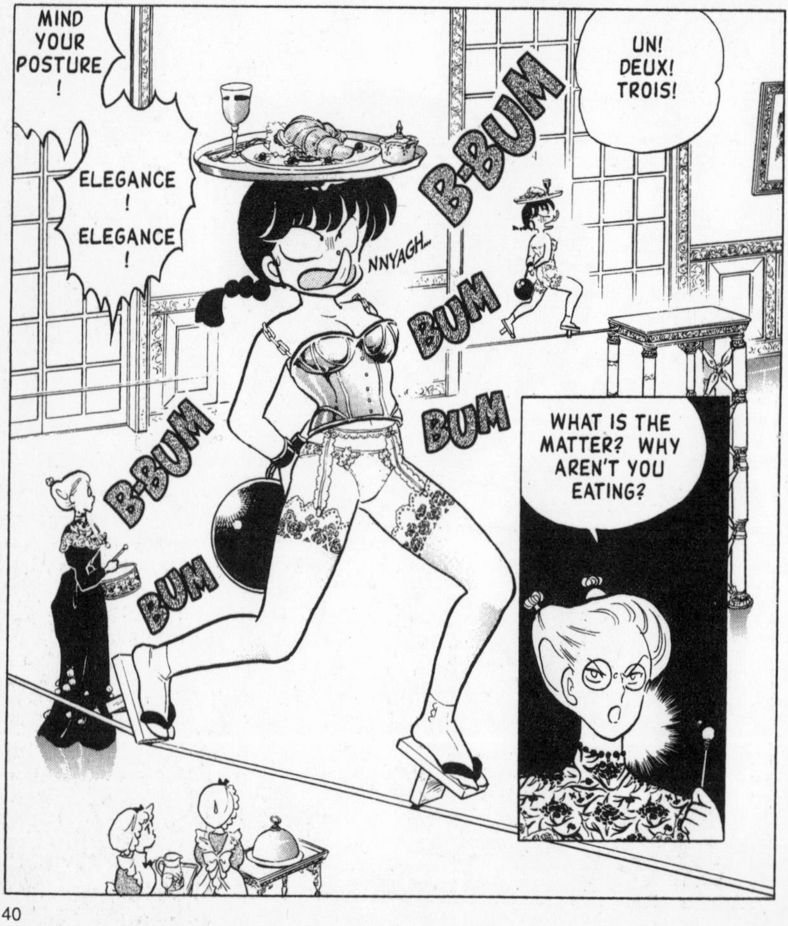
MIND YOUR POSTURE!
ELEGANCE! ELEGANCE!
B-BUM
NNYAGH...
UN! DEUX! TROIS!
BUM
BUM
B-BUM
BUM
WHAT IS THE MATTER? WHY AREN'T YOU EATING?

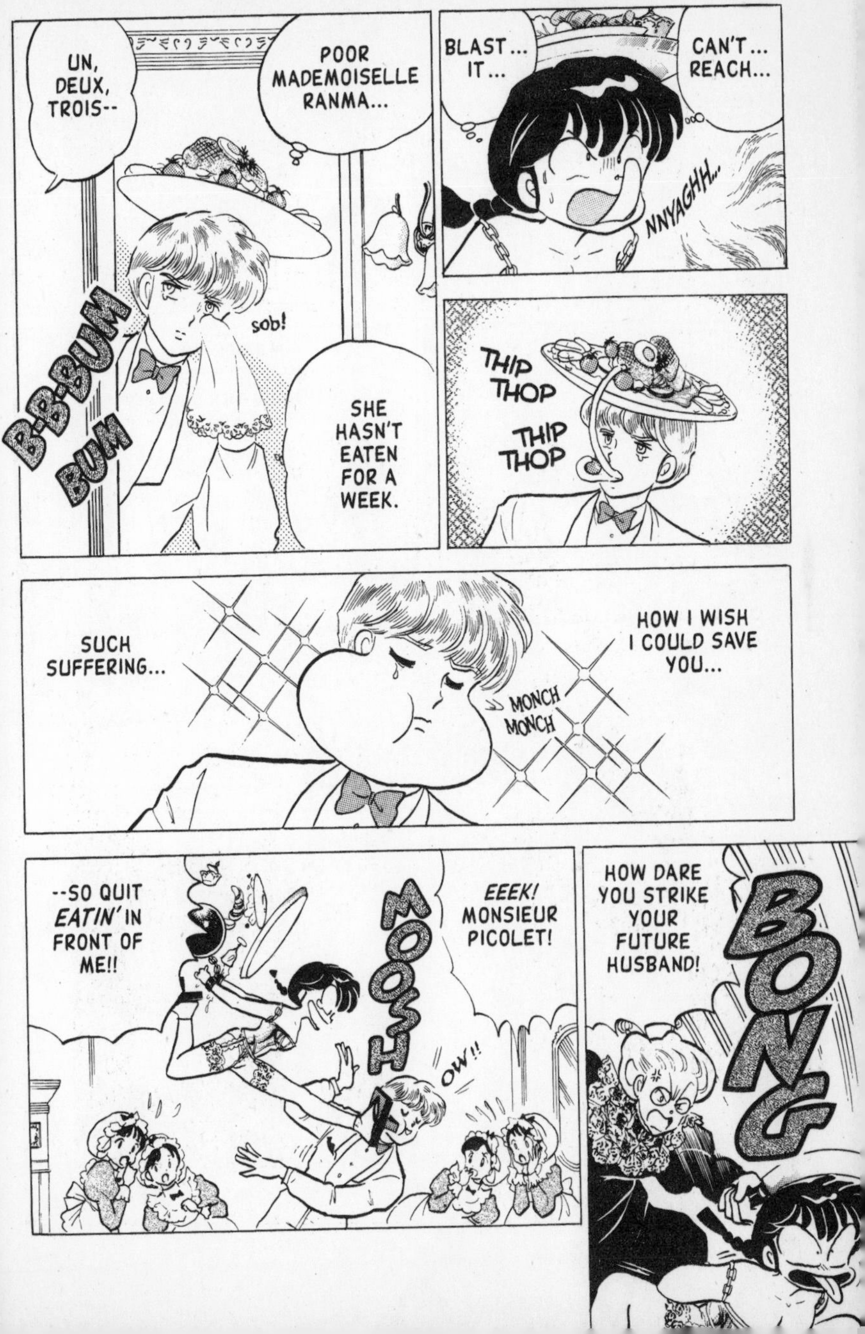
UN, DEUX, TROIS--
POOR MADEMOISELLE RANMA...
sob!
SHE HASN'T EATEN FOR A WEEK.
B-B-BUM BUM
BLAST... IT...
CAN'T... REACH...
NNYAGHH...
THIP THOP
THIP THOP
SUCH SUFFERING...
MONCH MONCH
HOW I WISH I COULD SAVE YOU...
--SO QUIT *EATIN'* IN FRONT OF ME!!
WOOSH
EEEK! MONSIEUR PICOLET!
OW!!
HOW DARE YOU STRIKE YOUR FUTURE HUSBAND!
BONG

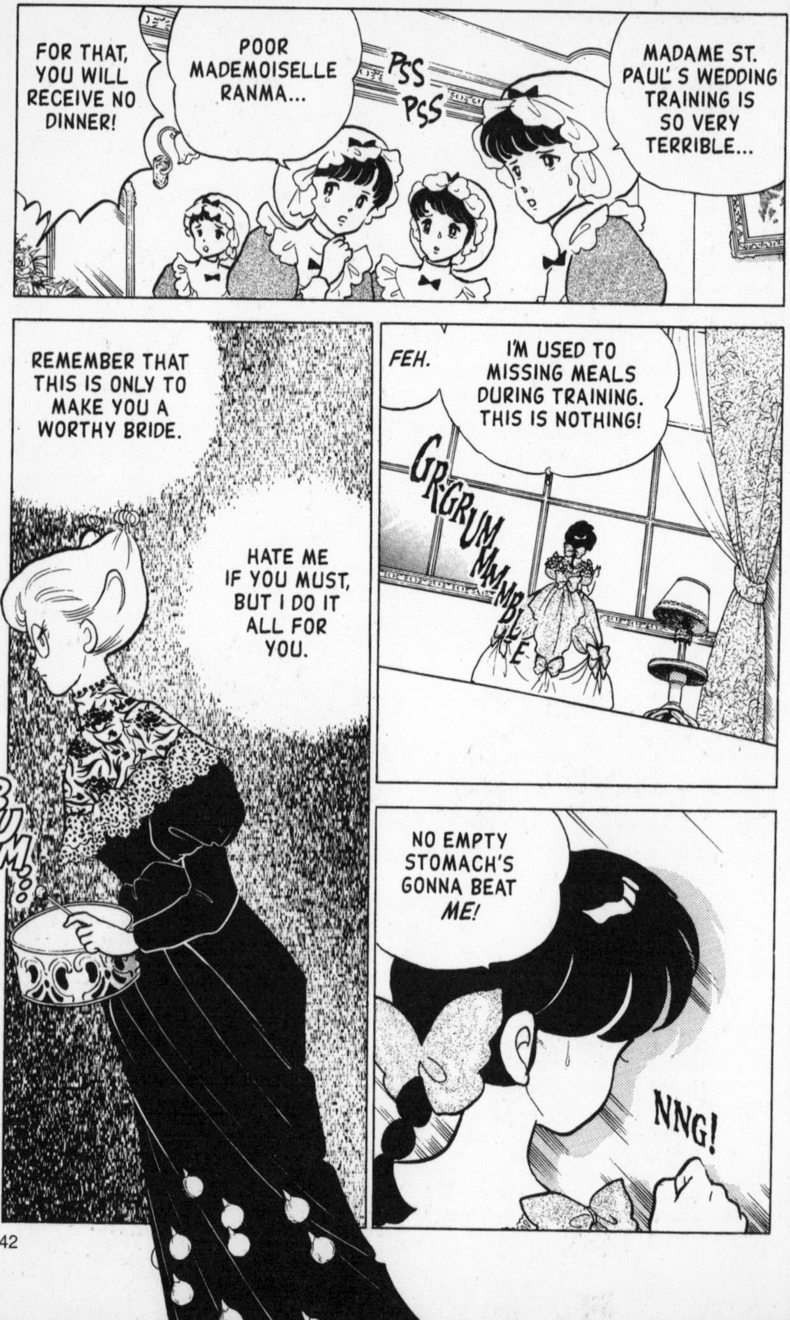
FOR THAT, YOU WILL RECEIVE NO DINNER!
POOR MADEMOISELLE RANMA...
PSS PSS
MADAME ST. PAUL'S WEDDING TRAINING IS SO VERY TERRIBLE...
REMEMBER THAT THIS IS ONLY TO MAKE YOU A WORTHY BRIDE.
HATE ME IF YOU MUST, BUT I DO IT ALL FOR YOU.
BUM...
FEH.
I'M USED TO MISSING MEALS DURING TRAINING. THIS IS NOTHING!
GR-GRUMMMMBLE
NO EMPTY STOMACH'S GONNA BEAT ME!
NNG!

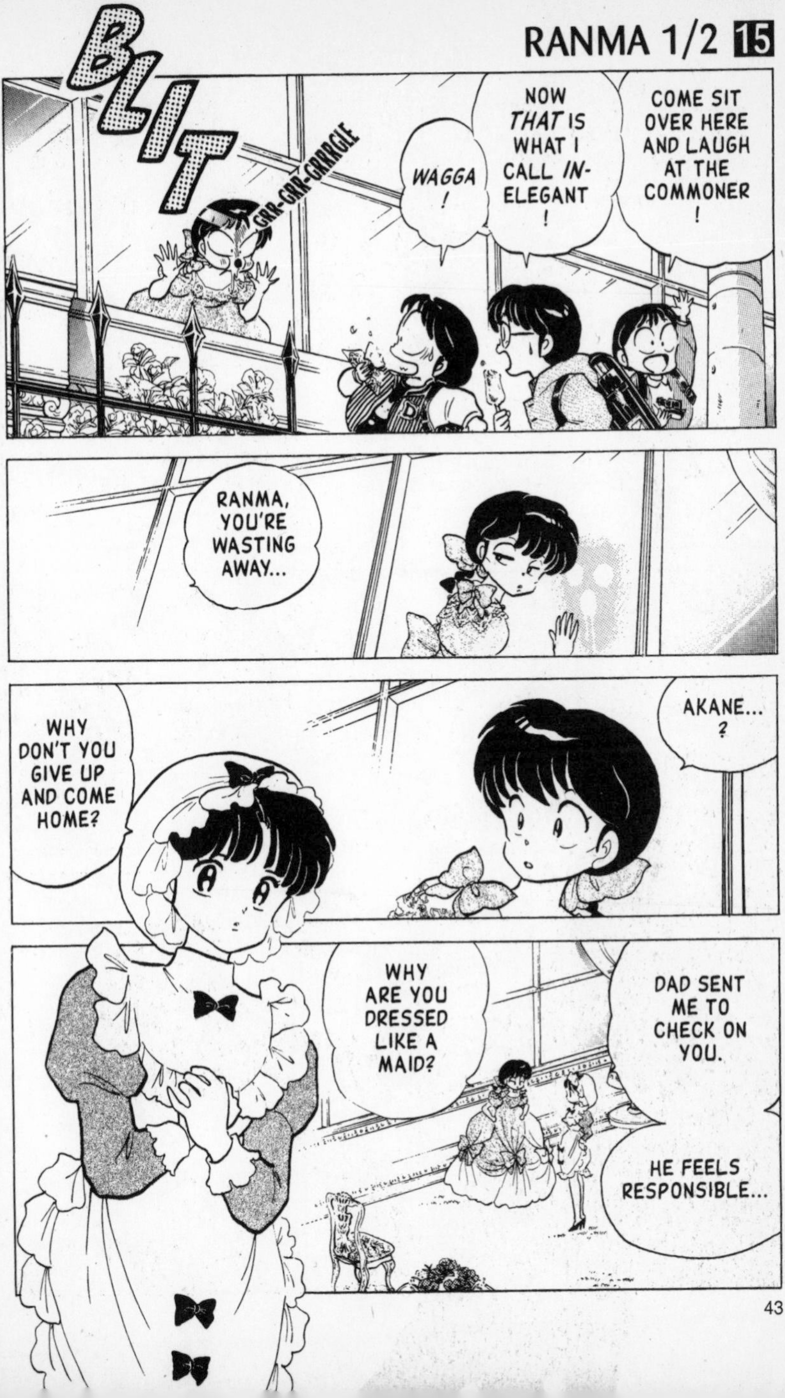
BLIT
GRR-GRR-GRRRGLE
WAGGA!
NOW THAT IS WHAT I CALL IN-ELEGANT!
COME SIT OVER HERE AND LAUGH AT THE COMMONER!
RANMA, YOU'RE WASTING AWAY...
WHY DON'T YOU GIVE UP AND COME HOME?
AKANE...?
WHY ARE YOU DRESSED LIKE A MAID?
DAD SENT ME TO CHECK ON YOU.
HE FEELS RESPONSIBLE...

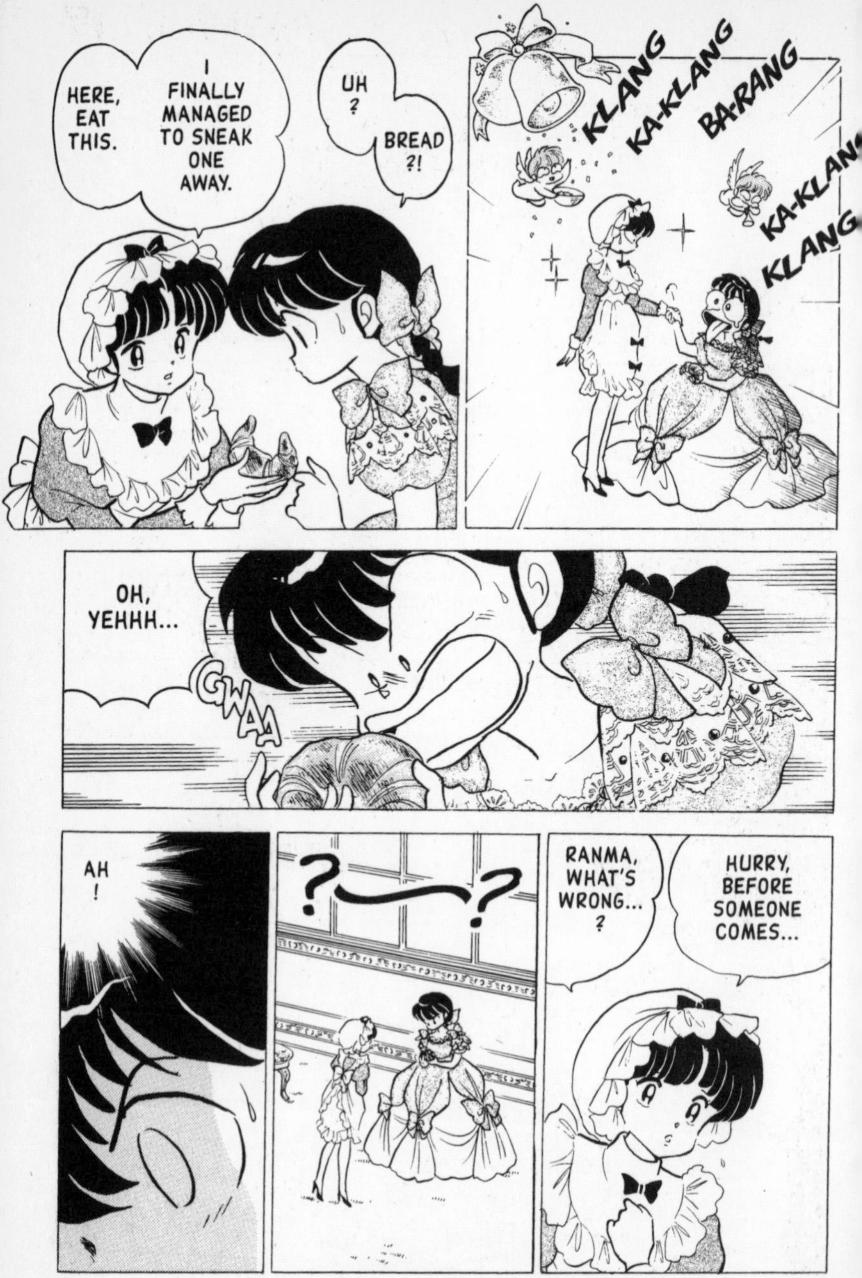
HERE, EAT THIS.
I FINALLY MANAGED TO SNEAK ONE AWAY.
UH? BREAD?!
KLANG
KA-KLANG
BA-RANG
KA-KLANG
KLANG
OH, YEHHH...
GWAA
AH!
?——?
RANMA, WHAT'S WRONG...?
HURRY, BEFORE SOMEONE COMES...

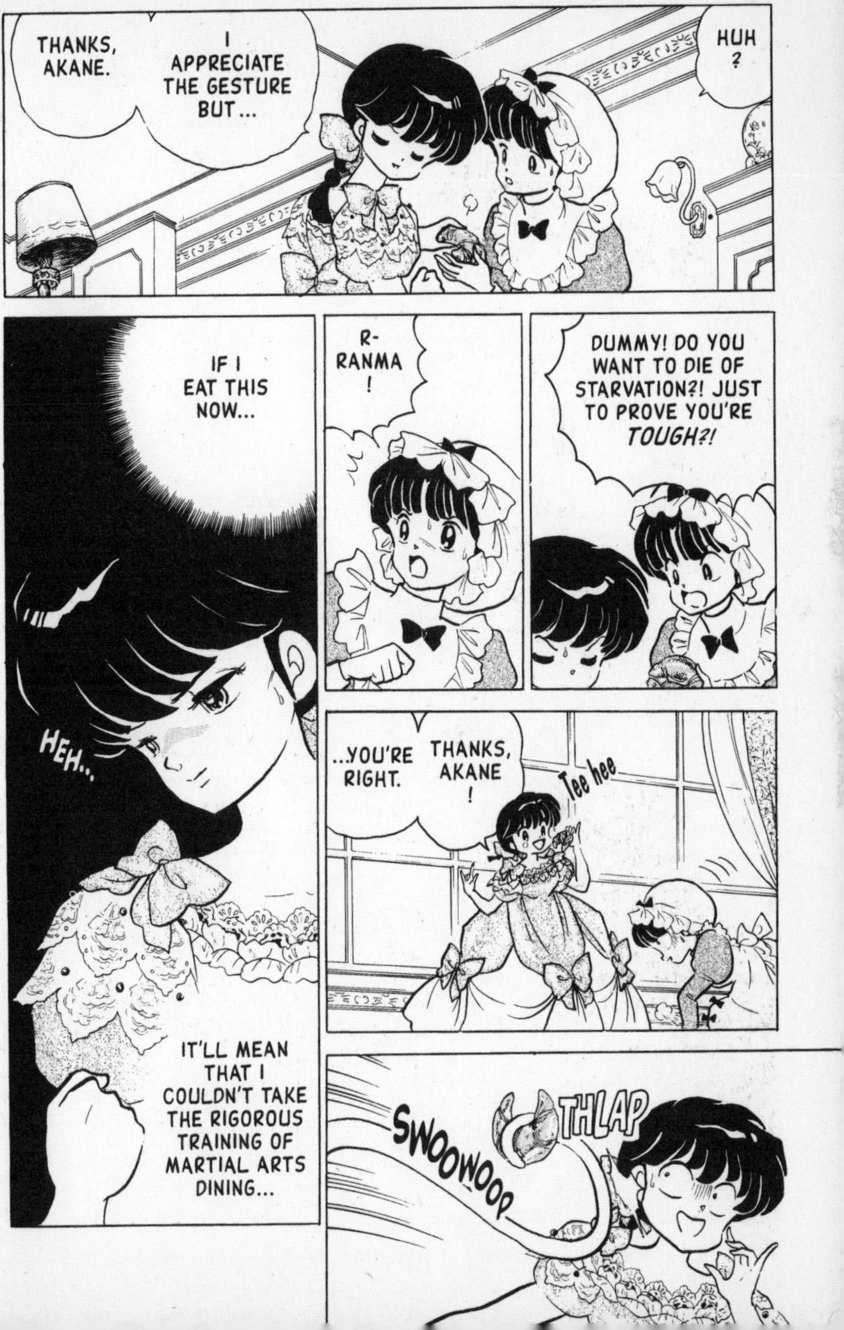
THANKS, AKANE.
I APPRECIATE THE GESTURE BUT...
HUH?
IF I EAT THIS NOW...
HEH...
IT'LL MEAN THAT I COULDN'T TAKE THE RIGOROUS TRAINING OF MARTIAL ARTS DINING...
R-RANMA!
DUMMY! DO YOU WANT TO DIE OF STARVATION?! JUST TO PROVE YOU'RE *TOUGH?!*
...YOU'RE RIGHT.
THANKS, AKANE!
Tee hee
SWOOWOOP
THLAP

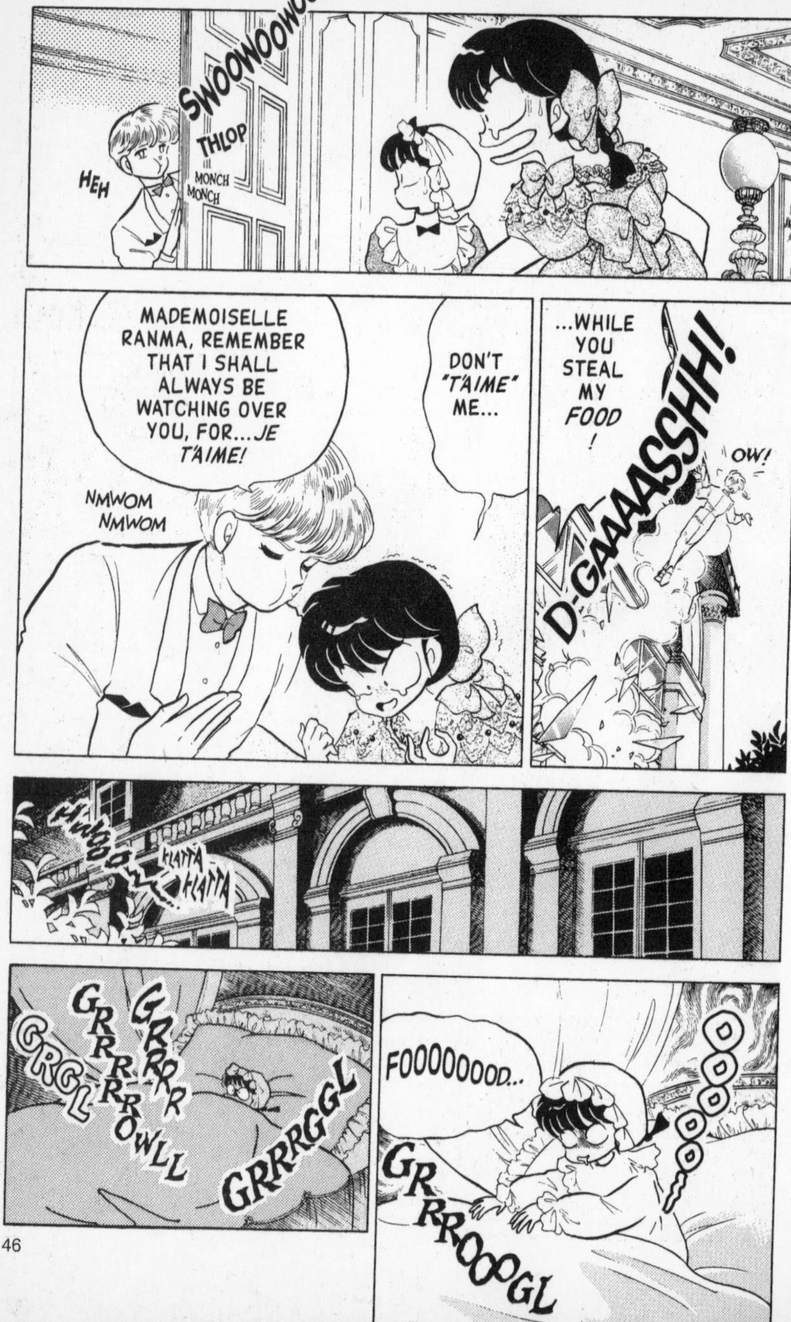
SWOOWOOWOOP
HEH
THLOP
MONCH MONCH
MADEMOISELLE RANMA, REMEMBER THAT I SHALL ALWAYS BE WATCHING OVER YOU, FOR...JE T'AIME!
DON'T "T'AIME" ME...
NMWOM NMWOM
...WHILE YOU STEAL MY FOOD!
D-GAAAASSHH!
OW!
KLATTA KLATTA
GRRRRR
GRRRRROWLL
GRGL
GRRRGGL
FOOOOOOOD...
GRRROOOGL
DOOOOOO...

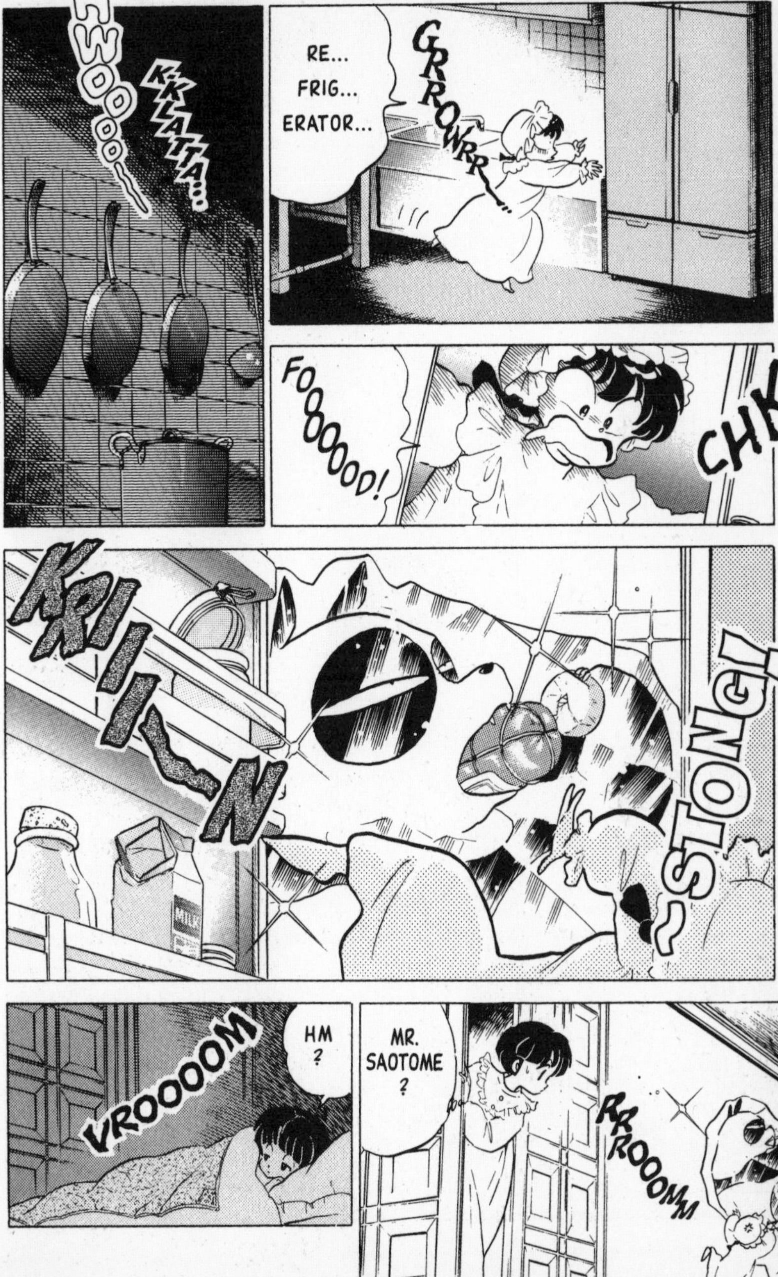
HWOOOO...
K-KLATTA...
RE... FRIG... ERATOR...
GRROWRR...
FOOOOOOOD!
CHK
KRIIIN
~STONG!
VROOOOM
HM ?
MR. SAOTOME ?
RRROOOMM

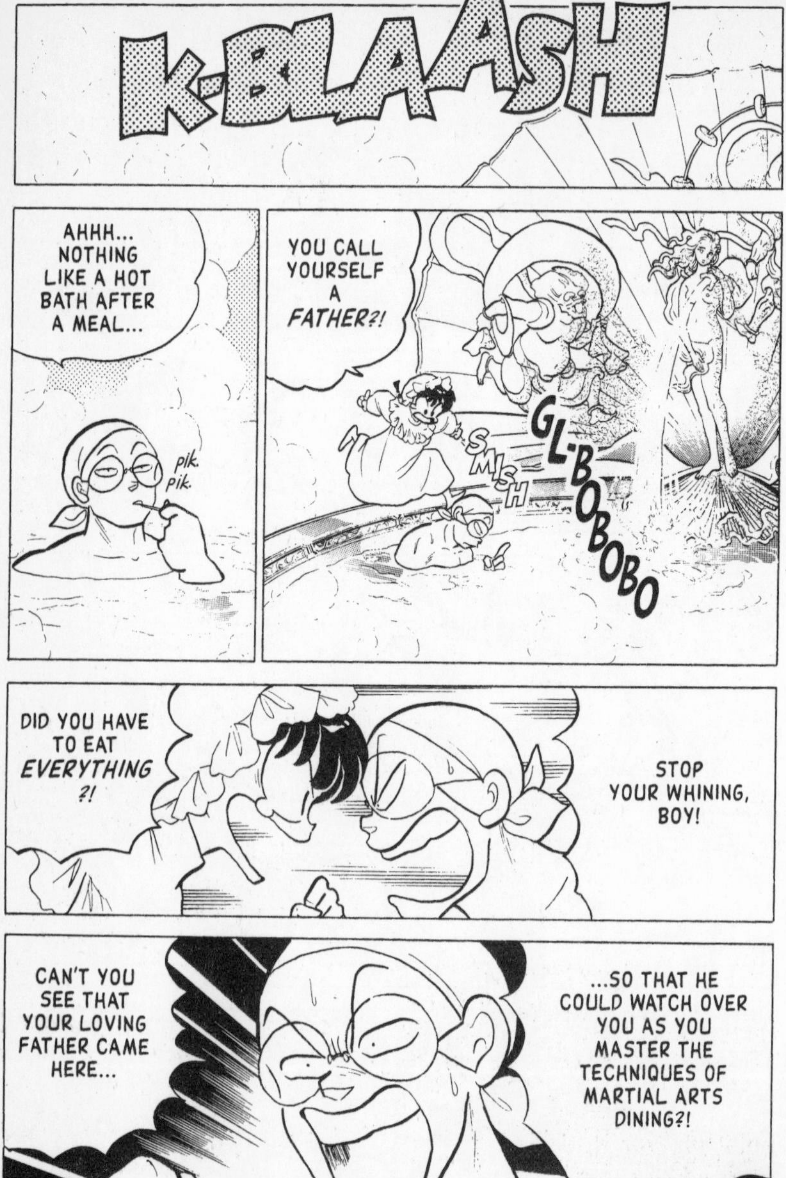
K-BLAASH
AHHH... NOTHING LIKE A HOT BATH AFTER A MEAL...
pik. pik.
YOU CALL YOURSELF A *FATHER*?!
SMISH
GL-BOBOBOBO
DID YOU HAVE TO EAT *EVERYTHING*?!
STOP YOUR WHINING, BOY!
CAN'T YOU SEE THAT YOUR LOVING FATHER CAME HERE...
...SO THAT HE COULD WATCH OVER YOU AS YOU MASTER THE TECHNIQUES OF MARTIAL ARTS DINING?!

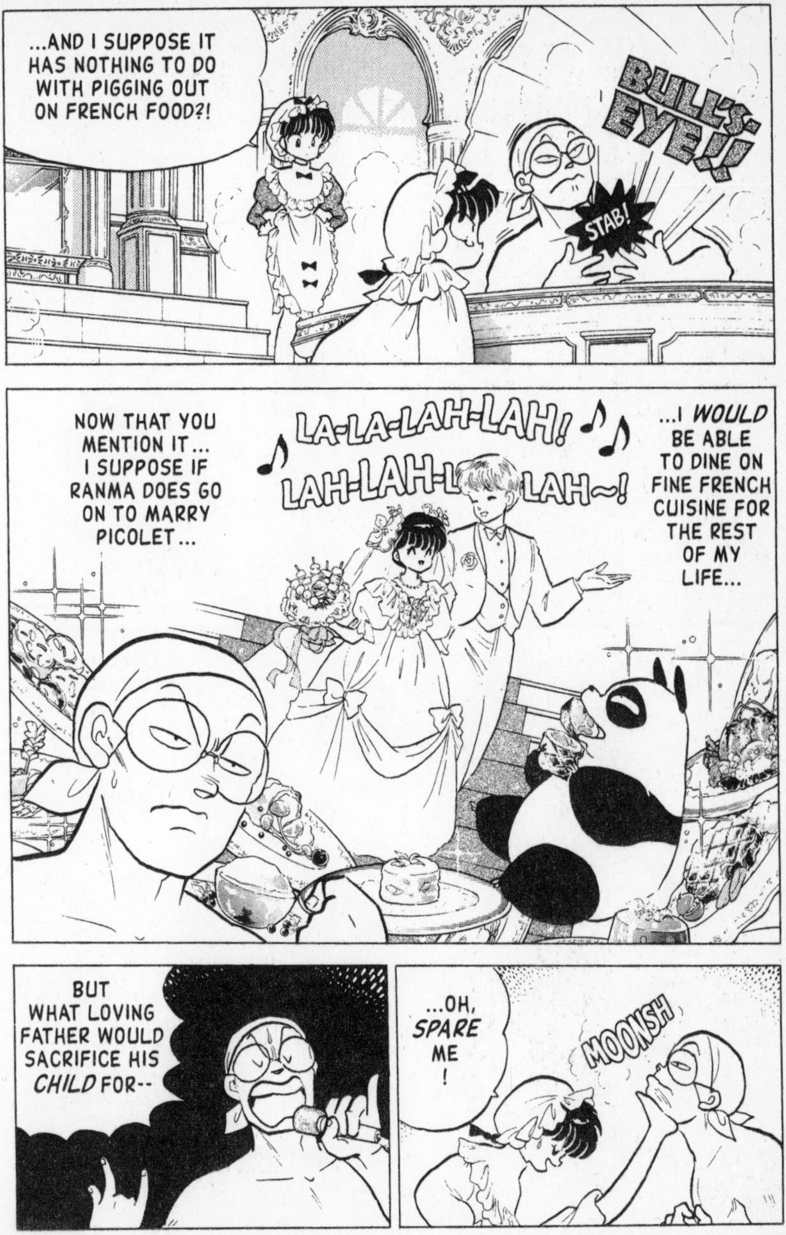
...AND I SUPPOSE IT HAS NOTHING TO DO WITH PIGGING OUT ON FRENCH FOOD?!
BULL'S-EYE!!
STAB!
NOW THAT YOU MENTION IT... I SUPPOSE IF RANMA DOES GO ON TO MARRY PICOLET...
LA-LA-LAH-LAH! ♪ ♪
♪ LAH-LAH-L LAH~!
...I *WOULD* BE ABLE TO DINE ON FINE FRENCH CUISINE FOR THE REST OF MY LIFE...
BUT WHAT LOVING FATHER WOULD SACRIFICE HIS *CHILD* FOR--
...OH, *SPARE* ME!
MOONSH

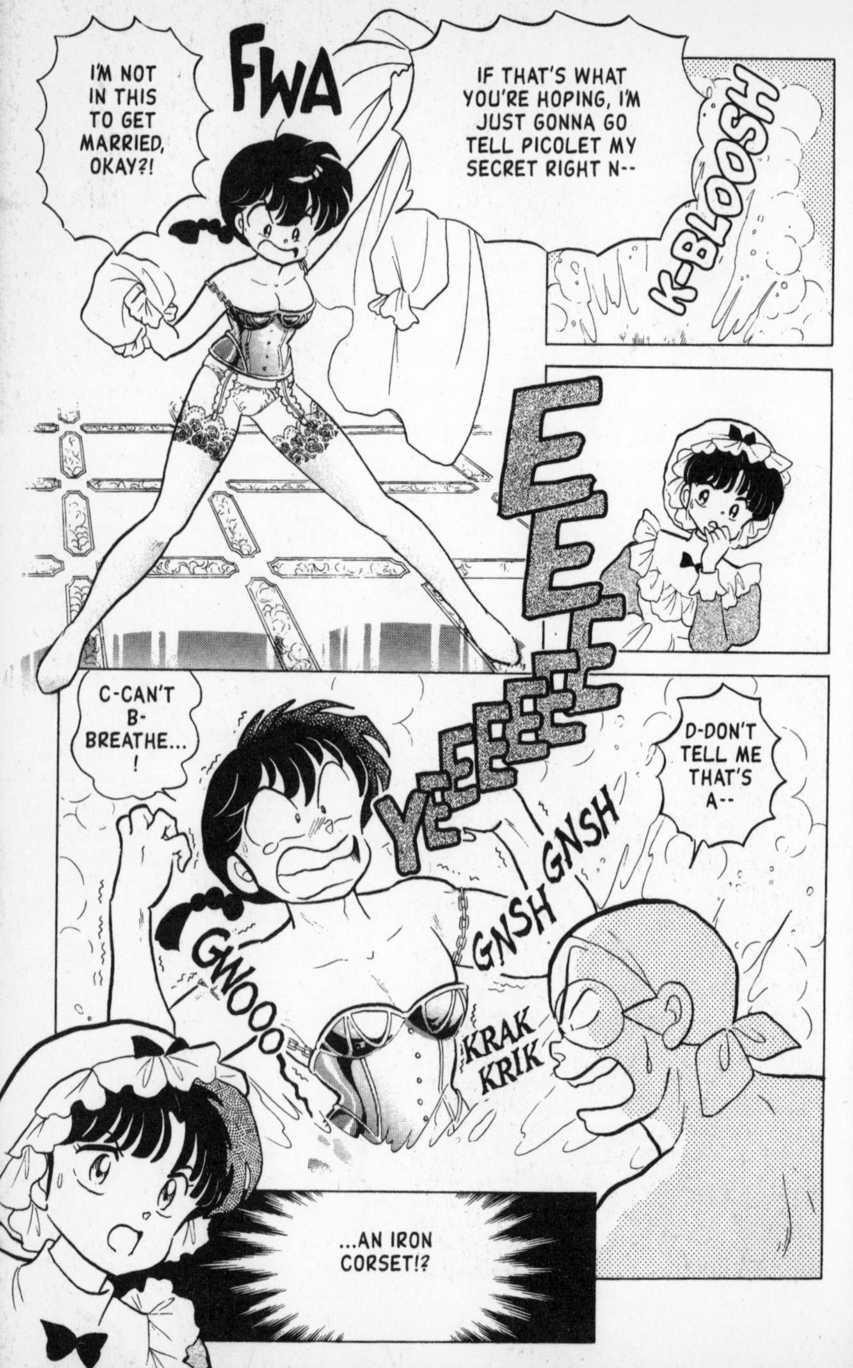
I'M NOT IN THIS TO GET MARRIED, OKAY?!
FWA
IF THAT'S WHAT YOU'RE HOPING, I'M JUST GONNA GO TELL PICOLET MY SECRET RIGHT N--
K-BLOOSH
EEEE
C-CAN'T B-BREATHE...!
YEEEEEE
D-DON'T TELL ME THAT'S A--
GNSH GNSH GNSH
GWOOO
KRAK KRIK
...AN IRON CORSET!?

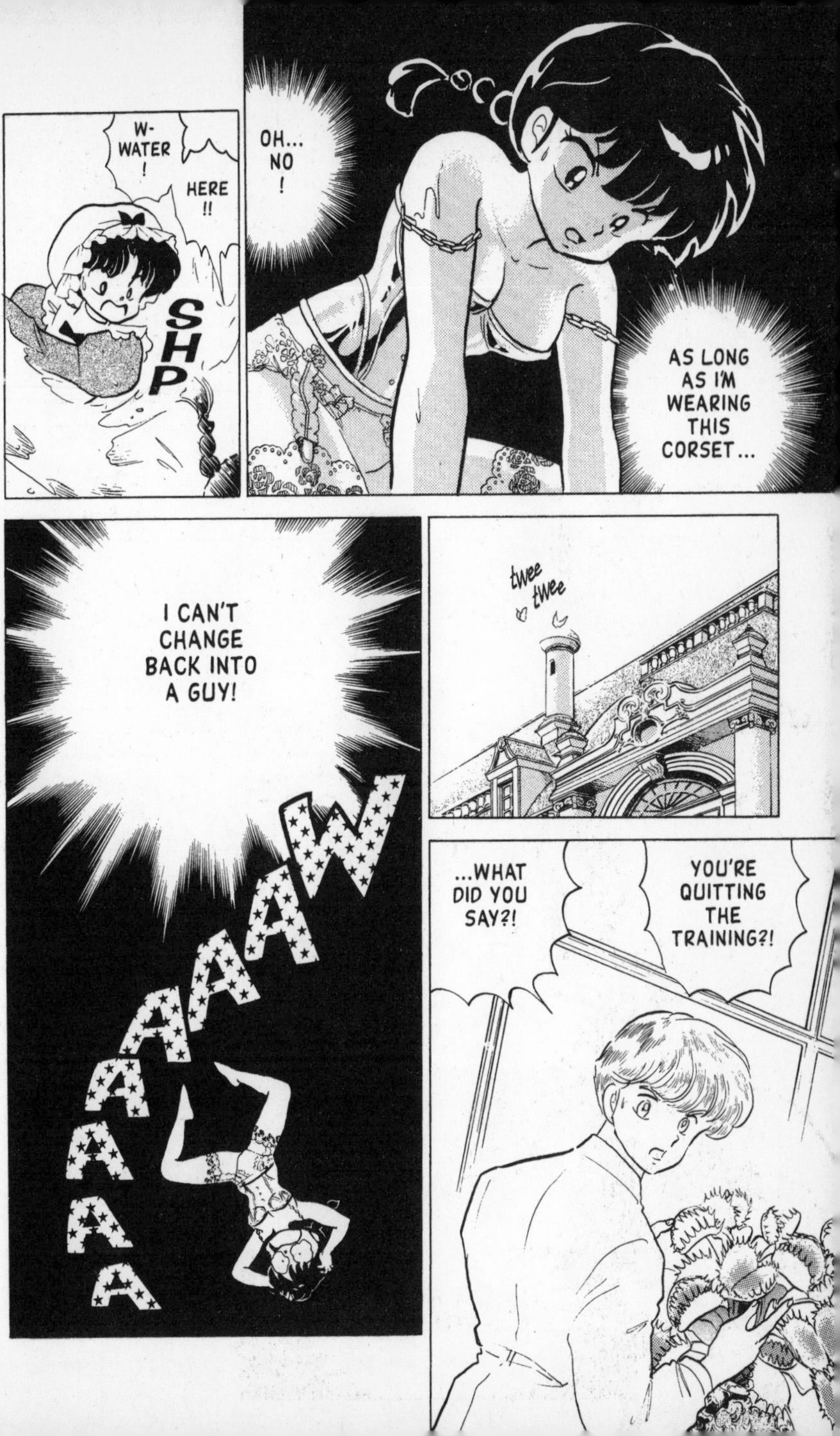
W-WATER!
HERE!!
SHP
OH... NO!
AS LONG AS I'M WEARING THIS CORSET...
I CAN'T CHANGE BACK INTO A GUY!
AAAAAAAW
twee twee
...WHAT DID YOU SAY?!
YOU'RE QUITTING THE TRAINING?!

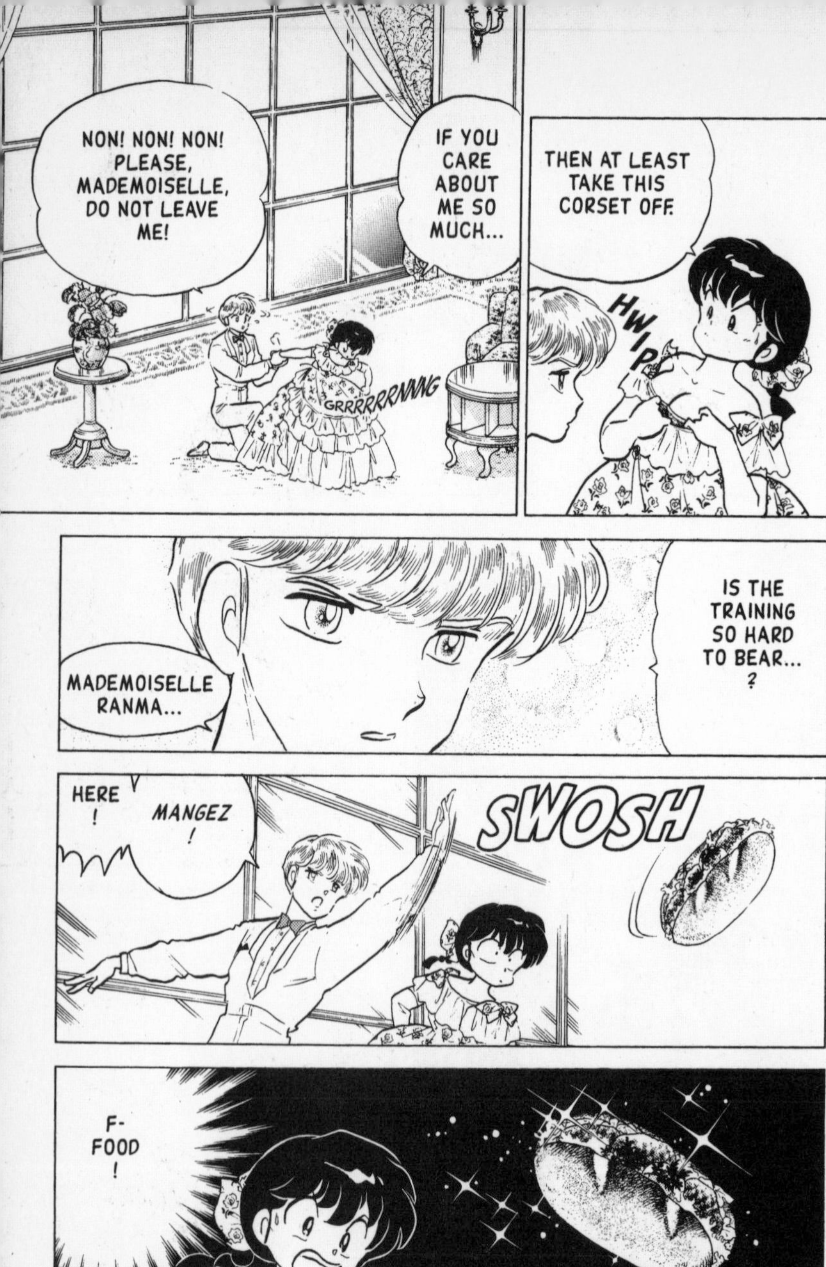
NON! NON! NON! PLEASE, MADEMOISELLE, DO NOT LEAVE ME!
GRRRRRRNNNG
IF YOU CARE ABOUT ME SO MUCH...
THEN AT LEAST TAKE THIS CORSET OFF.
HWIP
MADEMOISELLE RANMA...
IS THE TRAINING SO HARD TO BEAR...?
HERE! MANGEZ!
SWOSH
F-FOOD!

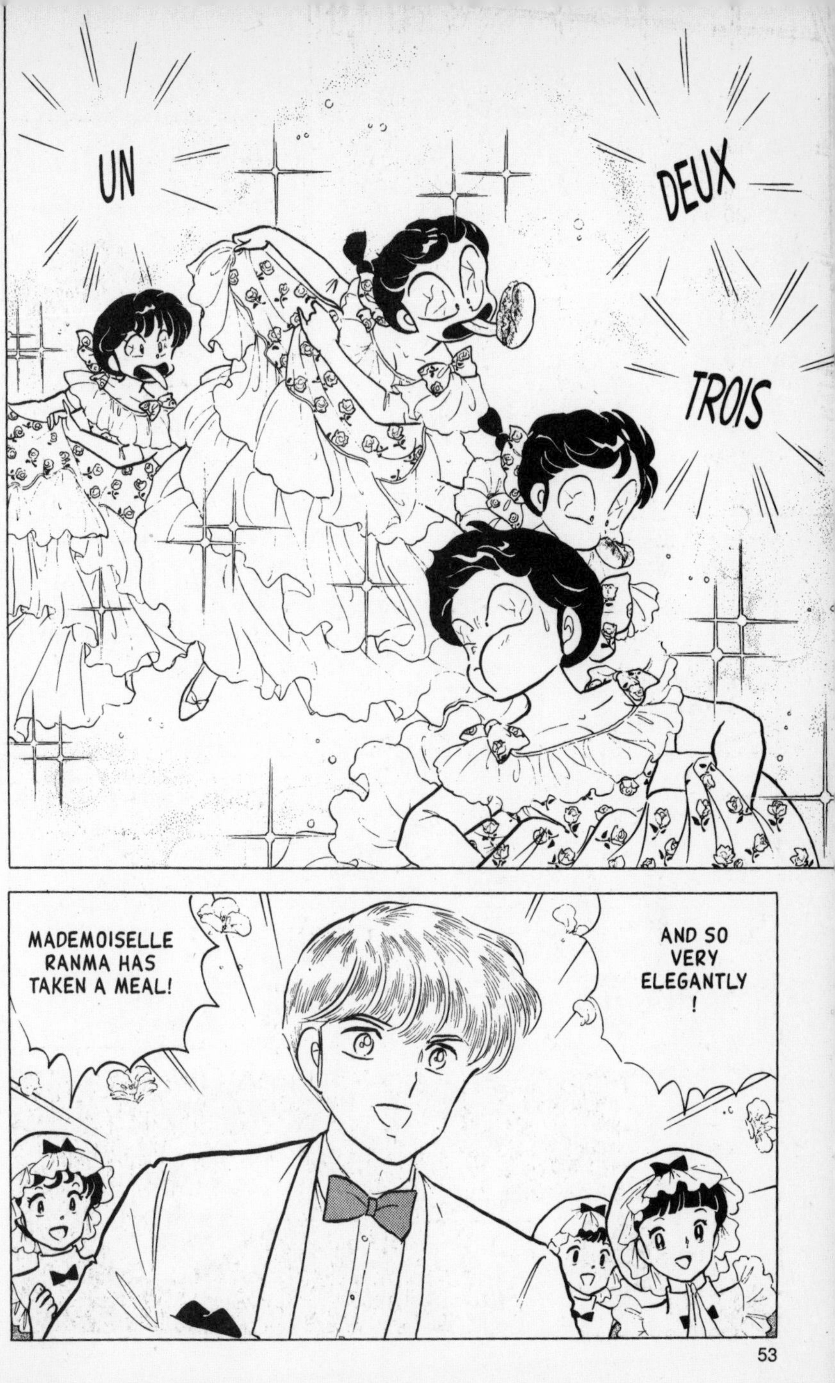
UN
DEUX
TROIS
MADEMOISELLE RANMA HAS TAKEN A MEAL!
AND SO VERY ELEGANTLY!

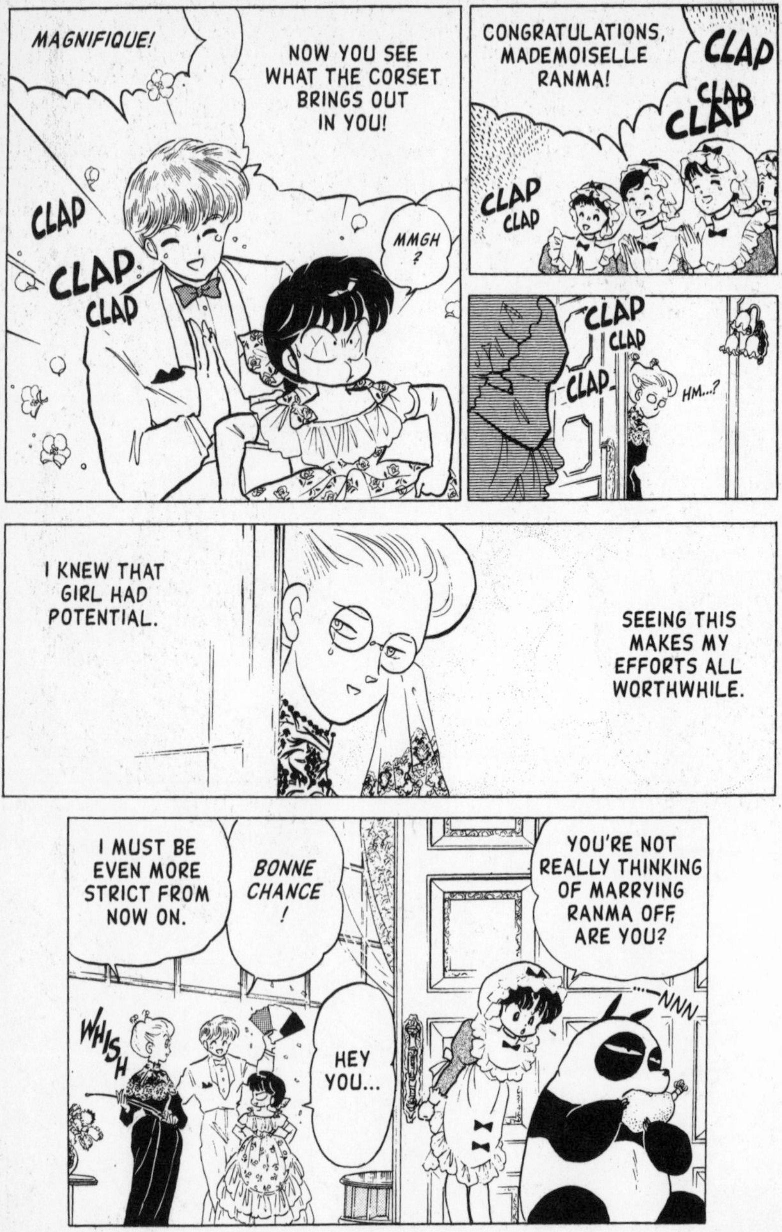
MAGNIFIQUE!
NOW YOU SEE WHAT THE CORSET BRINGS OUT IN YOU!
CLAP
CLAP
CLAP
MMGH ?
CONGRATULATIONS, MADEMOISELLE RANMA!
CLAP
CLAP
CLAP
CLAP
CLAP
CLAP
CLAP
CLAP
HM...?
I KNEW THAT GIRL HAD POTENTIAL.
SEEING THIS MAKES MY EFFORTS ALL WORTHWHILE.
I MUST BE EVEN MORE STRICT FROM NOW ON.
BONNE CHANCE !
WHISH
HEY YOU...
YOU'RE NOT REALLY THINKING OF MARRYING RANMA OFF, ARE YOU?
...NNN

Part 4
LEKARATÉ DE
FOIE GRAS

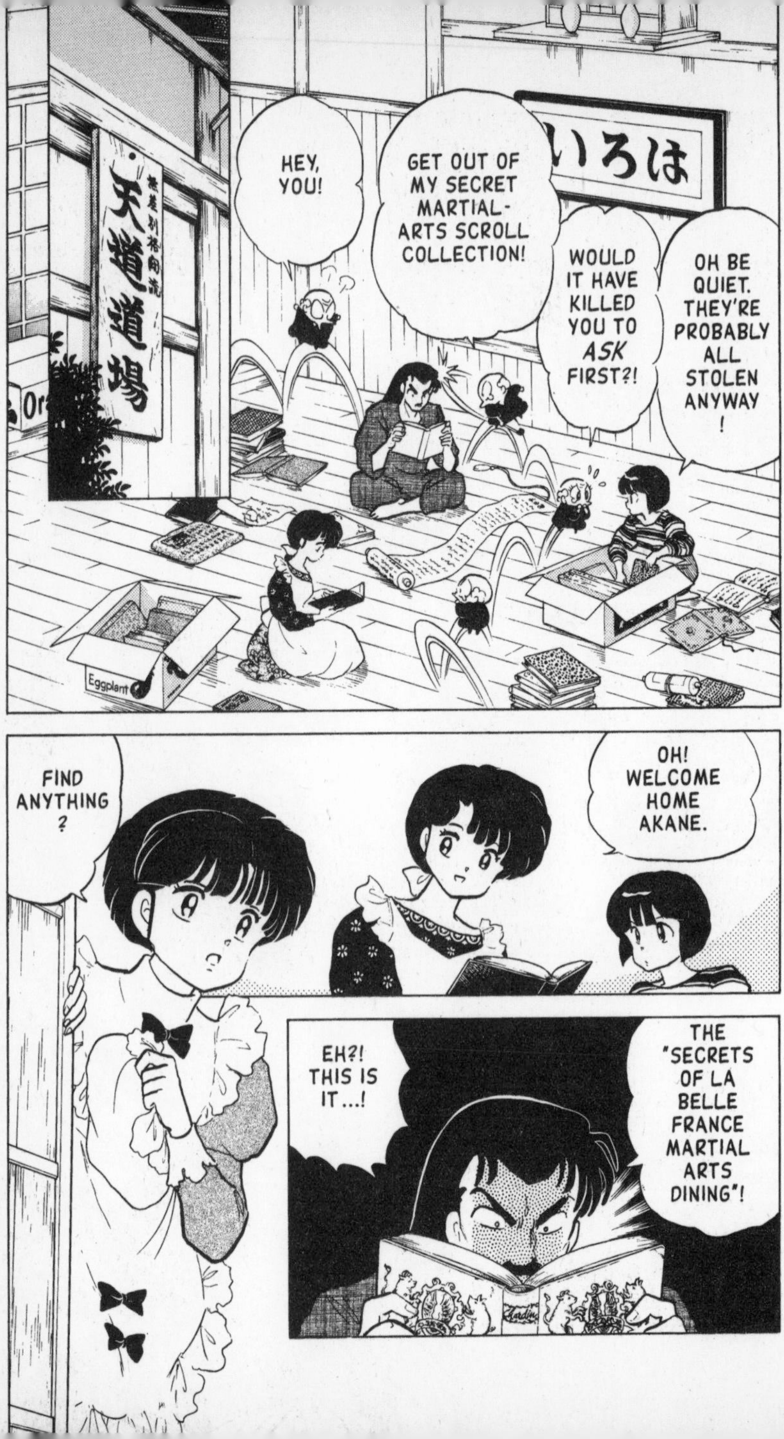
天道道場
いろは
HEY, YOU!
GET OUT OF MY SECRET MARTIAL-ARTS SCROLL COLLECTION!
WOULD IT HAVE KILLED YOU TO ASK FIRST?!
OH BE QUIET. THEY'RE PROBABLY ALL STOLEN ANYWAY!
Eggplant
FIND ANYTHING?
OH! WELCOME HOME AKANE.
EH?! THIS IS IT...!
THE "SECRETS OF LA BELLE FRANCE MARTIAL ARTS DINING"!

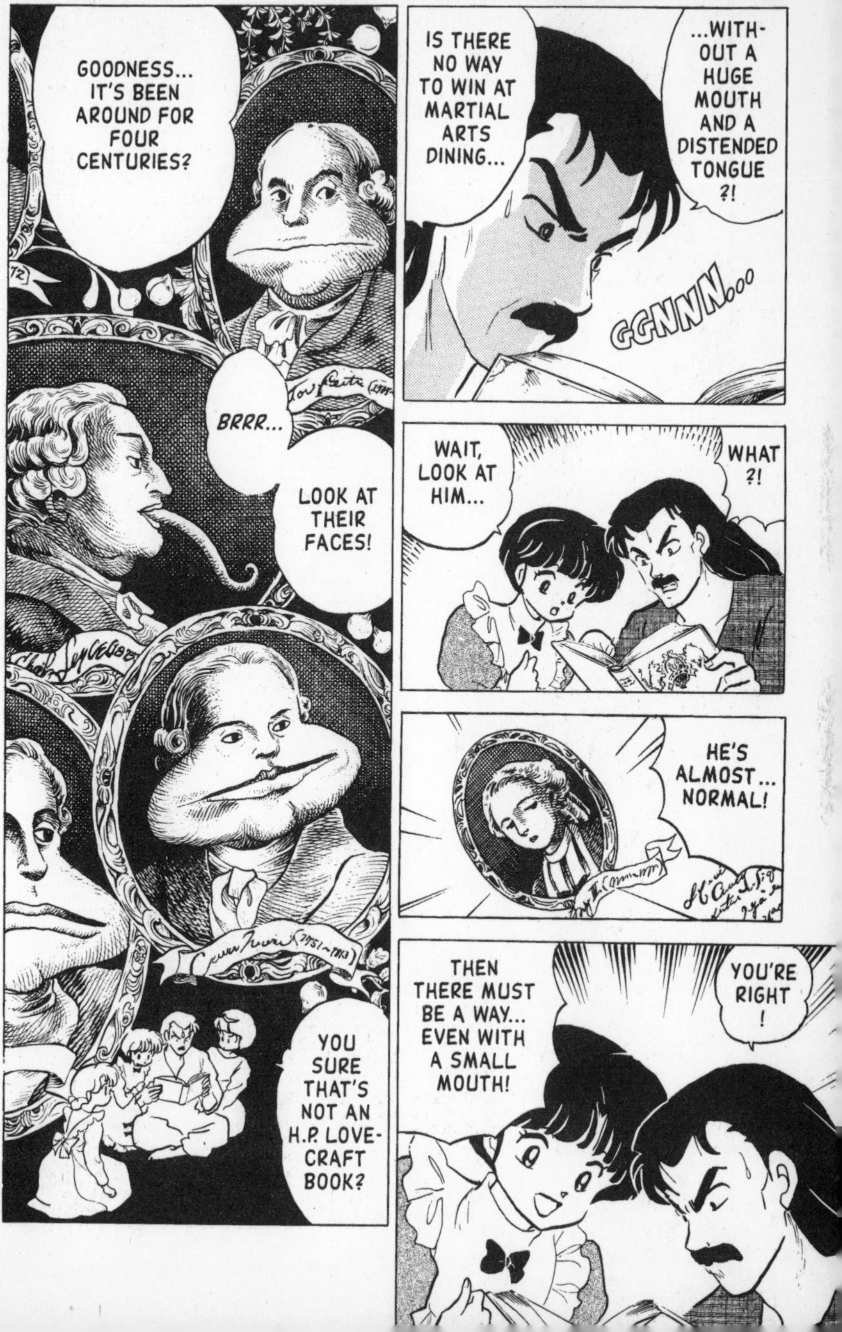
GOODNESS... IT'S BEEN AROUND FOR FOUR CENTURIES?
BRRR...
LOOK AT THEIR FACES!
YOU SURE THAT'S NOT AN H.P. LOVECRAFT BOOK?
IS THERE NO WAY TO WIN AT MARTIAL ARTS DINING...
...WITHOUT A HUGE MOUTH AND A DISTENDED TONGUE ?!
GGNNNooo
WAIT, LOOK AT HIM...
WHAT ?!
HE'S ALMOST... NORMAL!
THEN THERE MUST BE A WAY... EVEN WITH A SMALL MOUTH!
YOU'RE RIGHT !

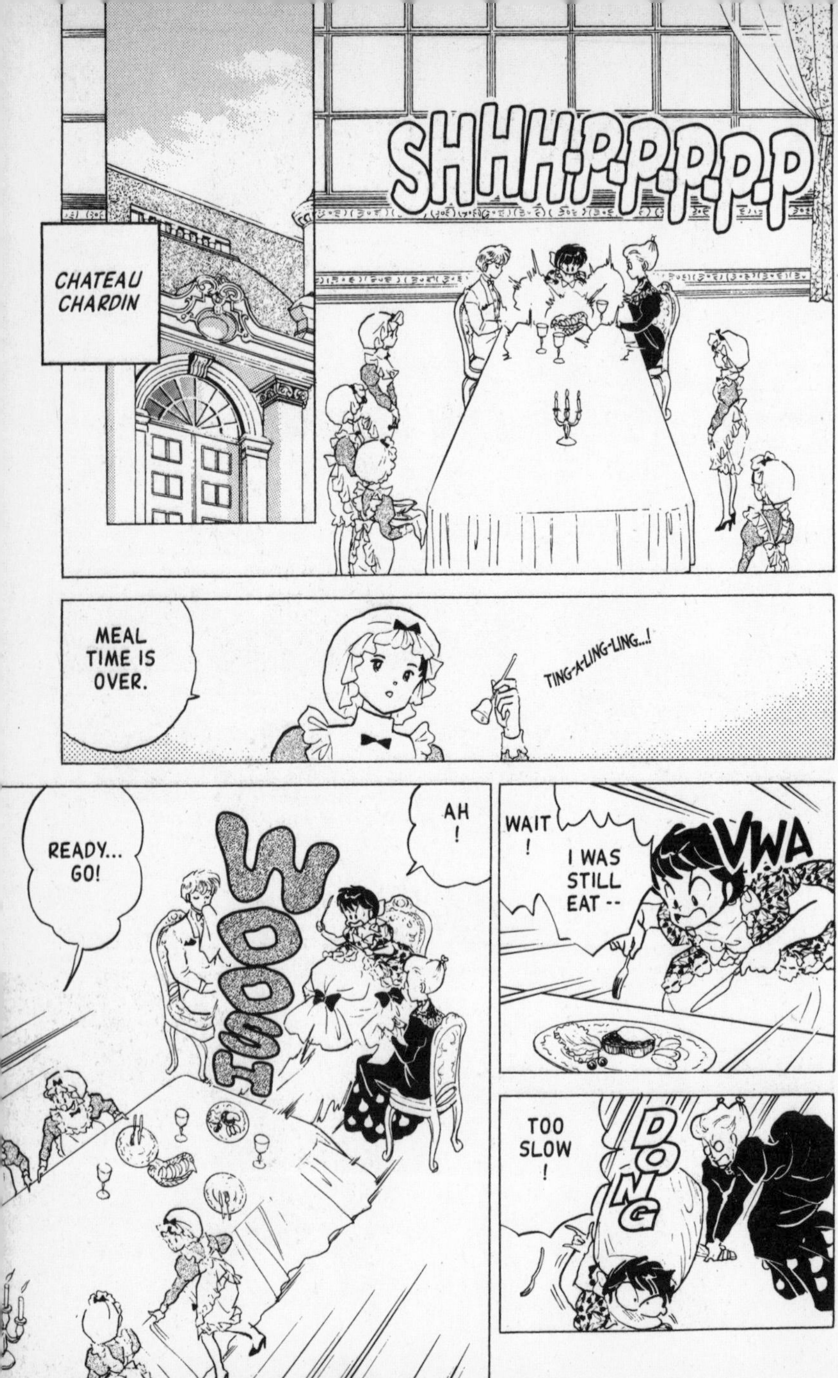
CHATEAU CHARDIN
SHHH-P-P-P-P-P
MEAL TIME IS OVER.
TING-A-LING-LING...!
READY... GO!
WOOSH
AH!
WAIT!
I WAS STILL EAT --
VWA
TOO SLOW!
DONG

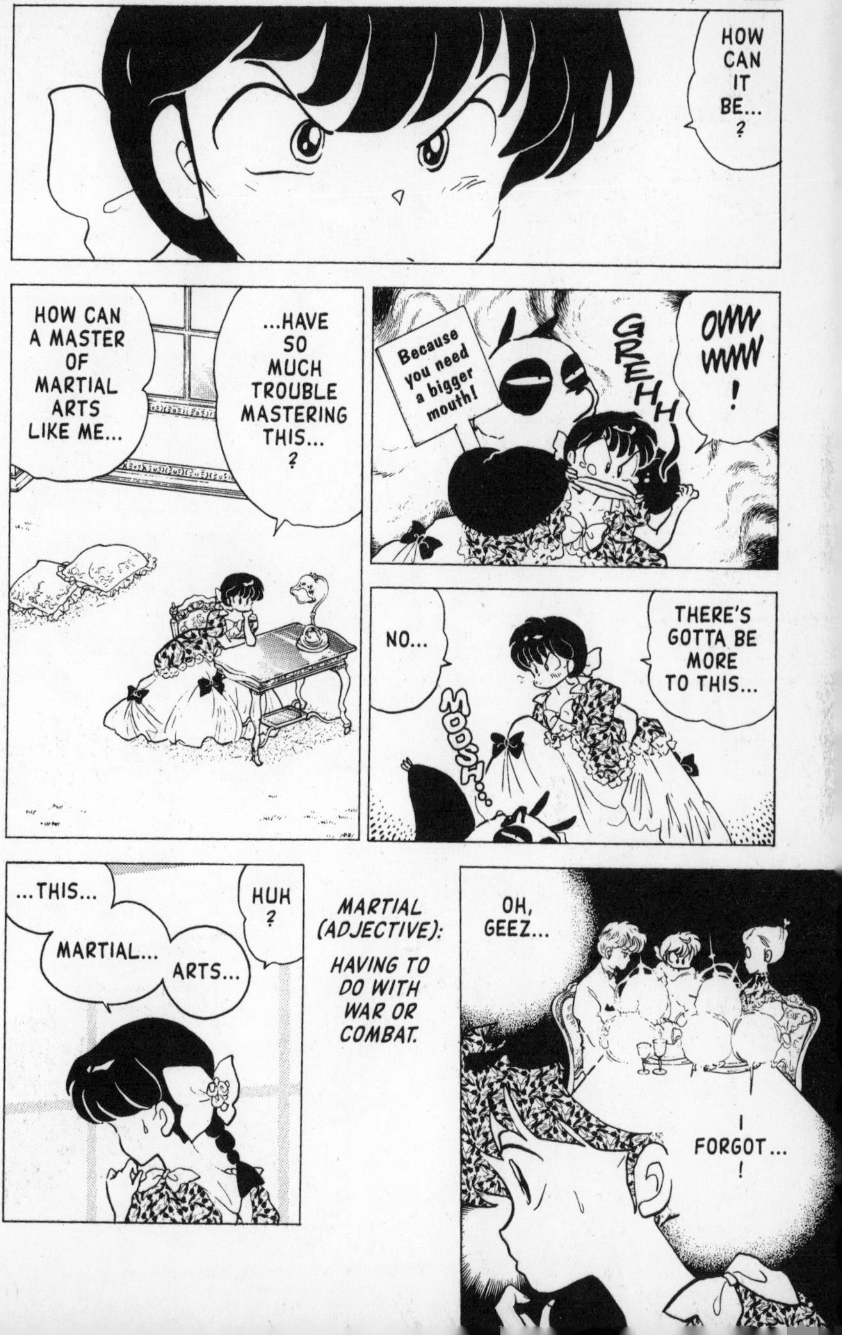
HOW CAN IT BE...?
HOW CAN A MASTER OF MARTIAL ARTS LIKE ME...
...HAVE SO MUCH TROUBLE MASTERING THIS...?
Because you need a bigger mouth!
GREHH
OWWWWW!
NO...
THERE'S GOTTA BE MORE TO THIS...
MOOSH...
...THIS...
HUH?
MARTIAL...
ARTS...
MARTIAL (ADJECTIVE):
HAVING TO DO WITH WAR OR COMBAT.
OH, GEEZ...
I FORGOT...!

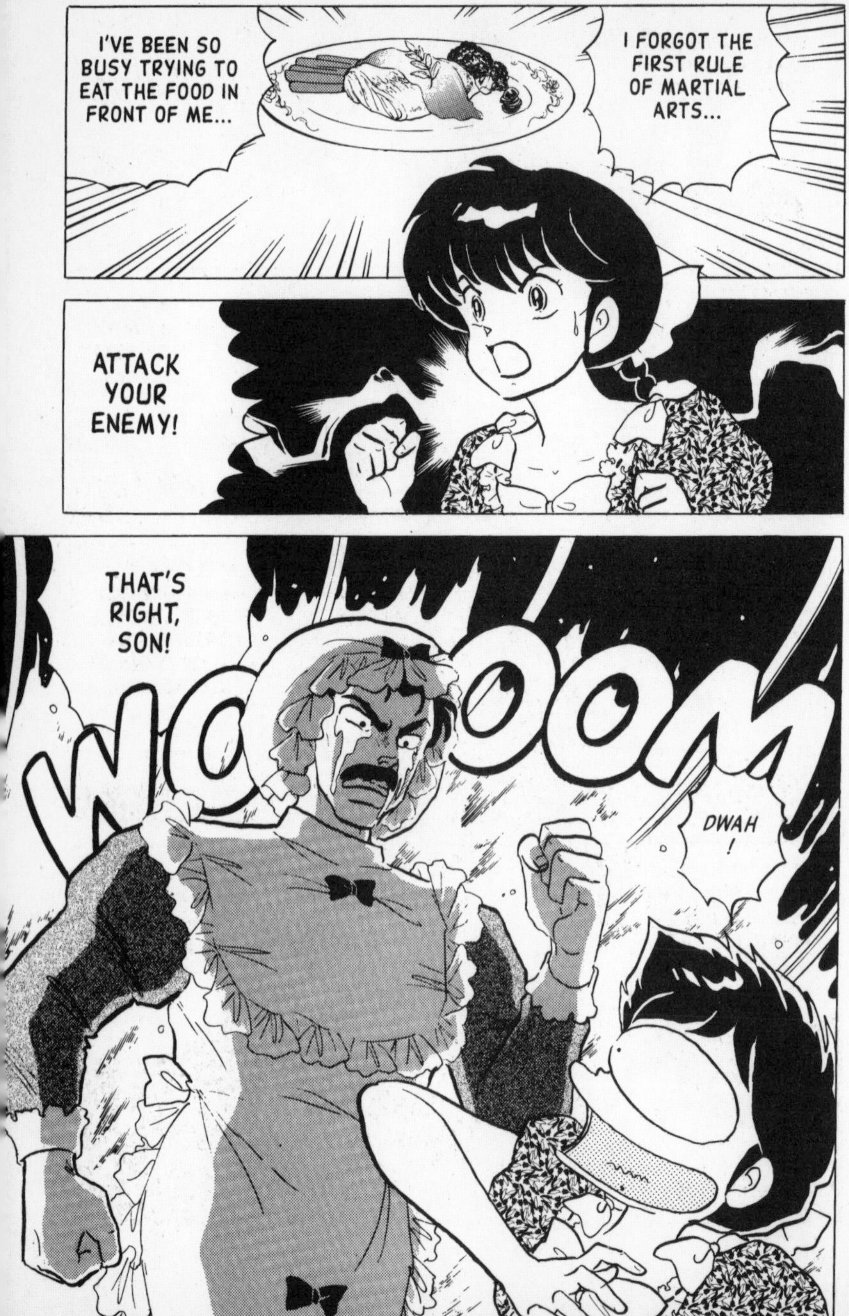
I'VE BEEN SO BUSY TRYING TO EAT THE FOOD IN FRONT OF ME...
I FORGOT THE FIRST RULE OF MARTIAL ARTS...
ATTACK YOUR ENEMY!
THAT'S RIGHT, SON!
WOOOOM
DWAH!

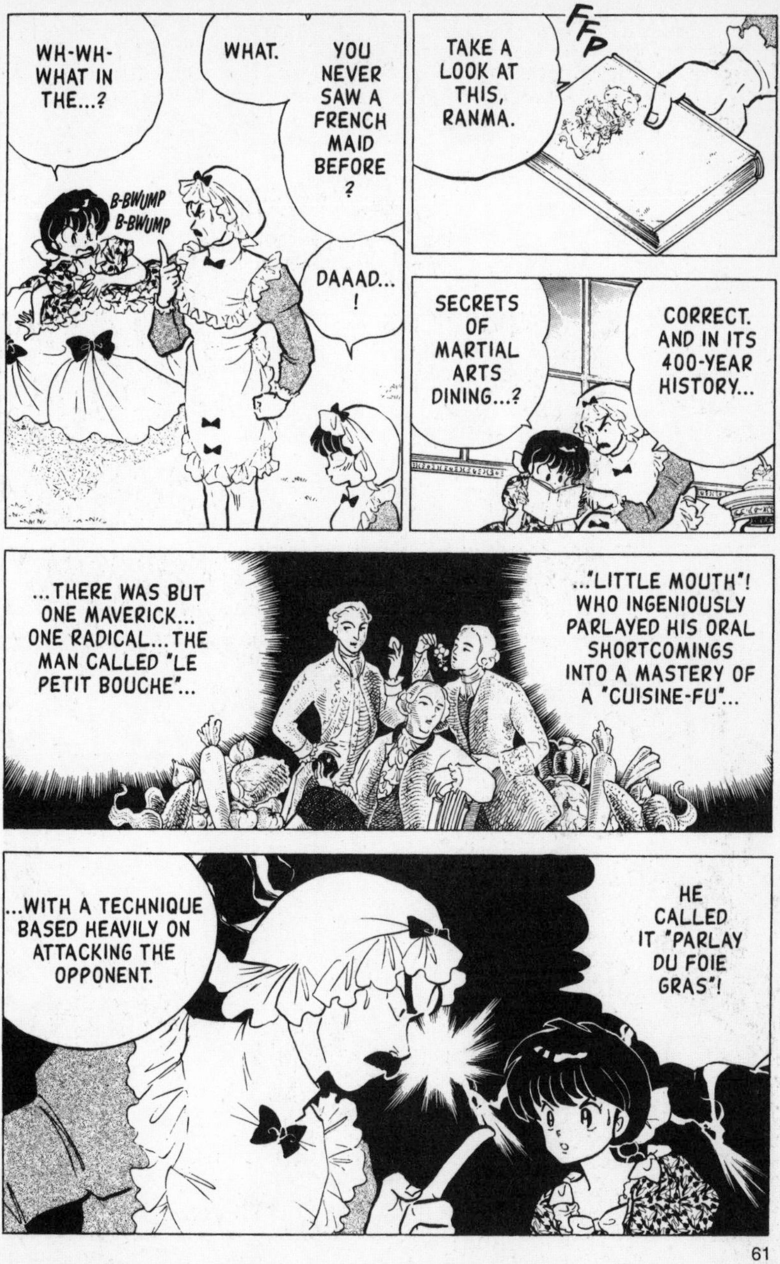
WH-WH-WHAT IN THE...?
B-BWUMP B-BWUMP
WHAT.
YOU NEVER SAW A FRENCH MAID BEFORE?
DAAAD...!
TAKE A LOOK AT THIS, RANMA.
FFP
SECRETS OF MARTIAL ARTS DINING...?
CORRECT. AND IN ITS 400-YEAR HISTORY...
...THERE WAS BUT ONE MAVERICK... ONE RADICAL...THE MAN CALLED "LE PETIT BOUCHE"...
..."LITTLE MOUTH"! WHO INGENIOUSLY PARLAYED HIS ORAL SHORTCOMINGS INTO A MASTERY OF A "CUISINE-FU"...
...WITH A TECHNIQUE BASED HEAVILY ON ATTACKING THE OPPONENT.
HE CALLED IT "PARLAY DU FOIE GRAS"!

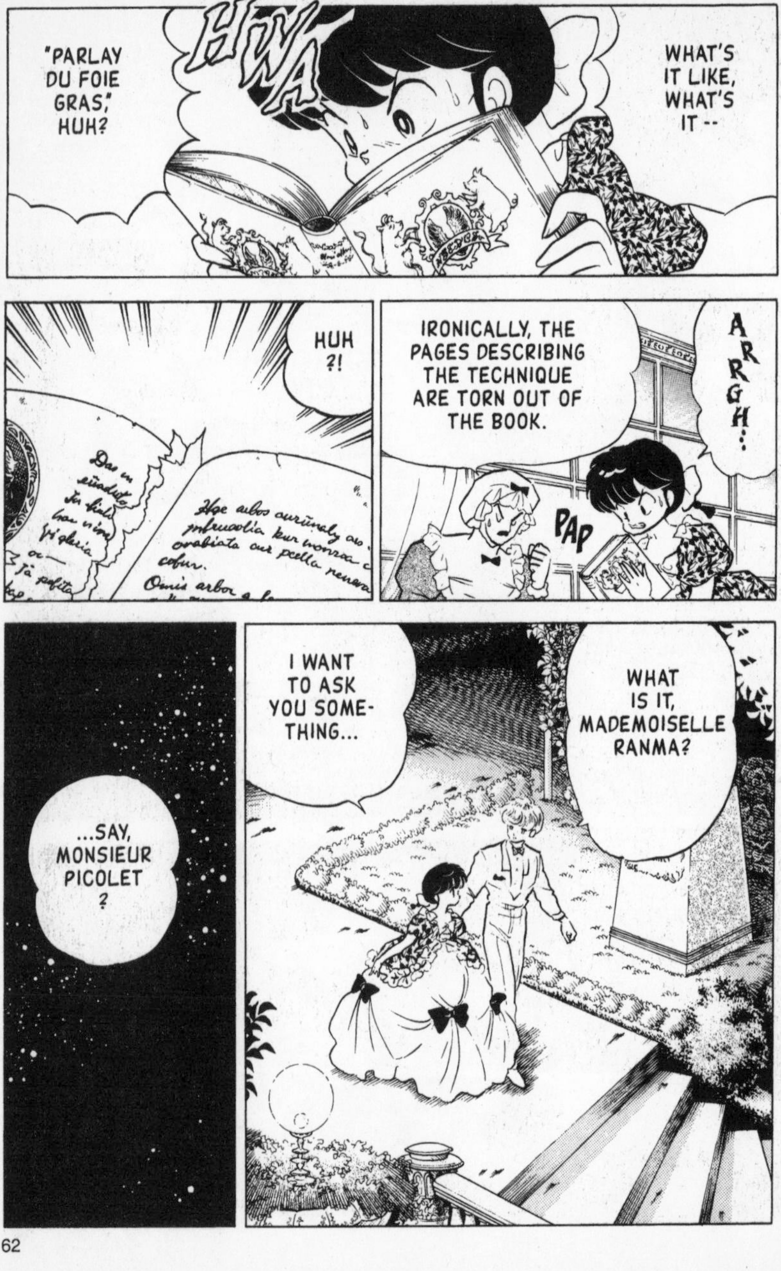
"PARLAY DU FOIE GRAS," HUH?
HWA
WHAT'S IT LIKE, WHAT'S IT --
HUH ?!
IRONICALLY, THE PAGES DESCRIBING THE TECHNIQUE ARE TORN OUT OF THE BOOK.
ARRGH!
PAP
...SAY, MONSIEUR PICOLET ?
I WANT TO ASK YOU SOMETHING...
WHAT IS IT, MADEMOISELLE RANMA?

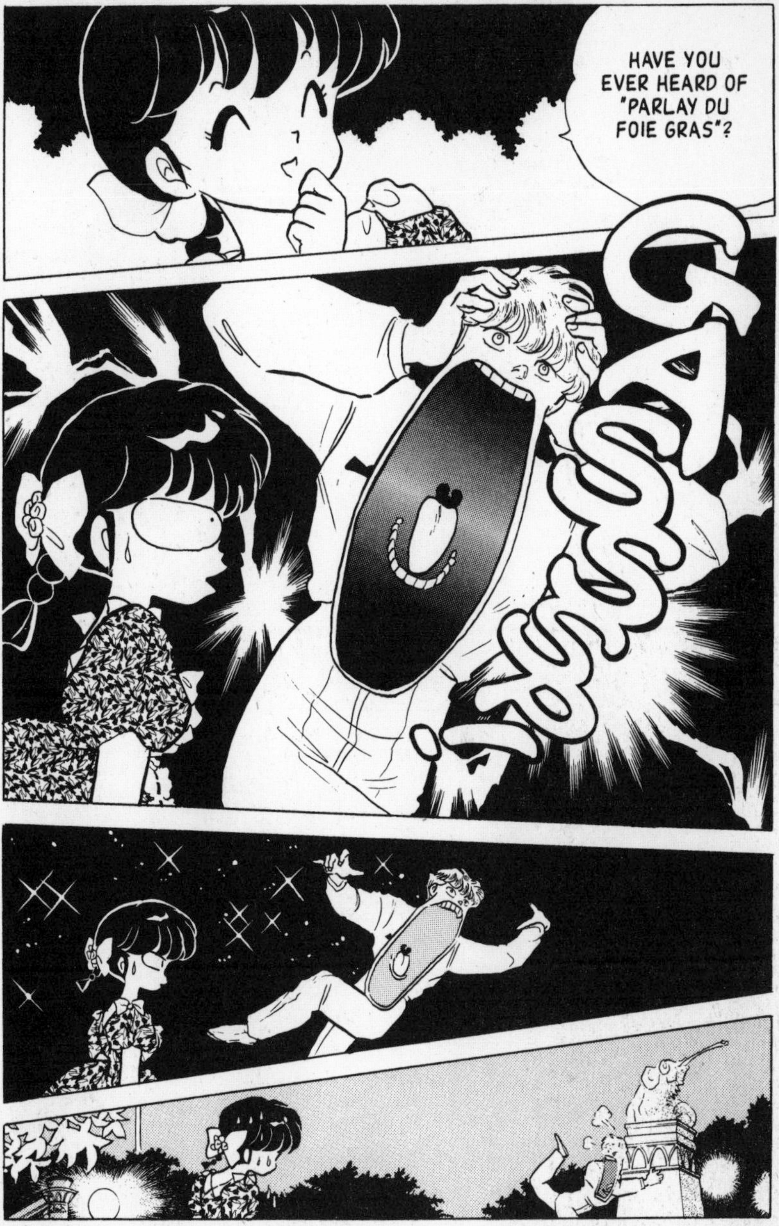
HAVE YOU EVER HEARD OF "PARLAY DU FOIE GRAS"?
GASHUP!

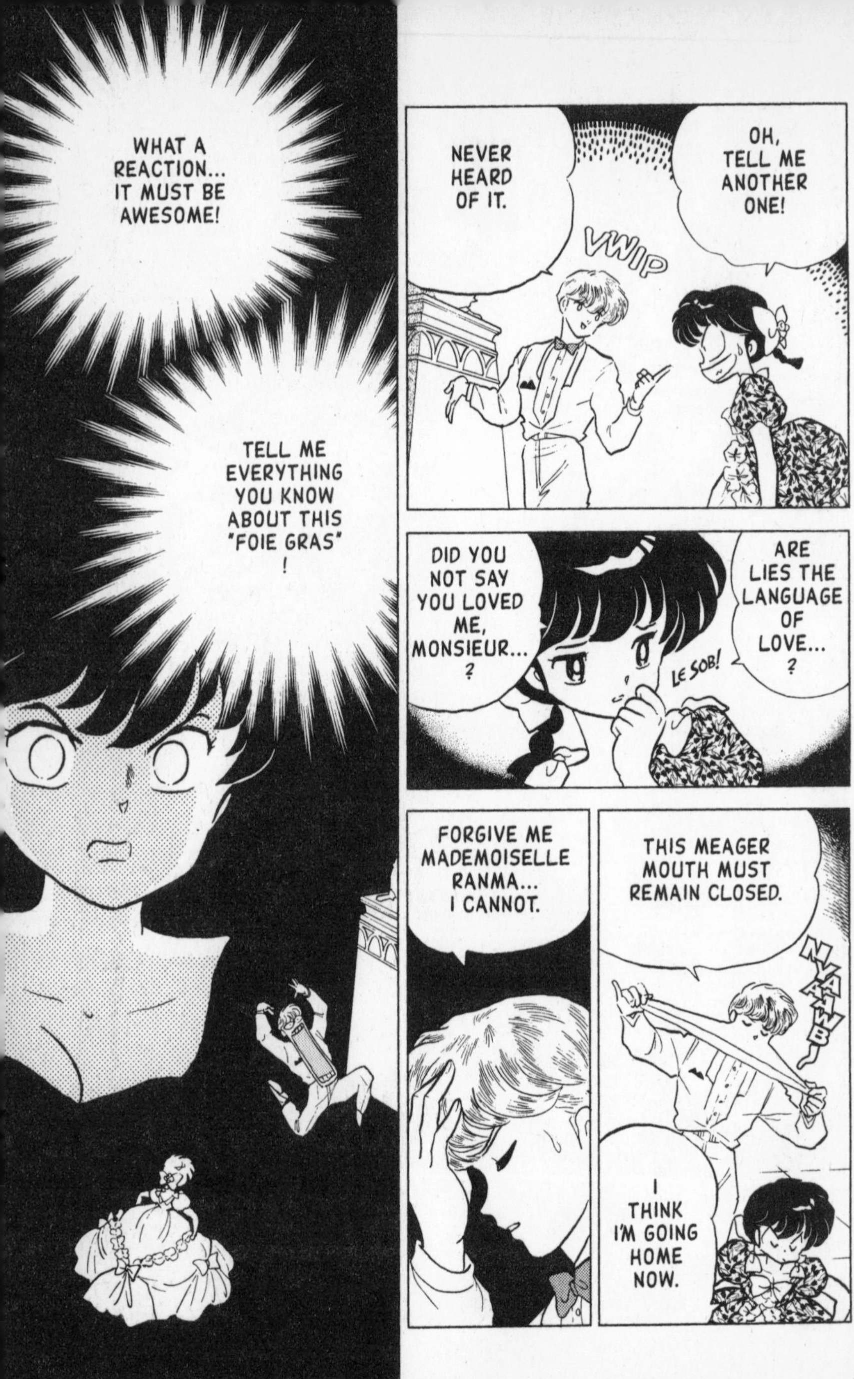
WHAT A REACTION... IT MUST BE AWESOME!
TELL ME EVERYTHING YOU KNOW ABOUT THIS "FOIE GRAS" !
NEVER HEARD OF IT.
VWIP
OH, TELL ME ANOTHER ONE!
DID YOU NOT SAY YOU LOVED ME, MONSIEUR... ?
LE SOB!
ARE LIES THE LANGUAGE OF LOVE... ?
FORGIVE ME MADEMOISELLE RANMA... I CANNOT.
THIS MEAGER MOUTH MUST REMAIN CLOSED.
NYAAWB
I THINK I'M GOING HOME NOW.

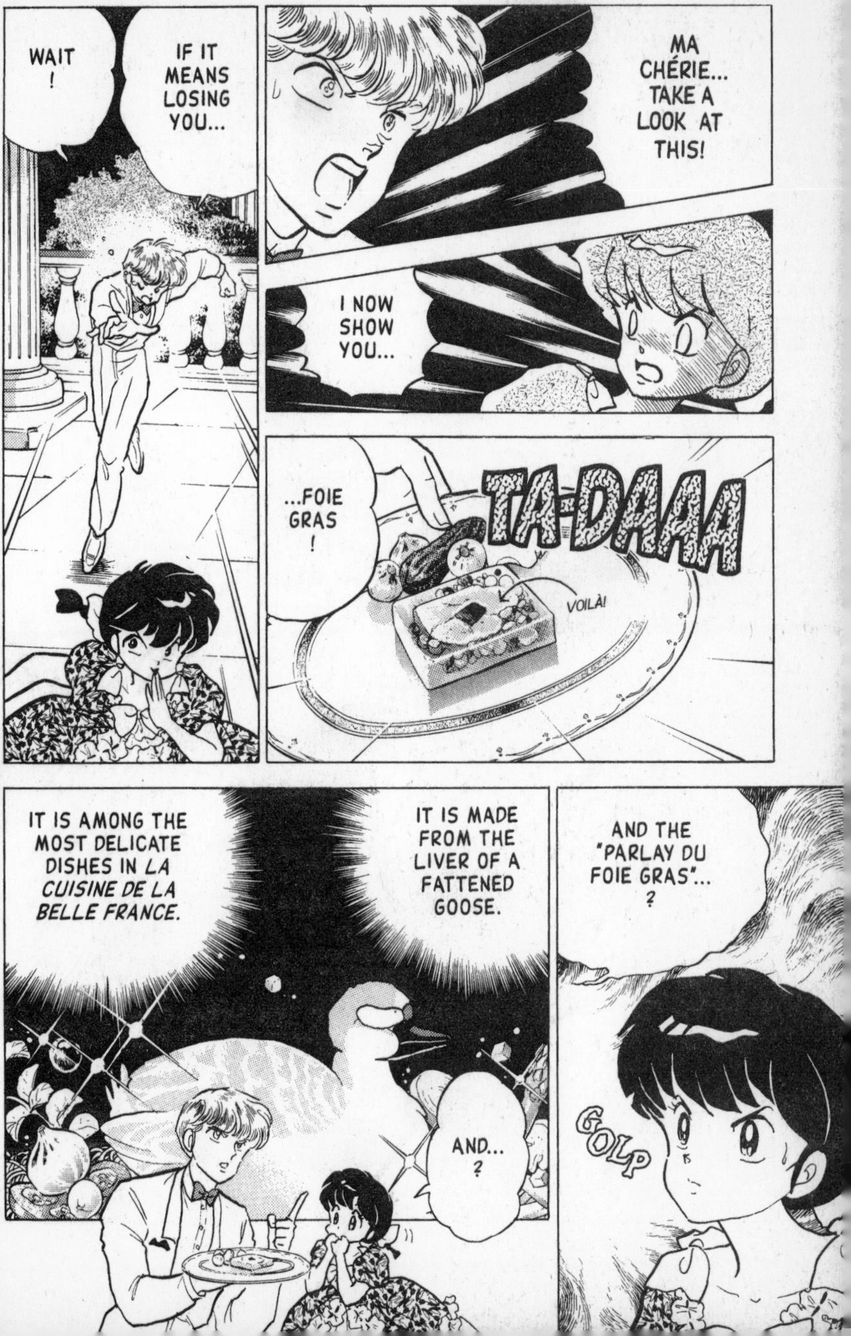
WAIT!
IF IT MEANS LOSING YOU...
MA CHÉRIE... TAKE A LOOK AT THIS!
I NOW SHOW YOU...
...FOIE GRAS!
TA-DAAA
VOILÀ!
IT IS AMONG THE MOST DELICATE DISHES IN *LA CUISINE DE LA BELLE FRANCE.*
IT IS MADE FROM THE LIVER OF A FATTENED GOOSE.
AND...?
AND THE "PARLAY DU FOIE GRAS"...?
GOLP

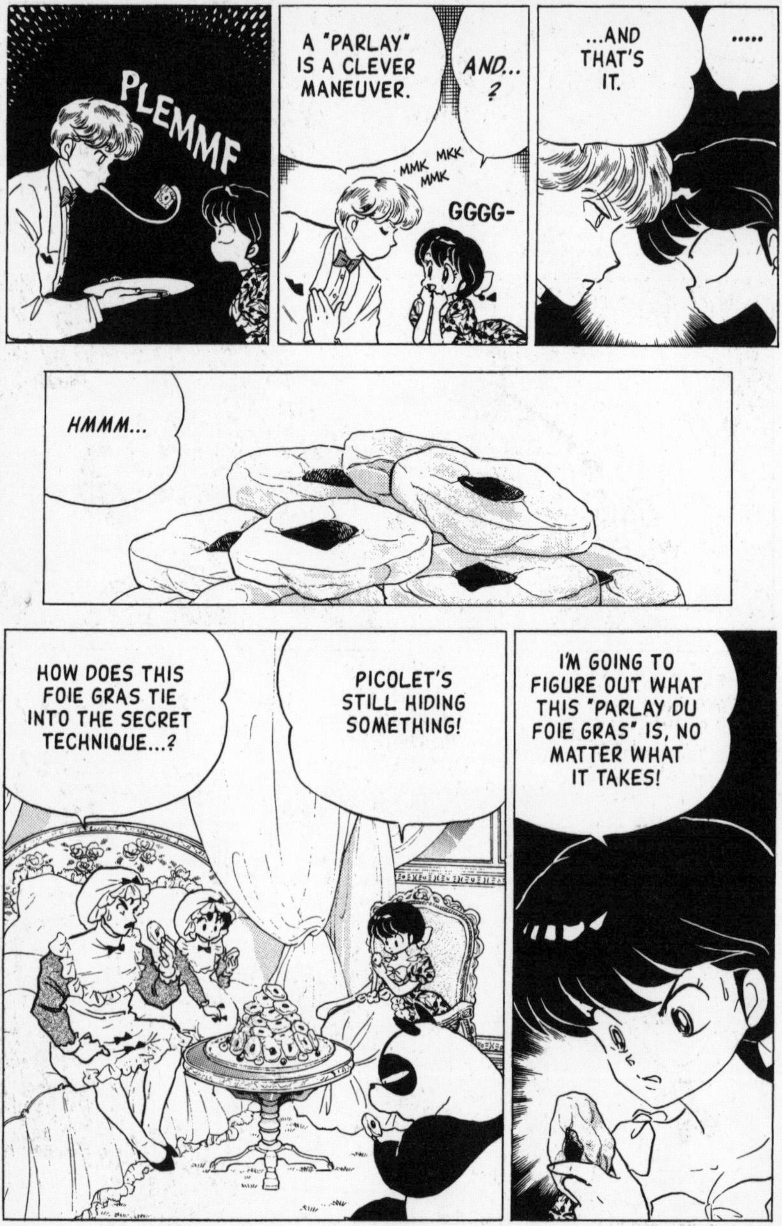
PLEMMF
A "PARLAY" IS A CLEVER MANEUVER.
AND...?
MMK MKK MMK
GGGG-
...AND THAT'S IT.
.....
HMMM...
HOW DOES THIS FOIE GRAS TIE INTO THE SECRET TECHNIQUE...?
PICOLET'S STILL HIDING SOMETHING!
I'M GOING TO FIGURE OUT WHAT THIS "PARLAY DU FOIE GRAS" IS, NO MATTER WHAT IT TAKES!

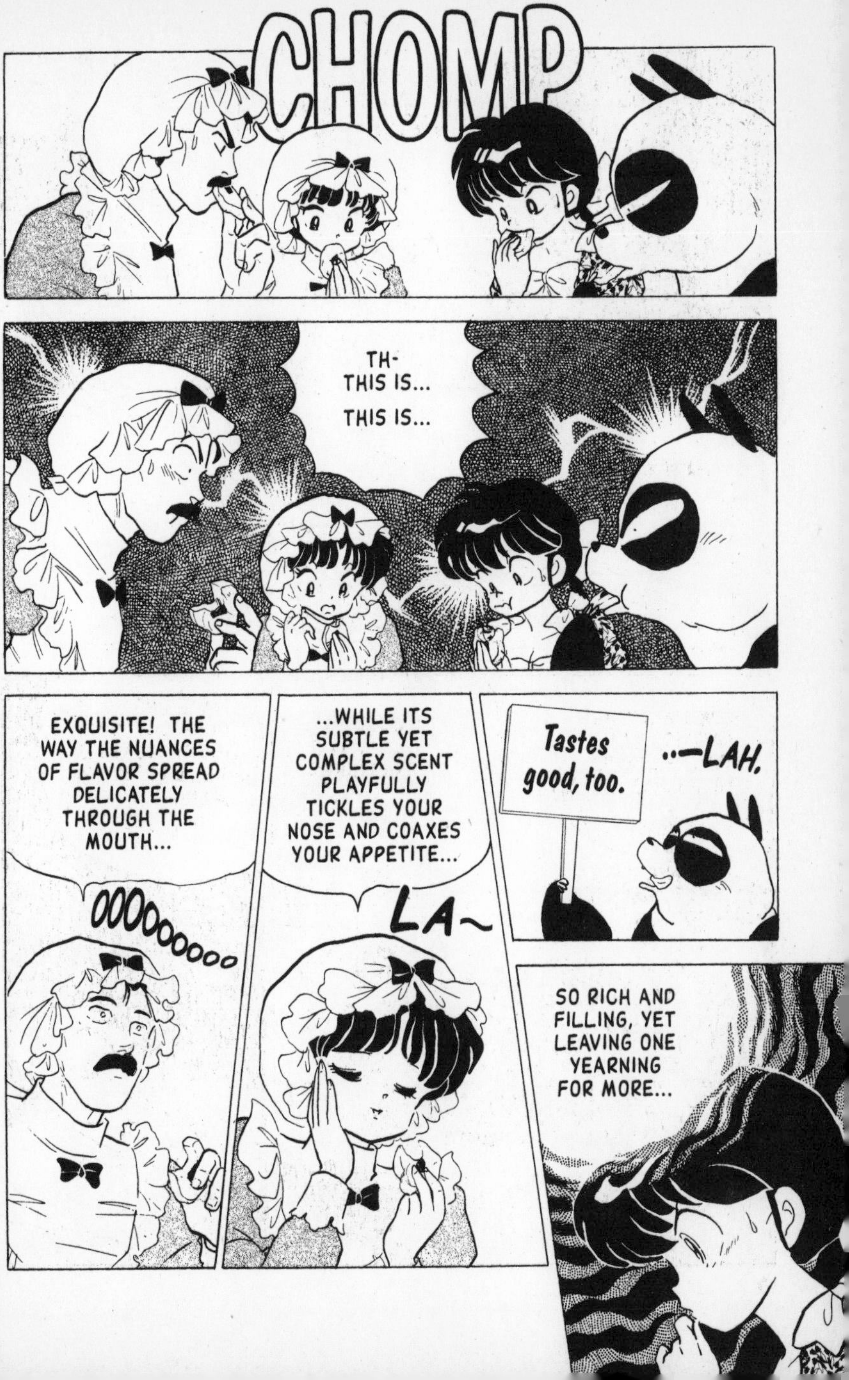
CHOMP
TH- THIS IS... THIS IS...
EXQUISITE! THE WAY THE NUANCES OF FLAVOR SPREAD DELICATELY THROUGH THE MOUTH...
OOOOOOOOOO
...WHILE ITS SUBTLE YET COMPLEX SCENT PLAYFULLY TICKLES YOUR NOSE AND COAXES YOUR APPETITE...
LA~
Tastes good, too.
...—LAH.
SO RICH AND FILLING, YET LEAVING ONE YEARNING FOR MORE...

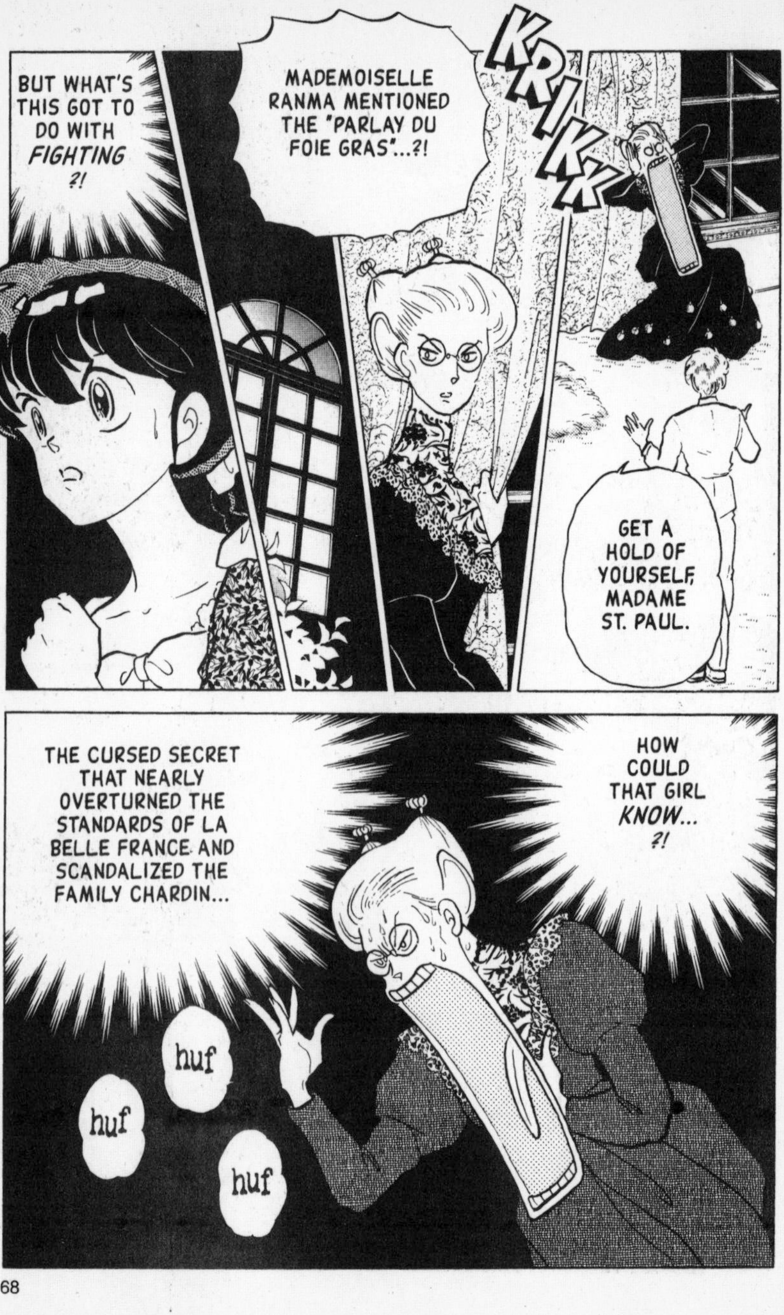
BUT WHAT'S THIS GOT TO DO WITH *FIGHTING* ?!
MADEMOISELLE RANMA MENTIONED THE "PARLAY DU FOIE GRAS"...?!
KRIKK
GET A HOLD OF YOURSELF, MADAME ST. PAUL.
THE CURSED SECRET THAT NEARLY OVERTURNED THE STANDARDS OF LA BELLE FRANCE AND SCANDALIZED THE FAMILY CHARDIN...
HOW COULD THAT GIRL *KNOW*... ?!
huf
huf
huf

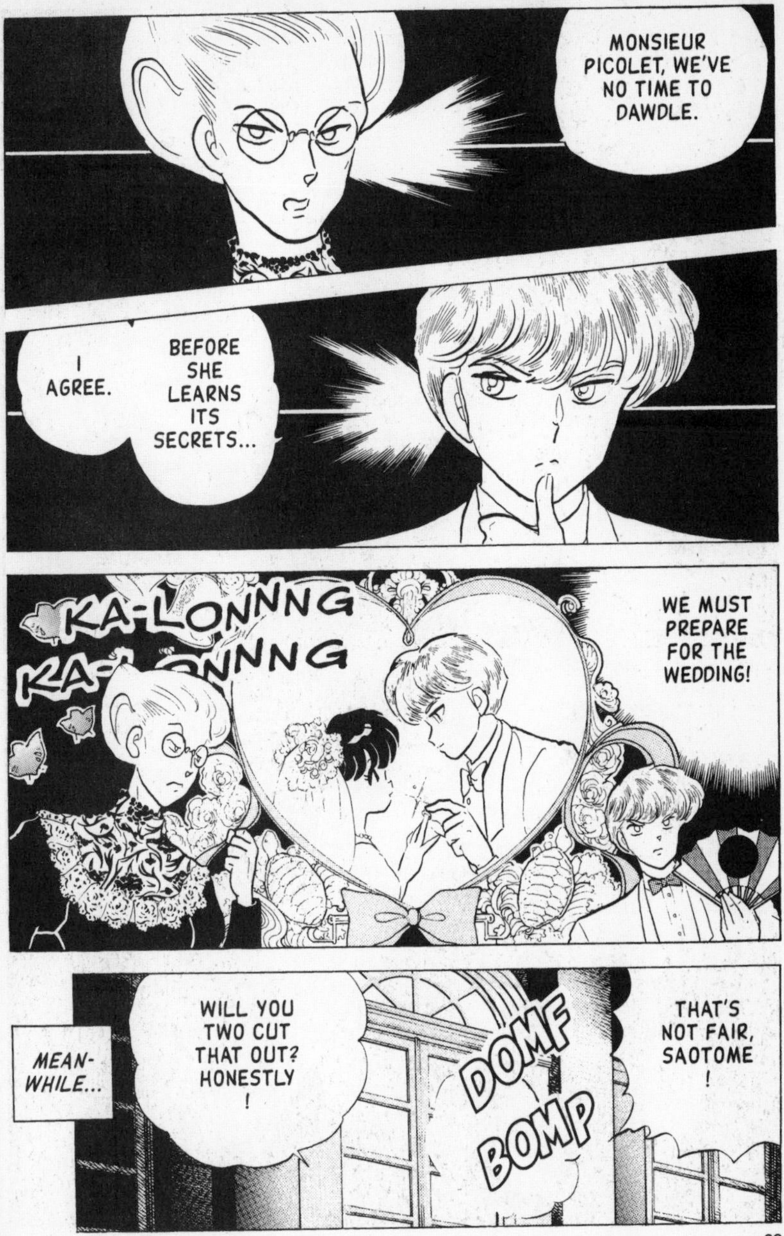
MONSIEUR PICOLET, WE'VE NO TIME TO DAWDLE.
I AGREE.
BEFORE SHE LEARNS ITS SECRETS...
KA-LONNNG
KA-LONNNG
WE MUST PREPARE FOR THE WEDDING!
MEAN-WHILE...
WILL YOU TWO CUT THAT OUT? HONESTLY!
DOMF
BOMP
THAT'S NOT FAIR, SAOTOME!

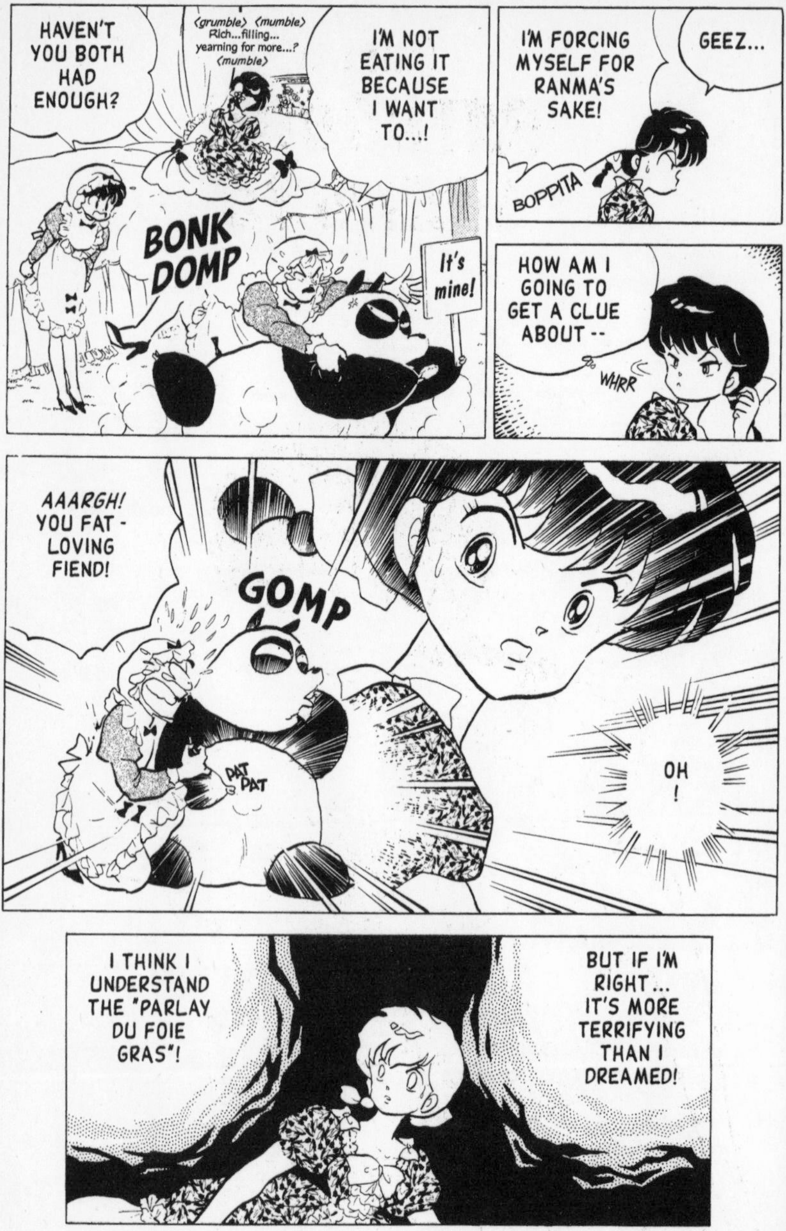

HAVEN'T YOU BOTH HAD ENOUGH?
<grumble> <mumble> Rich...filling... yearning for more...? <mumble>
I'M NOT EATING IT BECAUSE I WANT TO...!
BONK DOMP
It's mine!
I'M FORCING MYSELF FOR RANMA'S SAKE!
GEEZ...
BOPPITA
HOW AM I GOING TO GET A CLUE ABOUT --
WHRR
AAARGH! YOU FAT-LOVING FIEND!
GOMP
PAT PAT
OH!
I THINK I UNDERSTAND THE "PARLAY DU FOIE GRAS"!
BUT IF I'M RIGHT... IT'S MORE TERRIFYING THAN I DREAMED!

Part 5
BATHROOM TRAINING

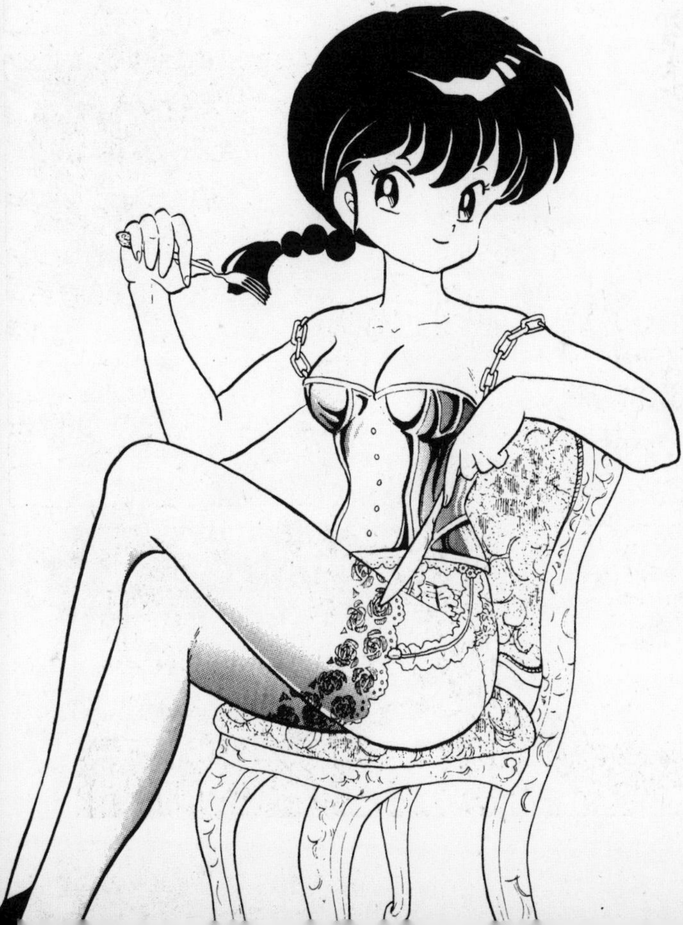

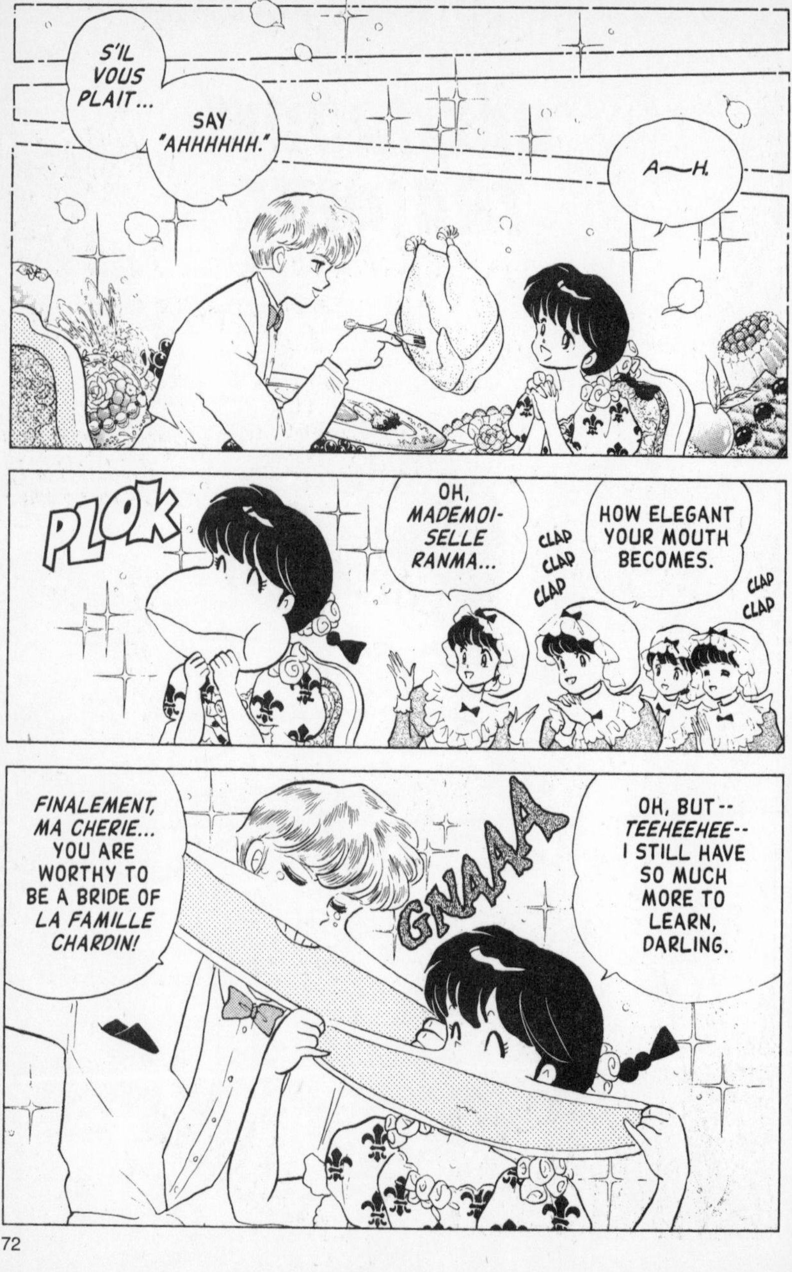
S'IL VOUS PLAIT...
SAY "AHHHHHH."
A—H.
PLOK
OH, MADEMOI-SELLE RANMA...
CLAP CLAP CLAP
HOW ELEGANT YOUR MOUTH BECOMES.
CLAP CLAP
FINALEMENT, MA CHERIE... YOU ARE WORTHY TO BE A BRIDE OF LA FAMILLE CHARDIN!
GNAAA
OH, BUT -- TEEHEEHEE -- I STILL HAVE SO MUCH MORE TO LEARN, DARLING.

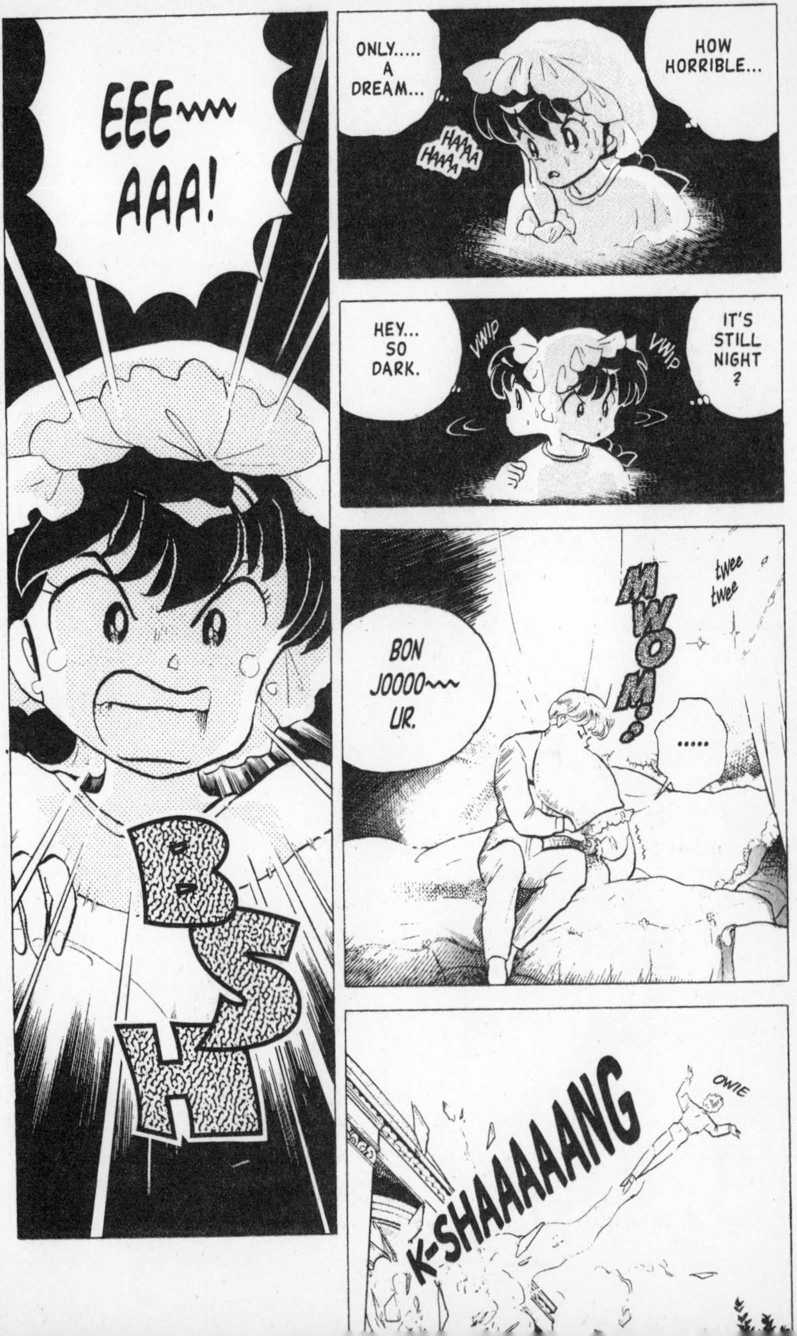
EEE~~ AAA!
BASH
ONLY..... A DREAM...
HAAAA HAAAA
HOW HORRIBLE...
HEY... SO DARK.
VWIP
VWIP
IT'S STILL NIGHT?
BON JOOOO~~ UR.
MWOM!
twee twee
.....
OWIE
K-SHAAAAANG

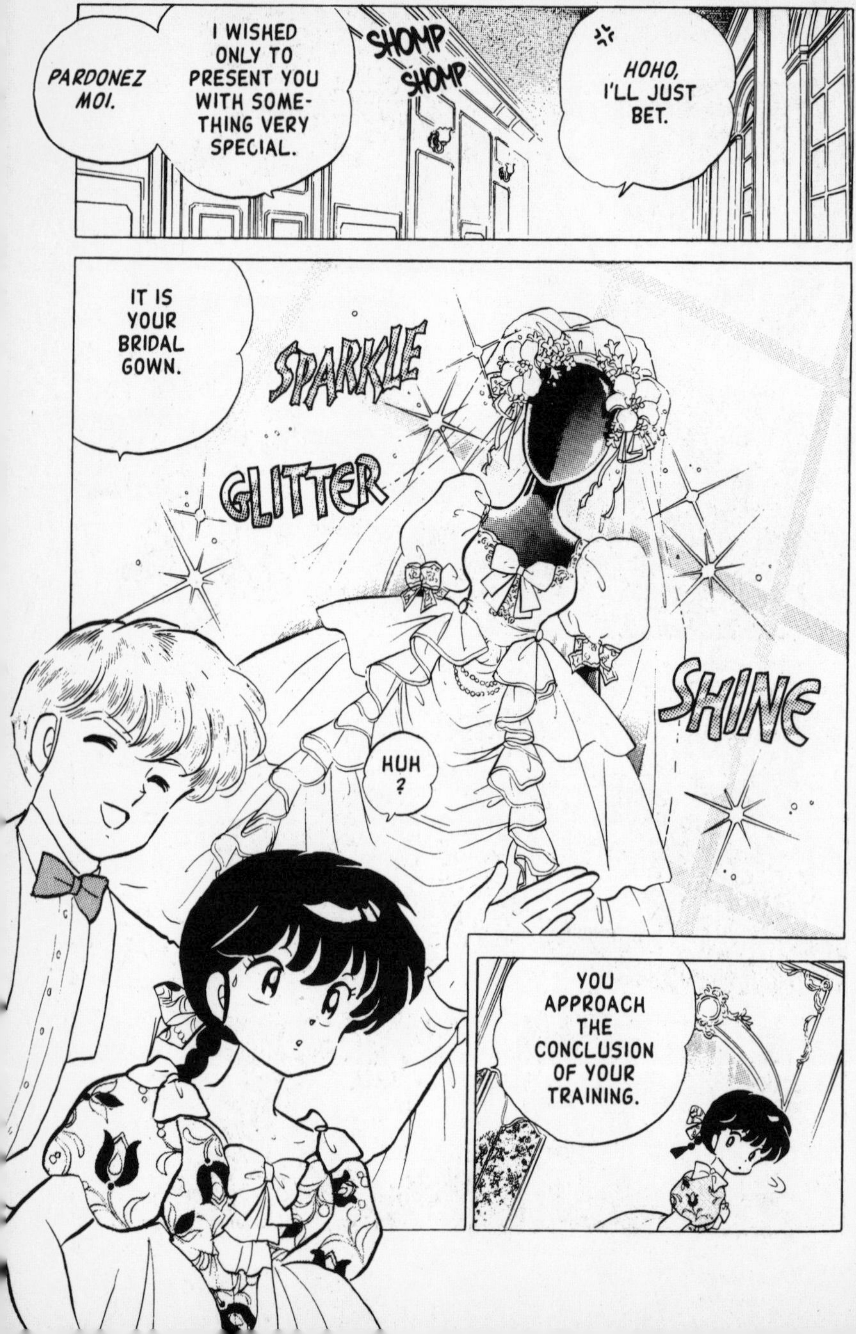
PARDONEZ MOI.
I WISHED ONLY TO PRESENT YOU WITH SOME-THING VERY SPECIAL.
SHOMP SHOMP
HOHO, I'LL JUST BET.
IT IS YOUR BRIDAL GOWN.
SPARKLE
GLITTER
SHINE
HUH?
YOU APPROACH THE CONCLUSION OF YOUR TRAINING.

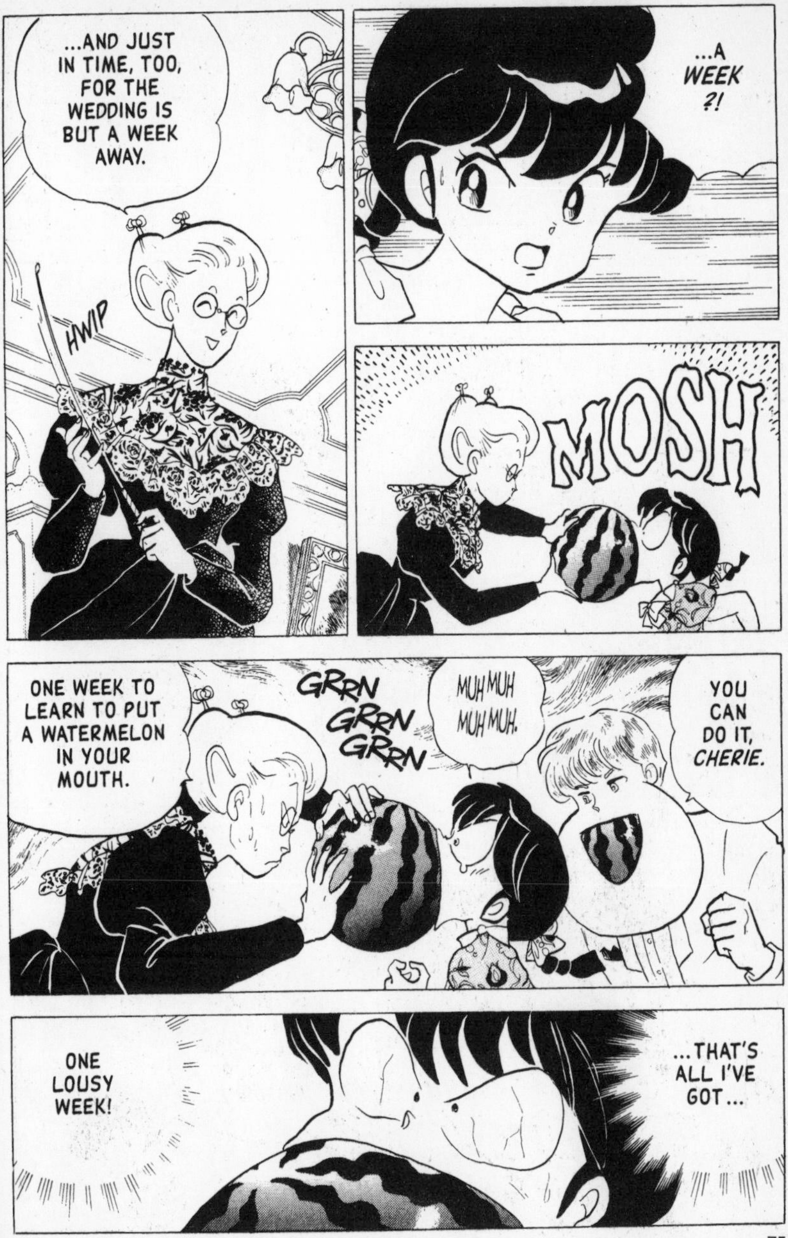
...AND JUST IN TIME, TOO, FOR THE WEDDING IS BUT A WEEK AWAY.
HWIP
...A WEEK ?!
MOSH
ONE WEEK TO LEARN TO PUT A WATERMELON IN YOUR MOUTH.
GRRN GRRN GRRN
MUH MUH MUH MUH.
YOU CAN DO IT, CHERIE.
ONE LOUSY WEEK!
...THAT'S ALL I'VE GOT...

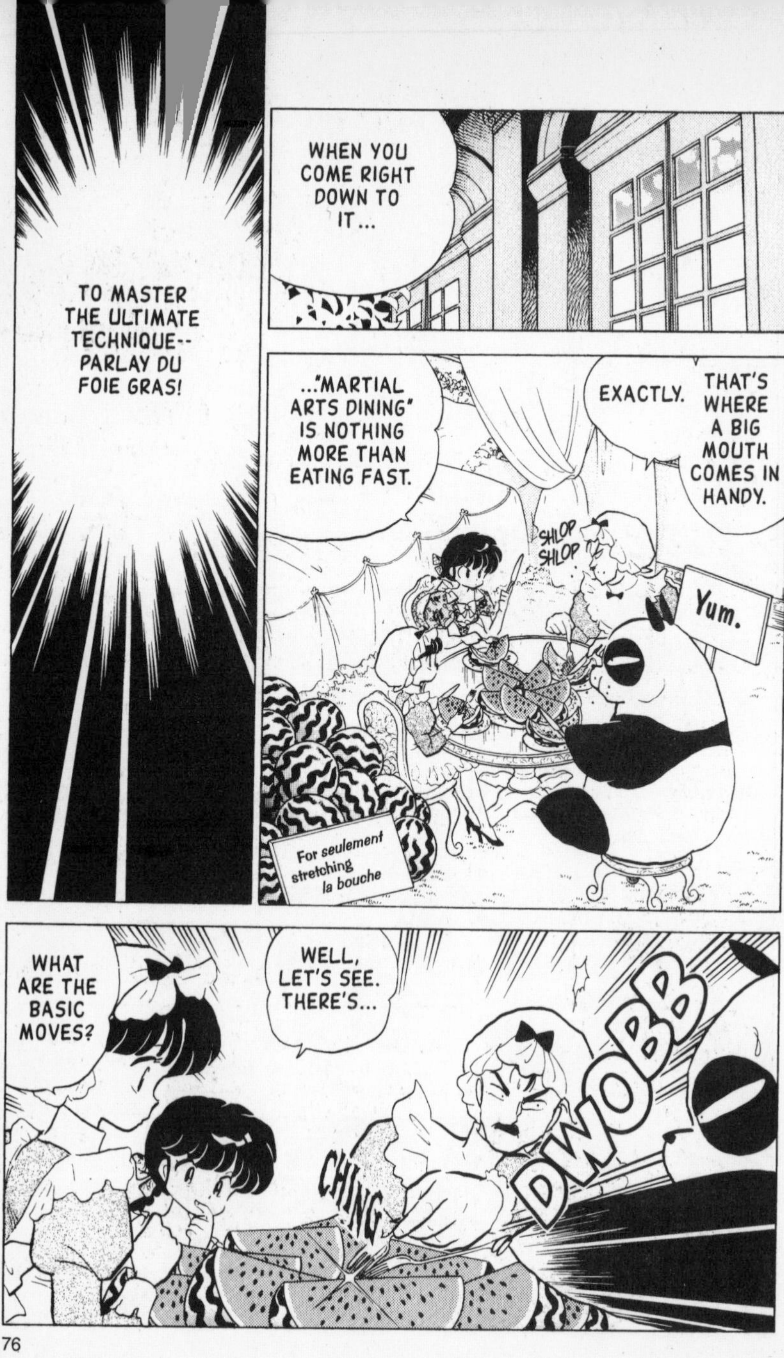
TO MASTER THE ULTIMATE TECHNIQUE-- PARLAY DU FOIE GRAS!
WHEN YOU COME RIGHT DOWN TO IT...
..."MARTIAL ARTS DINING" IS NOTHING MORE THAN EATING FAST.
EXACTLY.
THAT'S WHERE A BIG MOUTH COMES IN HANDY.
SHLOP SHLOP
Yum.
For seulement stretching la bouche
WHAT ARE THE BASIC MOVES?
WELL, LET'S SEE. THERE'S...
CHING
DWOBB

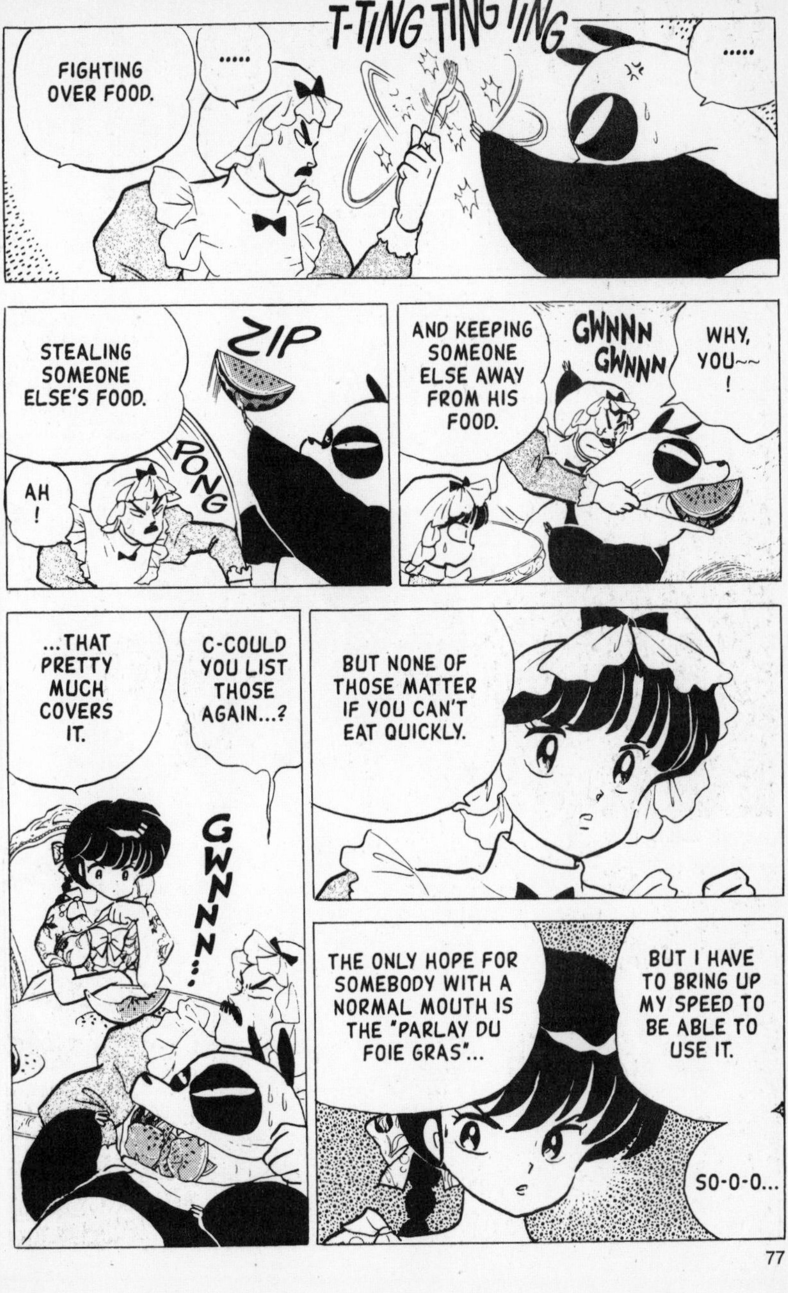
T-TING TING TING
FIGHTING OVER FOOD.
.....
.....
STEALING SOMEONE ELSE'S FOOD.
ZIP
PONG
AH !
AND KEEPING SOMEONE ELSE AWAY FROM HIS FOOD.
GWNNN GWNNN
WHY, YOU~~ !
...THAT PRETTY MUCH COVERS IT.
C-COULD YOU LIST THOSE AGAIN...?
GWNNN...
BUT NONE OF THOSE MATTER IF YOU CAN'T EAT QUICKLY.
THE ONLY HOPE FOR SOMEBODY WITH A NORMAL MOUTH IS THE "PARLAY DU FOIE GRAS"...
BUT I HAVE TO BRING UP MY SPEED TO BE ABLE TO USE IT.
SO-O-O...

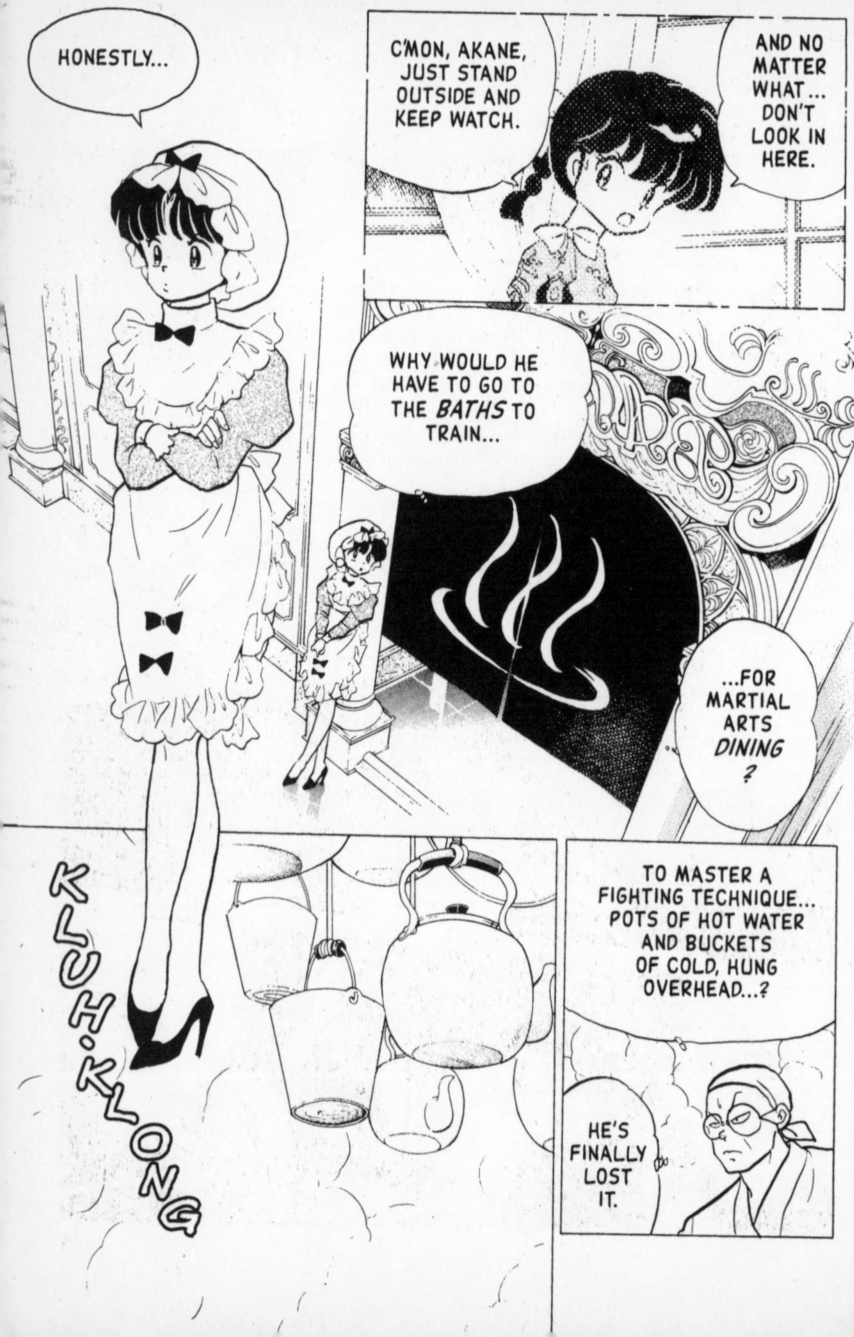
HONESTLY...
C'MON, AKANE, JUST STAND OUTSIDE AND KEEP WATCH.
AND NO MATTER WHAT... DON'T LOOK IN HERE.
WHY WOULD HE HAVE TO GO TO THE *BATHS* TO TRAIN...
...FOR MARTIAL ARTS *DINING* ?
KLUH KLONG
TO MASTER A FIGHTING TECHNIQUE... POTS OF HOT WATER AND BUCKETS OF COLD, HUNG OVERHEAD...?
HE'S FINALLY LOST IT.

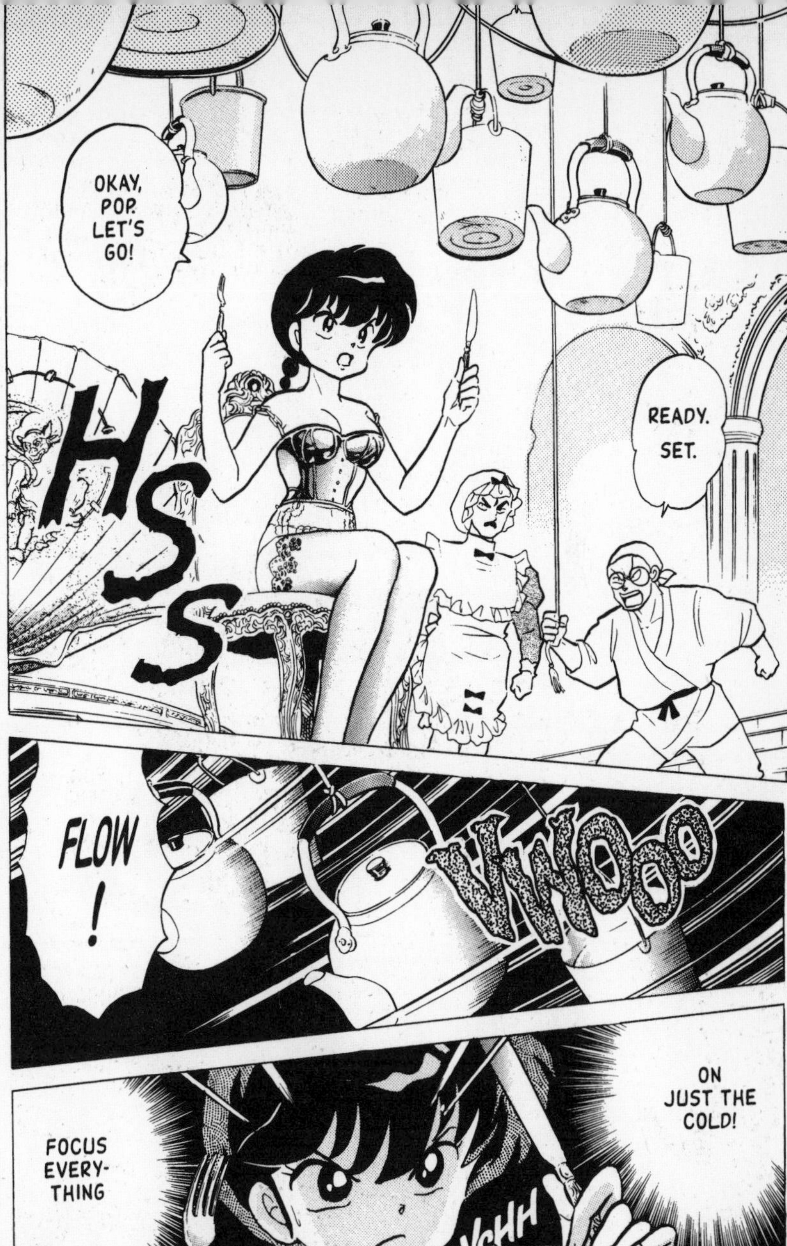
OKAY, POP. LET'S GO!
HSS
READY. SET.
FLOW!
VWOOP
FOCUS EVERY-THING
ON JUST THE COLD!
VSHH

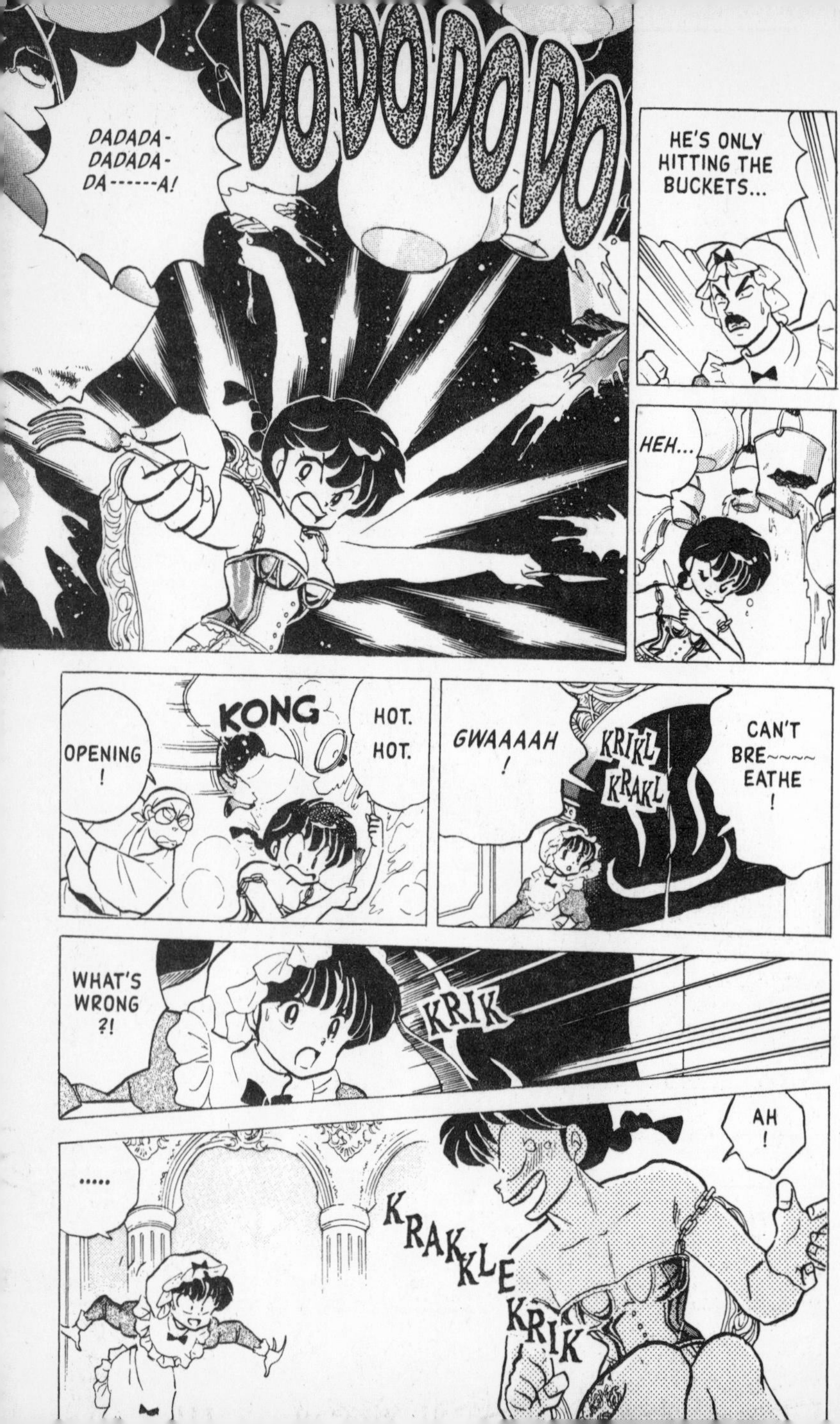
DADADA-
DADADA-
DA------A!
DO DO DO DO DO DO
HE'S ONLY HITTING THE BUCKETS...
HEH...
OPENING!
KONG
HOT. HOT.
GWAAAAH!
KRIKL KRAKL
CAN'T BRE~~~~EATHE!
WHAT'S WRONG?!
KRIK
......
KRAKKLE
KRIK
AH!

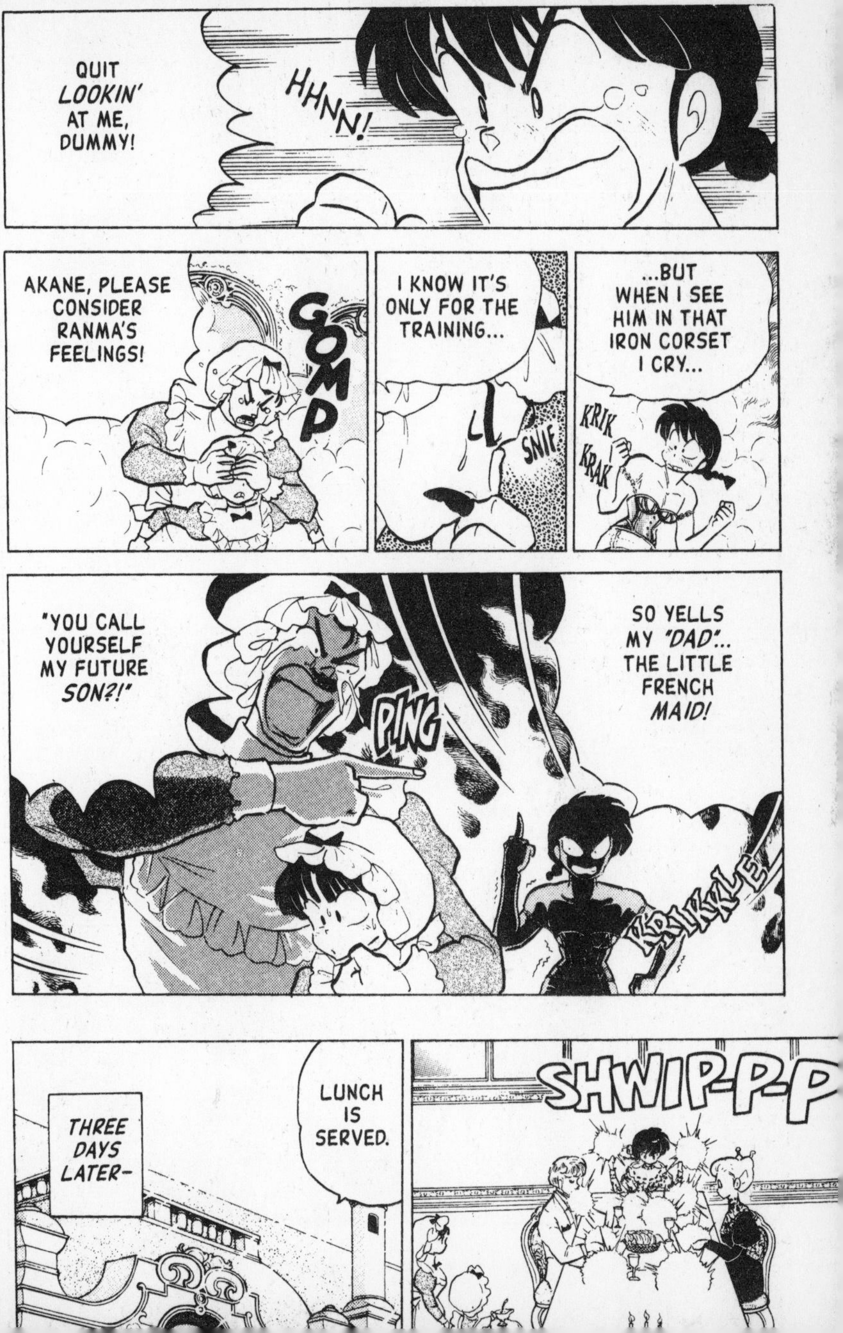
QUIT LOOKIN' AT ME, DUMMY!
HHNNN!
AKANE, PLEASE CONSIDER RANMA'S FEELINGS!
GOMP
I KNOW IT'S ONLY FOR THE TRAINING...
SNIF
...BUT WHEN I SEE HIM IN THAT IRON CORSET I CRY...
KRIK KRAK
"YOU CALL YOURSELF MY FUTURE SON?!"
PING
SO YELLS MY "DAD"... THE LITTLE FRENCH MAID!
KRIKKLE
THREE DAYS LATER–
LUNCH IS SERVED.
SHWIP-P-P

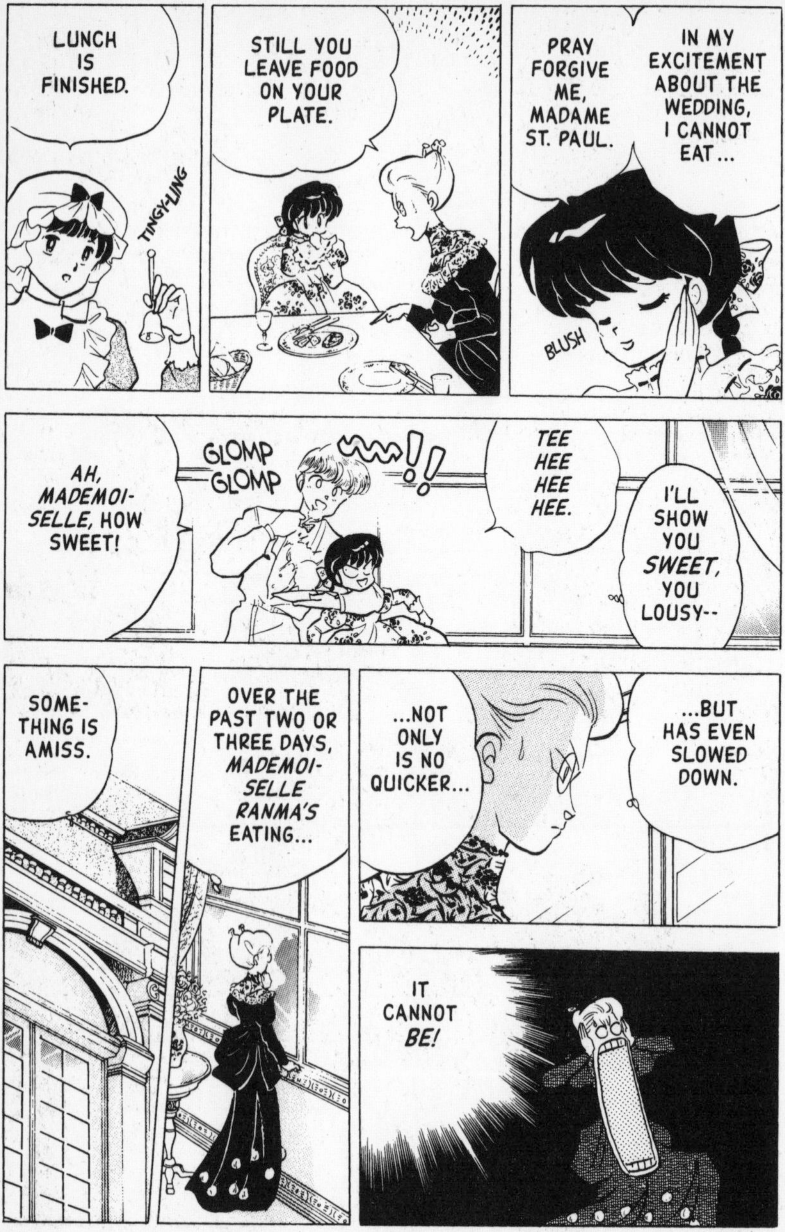

LUNCH IS FINISHED.
TINGY-LING
STILL YOU LEAVE FOOD ON YOUR PLATE.
PRAY FORGIVE ME, MADAME ST. PAUL.
IN MY EXCITEMENT ABOUT THE WEDDING, I CANNOT EAT...
BLUSH
AH, *MADEMOISELLE*, HOW SWEET!
GLOMP GLOMP
TEE HEE HEE HEE.
I'LL SHOW YOU *SWEET*, YOU LOUSY--
SOMETHING IS AMISS.
OVER THE PAST TWO OR THREE DAYS, *MADEMOISELLE RANMA'S* EATING...
...NOT ONLY IS NO QUICKER...
...BUT HAS EVEN SLOWED DOWN.
IT CANNOT *BE!*

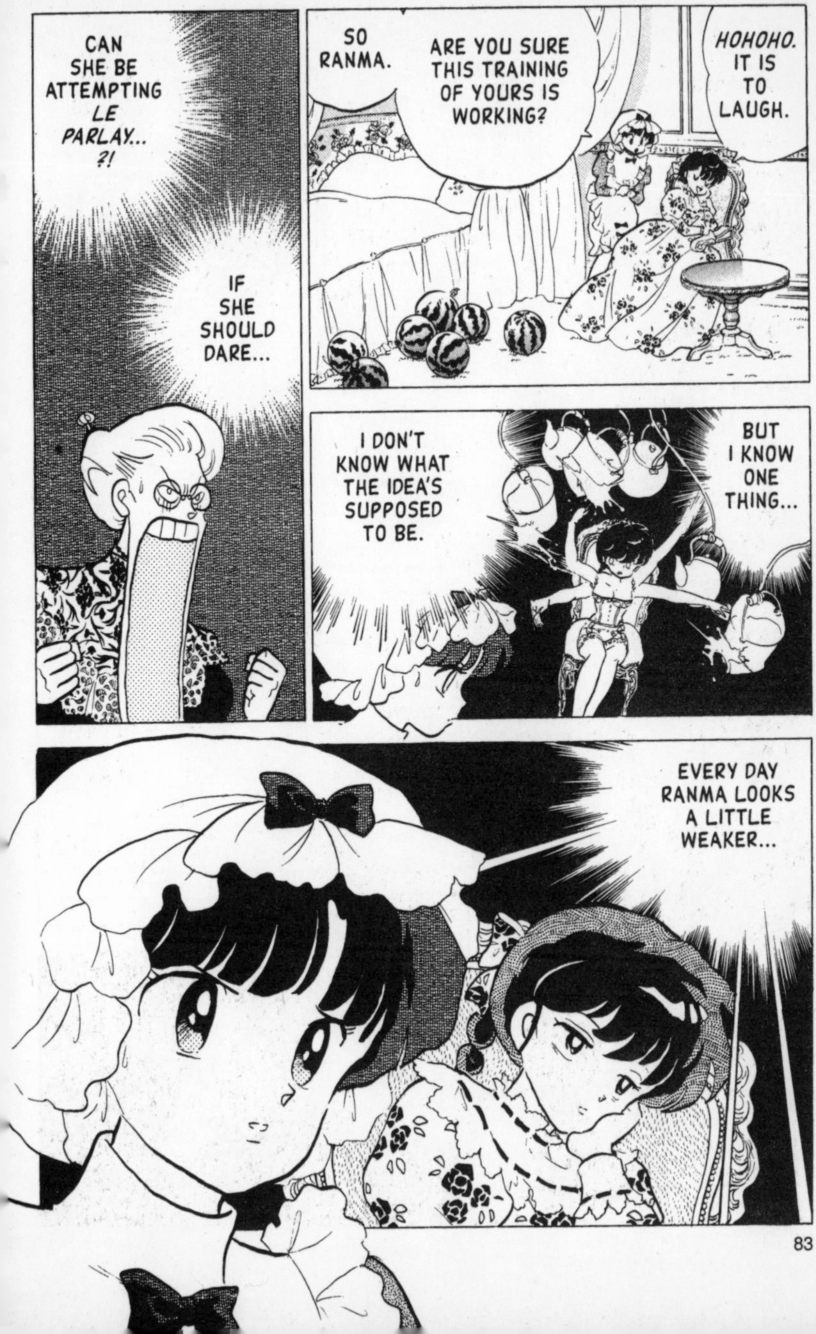
CAN SHE BE ATTEMPTING *LE PARLAY...* ?!
IF SHE SHOULD DARE...
SO RANMA.
ARE YOU SURE THIS TRAINING OF YOURS IS WORKING?
HOHOHO. IT IS TO LAUGH.
I DON'T KNOW WHAT THE IDEA'S SUPPOSED TO BE.
BUT I KNOW ONE THING...
EVERY DAY RANMA LOOKS A LITTLE WEAKER...

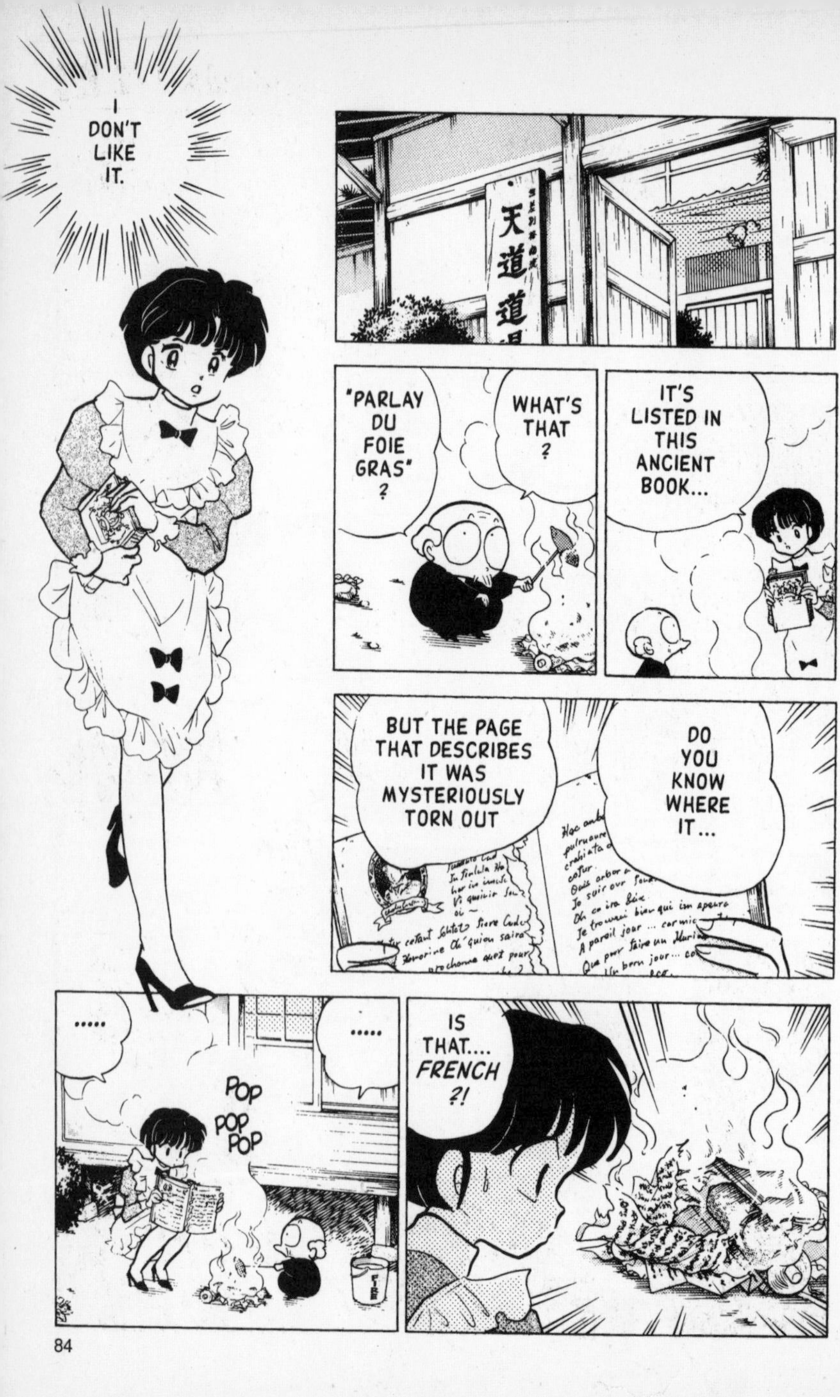
I DON'T LIKE IT.
"PARLAY DU FOIE GRAS" ?
WHAT'S THAT ?
IT'S LISTED IN THIS ANCIENT BOOK...
BUT THE PAGE THAT DESCRIBES IT WAS MYSTERIOUSLY TORN OUT
DO YOU KNOW WHERE IT...
.....
.....
POP
POP POP
IS THAT.... *FRENCH* ?!

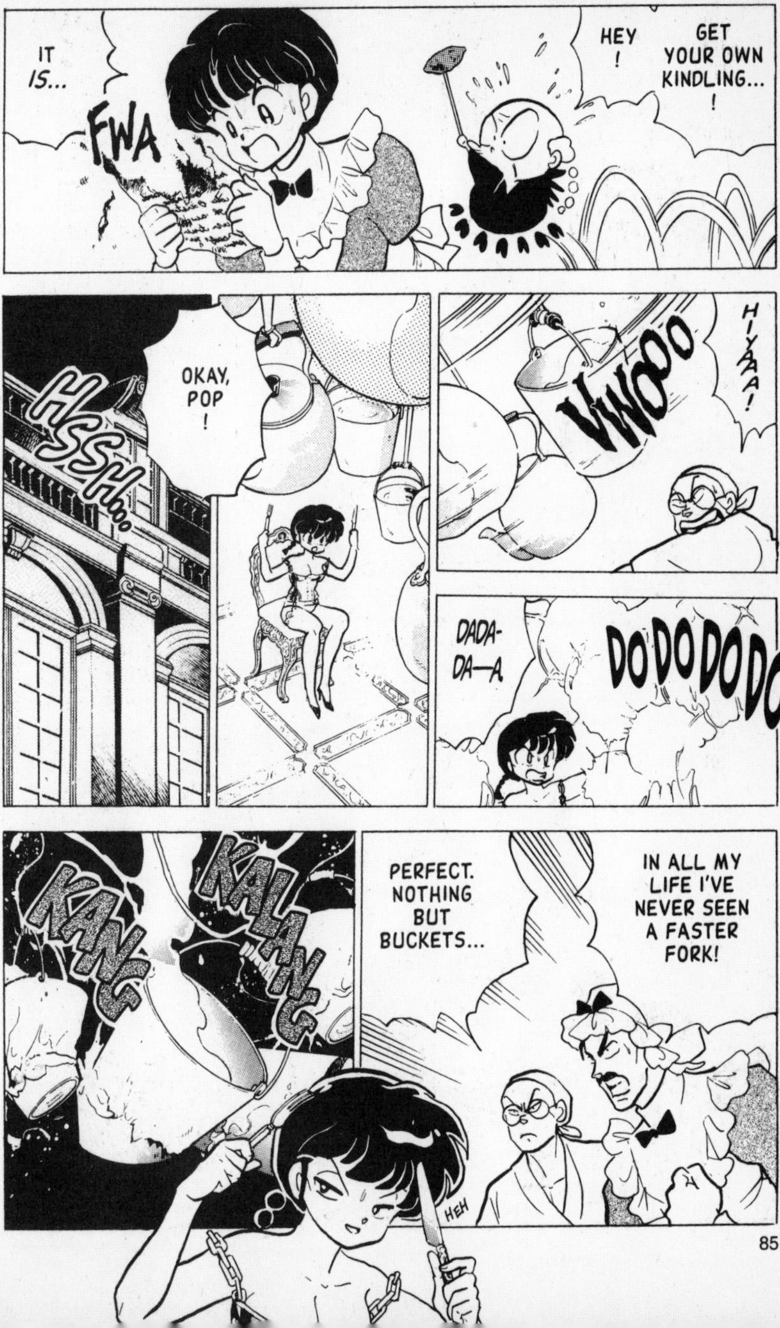
IT IS...
FWA
HEY !
GET YOUR OWN KINDLING... !
HSSH...
OKAY, POP !
VWOOO
HIYAAA!
DADA-DA—A.
DODODODODO
KANG
KALANG
PERFECT. NOTHING BUT BUCKETS...
IN ALL MY LIFE I'VE NEVER SEEN A FASTER FORK!
HEH

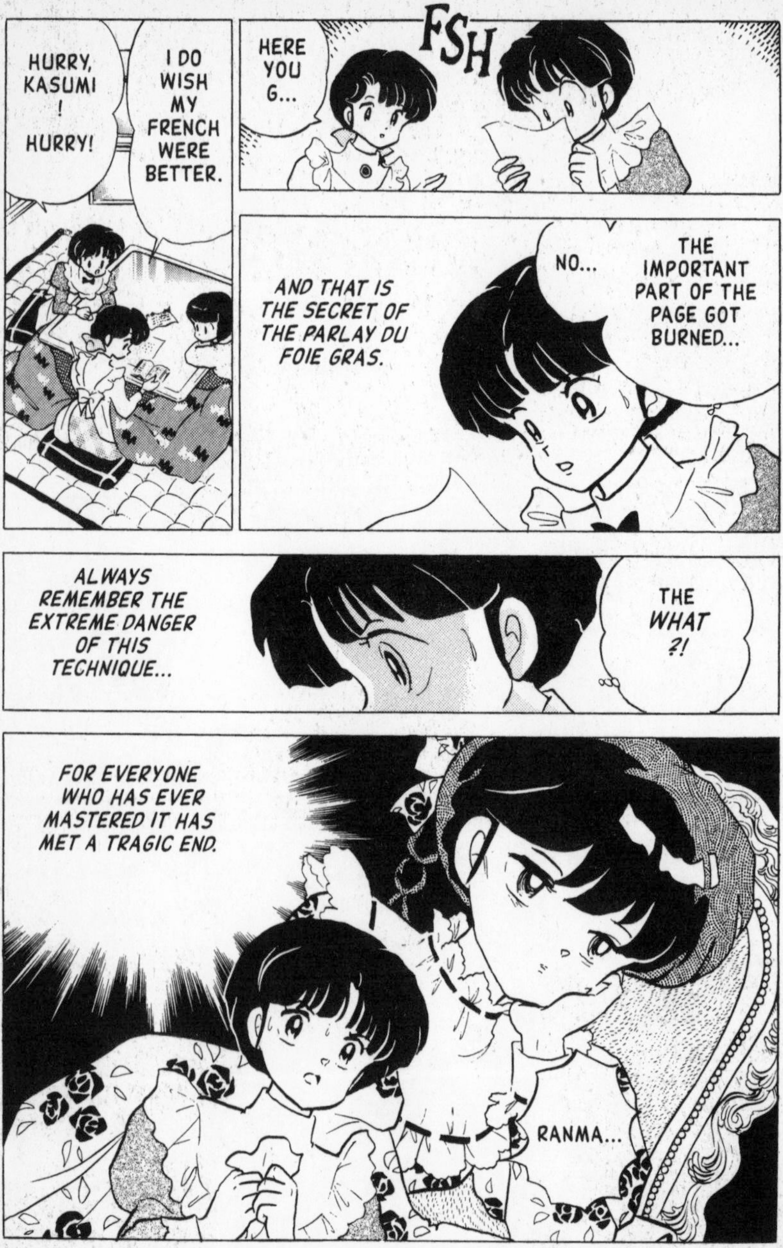
HURRY, KASUMI! HURRY!
I DO WISH MY FRENCH WERE BETTER.
HERE YOU G...
FSH
AND THAT IS THE SECRET OF THE PARLAY DU FOIE GRAS.
NO...
THE IMPORTANT PART OF THE PAGE GOT BURNED...
ALWAYS REMEMBER THE EXTREME DANGER OF THIS TECHNIQUE...
THE WHAT ?!
FOR EVERYONE WHO HAS EVER MASTERED IT HAS MET A TRAGIC END.
RANMA...

Part 6
WHO MASTERS WHAT?

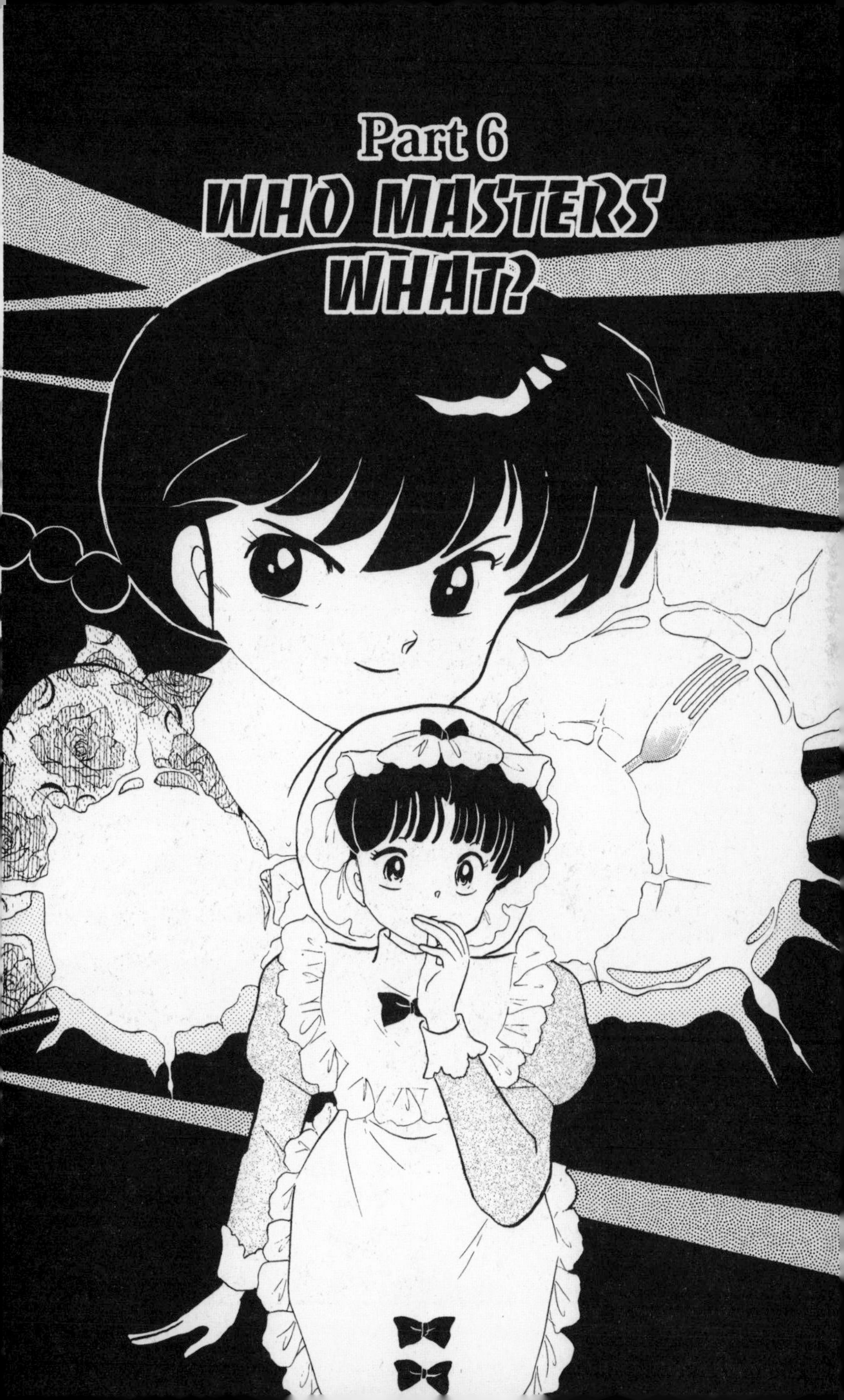

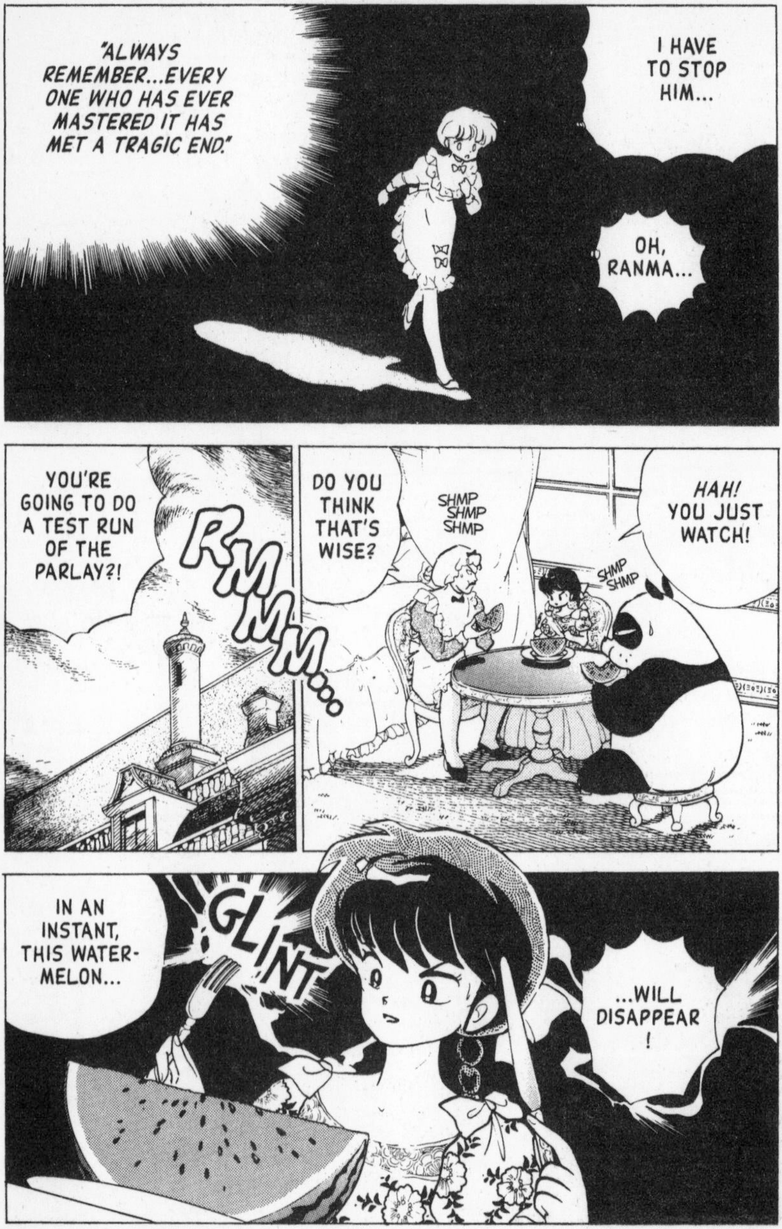

"ALWAYS REMEMBER...EVERY ONE WHO HAS EVER MASTERED IT HAS MET A TRAGIC END."
I HAVE TO STOP HIM...
OH, RANMA...
YOU'RE GOING TO DO A TEST RUN OF THE PARLAY?!
RMMM...
DO YOU THINK THAT'S WISE?
SHMP SHMP SHMP
SHMP SHMP
HAH! YOU JUST WATCH!
IN AN INSTANT, THIS WATER-MELON...
GLINT
...WILL DISAPPEAR!

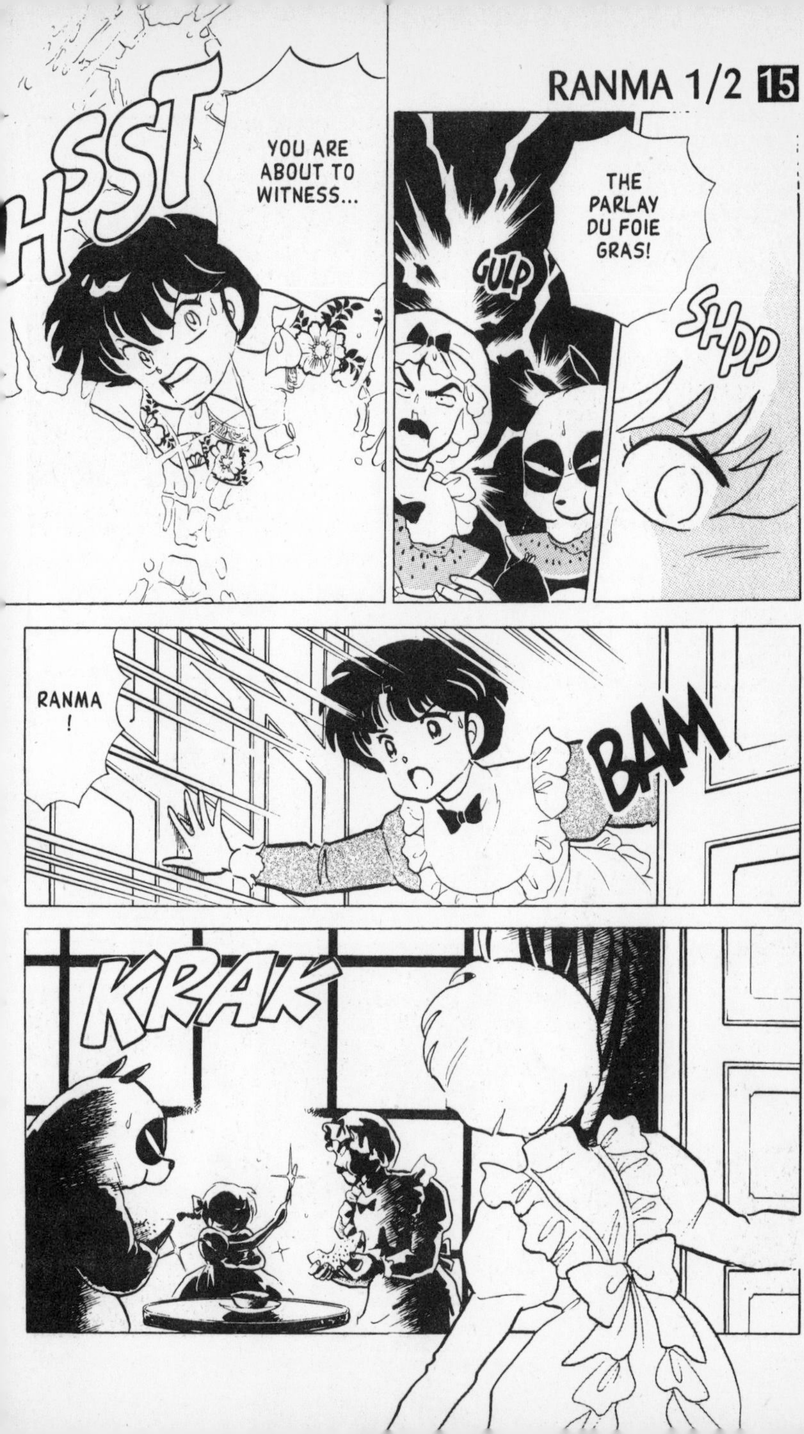
HSST
YOU ARE ABOUT TO WITNESS...
GULP
THE PARLAY DU FOIE GRAS!
SHPP
RANMA!
BAM
KRAK

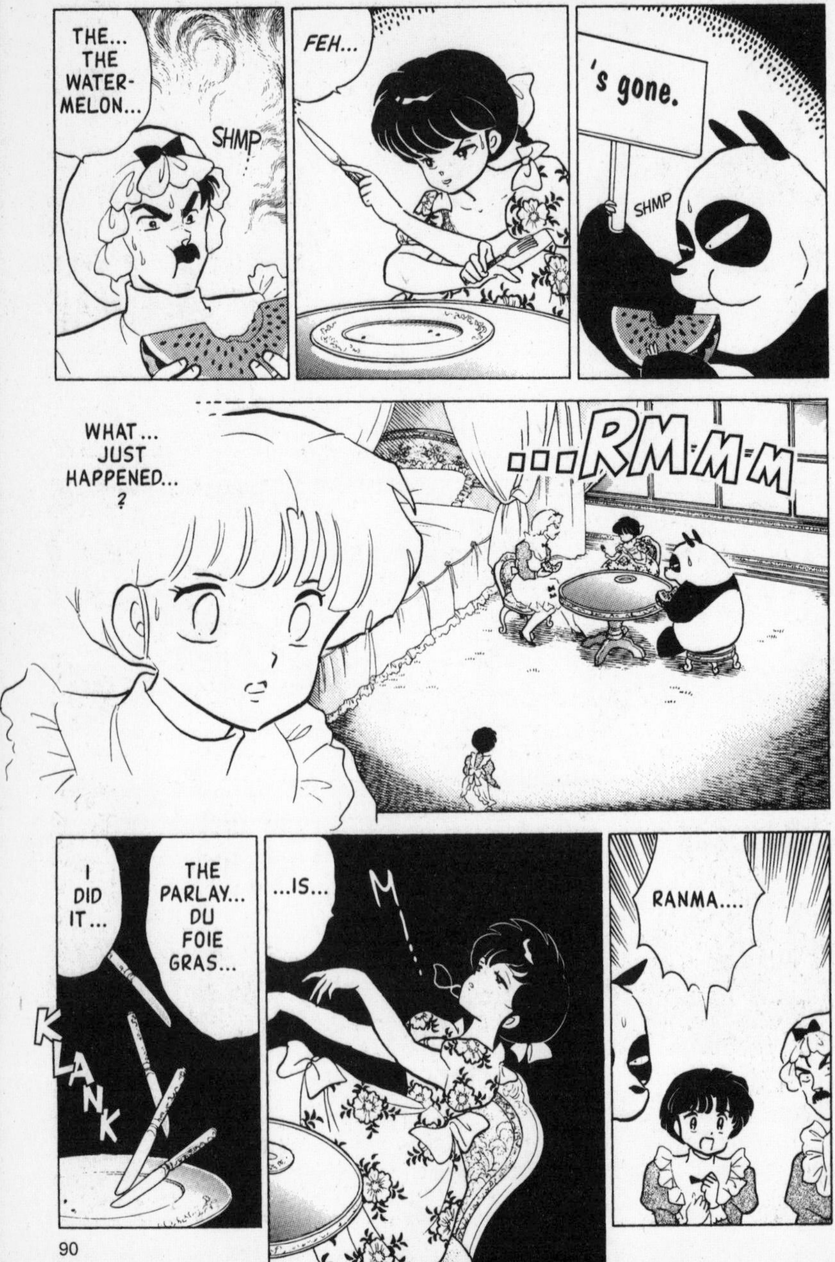
THE... THE WATER-MELON...
SHMP
FEH...
'S gone.
SHMP
WHAT... JUST HAPPENED... ?
...RMMMM
I DID IT...
THE PARLAY... DU FOIE GRAS...
...IS...
M...
KLANK
RANMA....

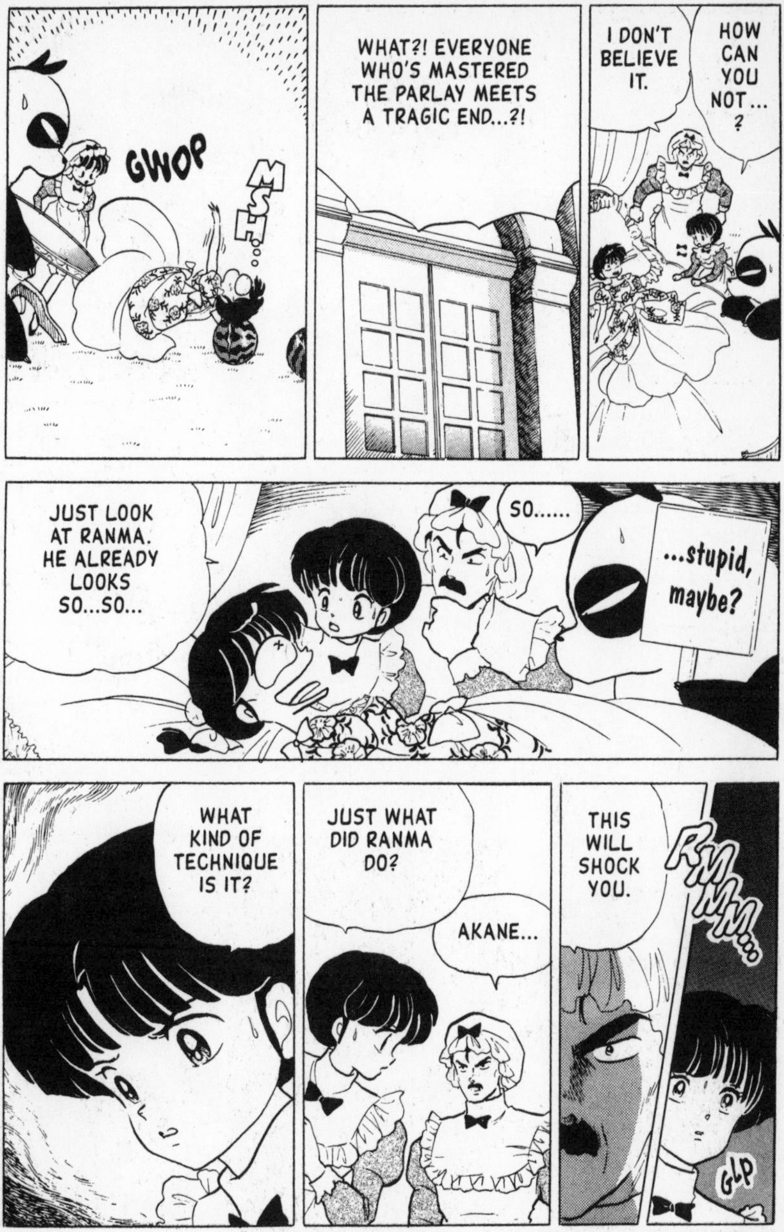
GWOP
MSH...
WHAT?! EVERYONE WHO'S MASTERED THE PARLAY MEETS A TRAGIC END...?!
I DON'T BELIEVE IT.
HOW CAN YOU NOT... ?
JUST LOOK AT RANMA. HE ALREADY LOOKS SO...SO...
SO......
...stupid, maybe?
WHAT KIND OF TECHNIQUE IS IT?
JUST WHAT DID RANMA DO?
AKANE...
THIS WILL SHOCK YOU.
RMMM...
GLP

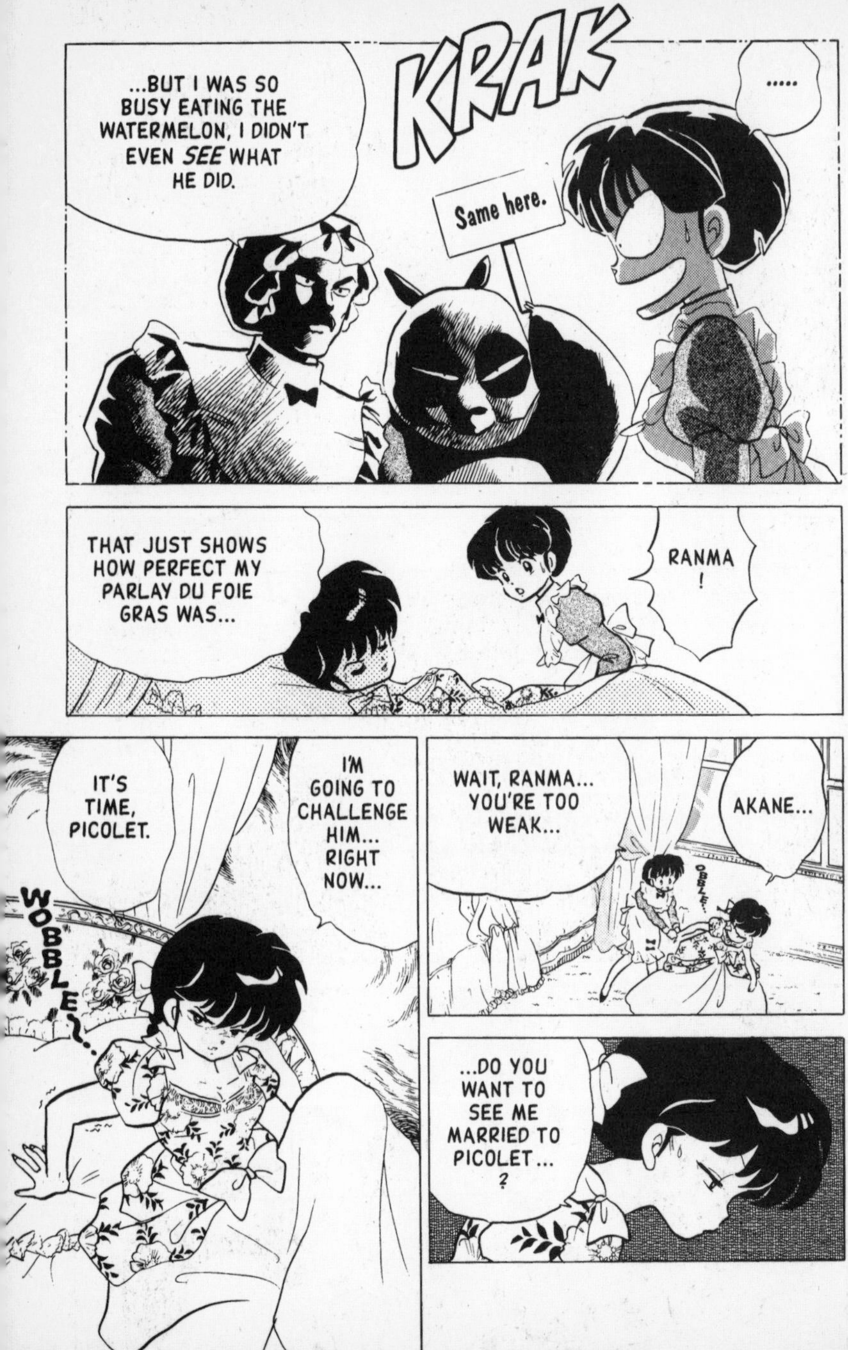
...BUT I WAS SO BUSY EATING THE WATERMELON, I DIDN'T EVEN SEE WHAT HE DID.
KRAK
Same here.
.....
THAT JUST SHOWS HOW PERFECT MY PARLAY DU FOIE GRAS WAS...
RANMA !
IT'S TIME, PICOLET.
I'M GOING TO CHALLENGE HIM... RIGHT NOW...
WOBBLE~...
WAIT, RANMA... YOU'RE TOO WEAK...
AKANE...
OBBLE...
...DO YOU WANT TO SEE ME MARRIED TO PICOLET... ?

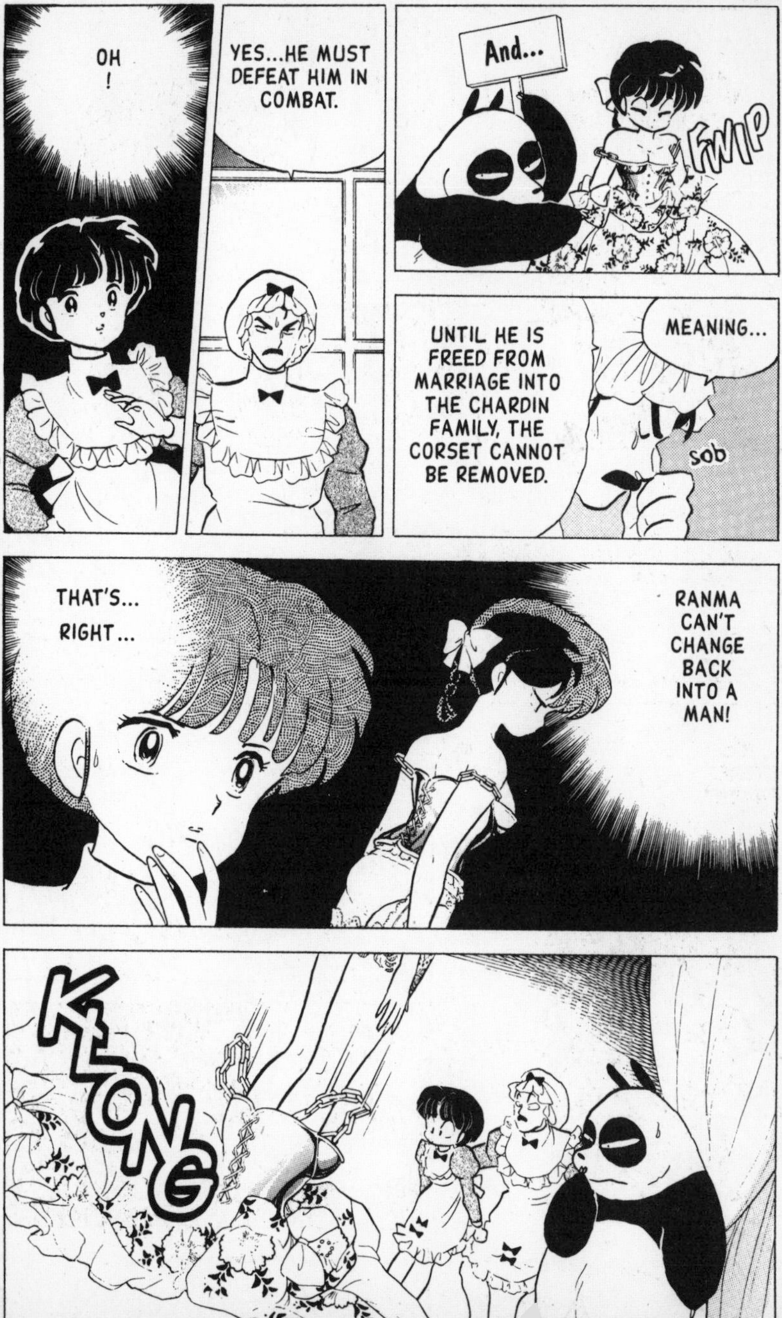
OH !
YES...HE MUST DEFEAT HIM IN COMBAT.
And...
FWIP
MEANING...
UNTIL HE IS FREED FROM MARRIAGE INTO THE CHARDIN FAMILY, THE CORSET CANNOT BE REMOVED.
sob
THAT'S... RIGHT...
RANMA CAN'T CHANGE BACK INTO A MAN!
KLONG

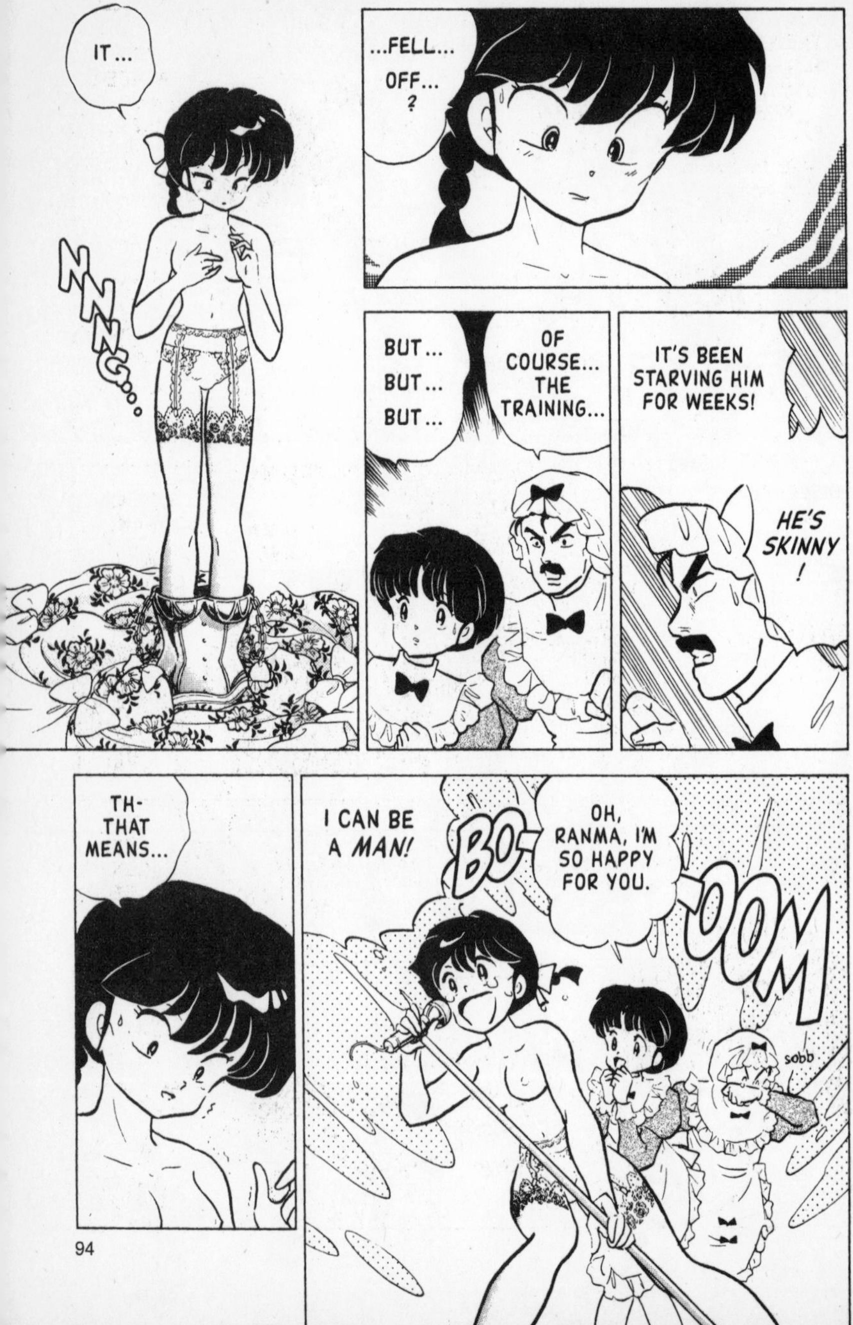
IT...
NNNG...
...FELL... OFF... ?
BUT... BUT... BUT...
OF COURSE... THE TRAINING...
IT'S BEEN STARVING HIM FOR WEEKS!
HE'S SKINNY!
TH- THAT MEANS...
I CAN BE A MAN!
BO-
OH, RANMA, I'M SO HAPPY FOR YOU.
-OOM
sobb

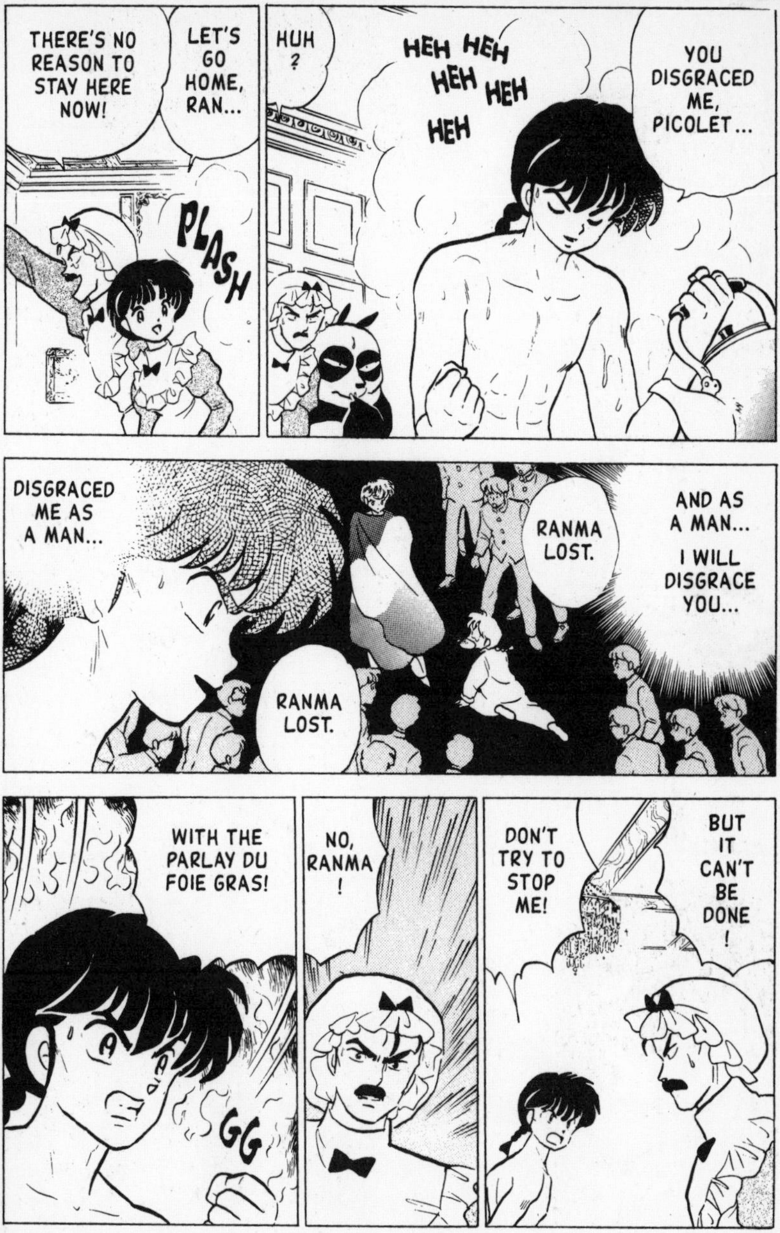
THERE'S NO REASON TO STAY HERE NOW!
LET'S GO HOME, RAN...
PLASH
HUH?
HEH HEH HEH HEH HEH
YOU DISGRACED ME, PICOLET...
DISGRACED ME AS A MAN...
RANMA LOST.
RANMA LOST.
AND AS A MAN...
I WILL DISGRACE YOU...
WITH THE PARLAY DU FOIE GRAS!
GG
NO, RANMA!
DON'T TRY TO STOP ME!
BUT IT CAN'T BE DONE!

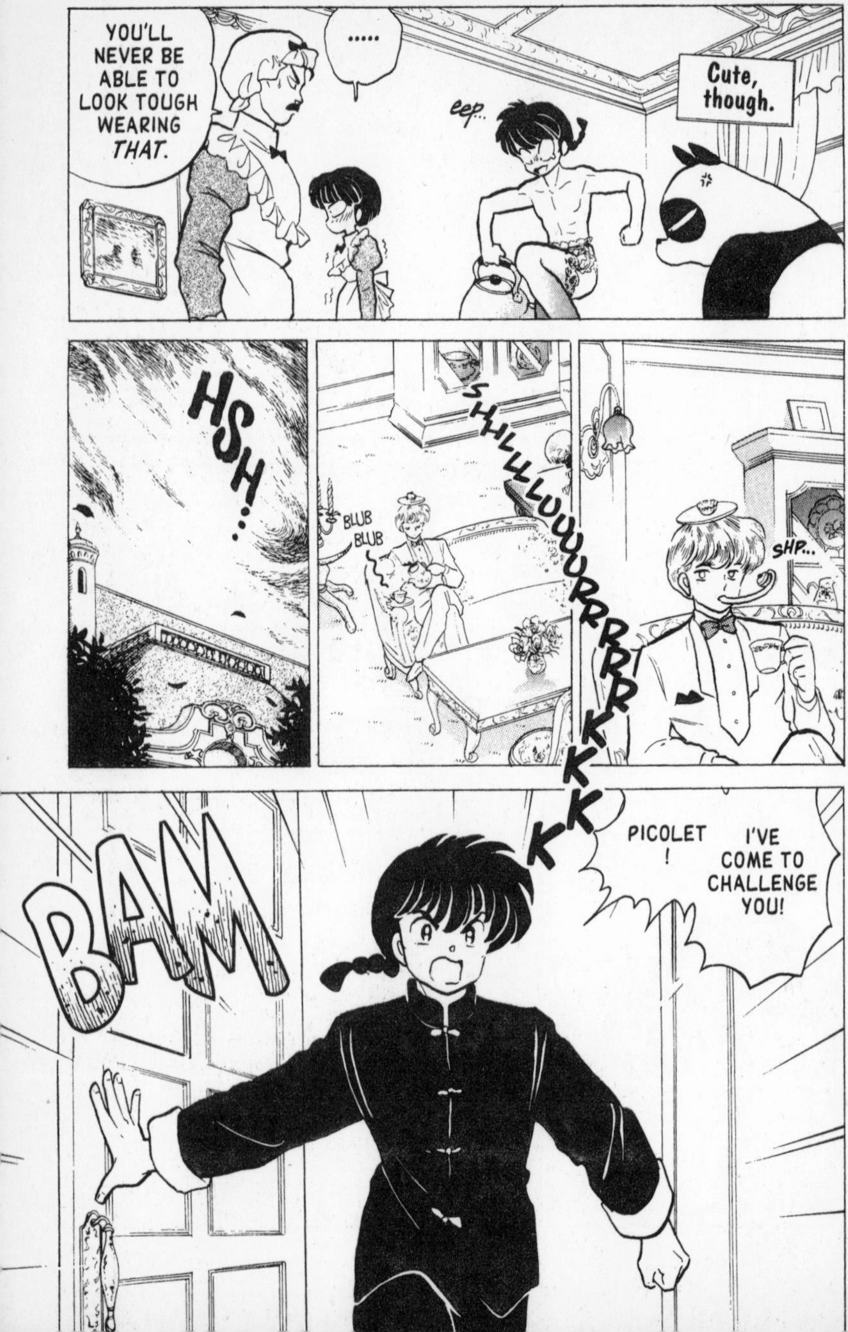
YOU'LL NEVER BE ABLE TO LOOK TOUGH WEARING THAT.
.....
eep...
Cute, though.
HSH...
SHHLLLUUURRRRRKKKKK
BLUB BLUB
SHP...
BAM
PICOLET!
I'VE COME TO CHALLENGE YOU!

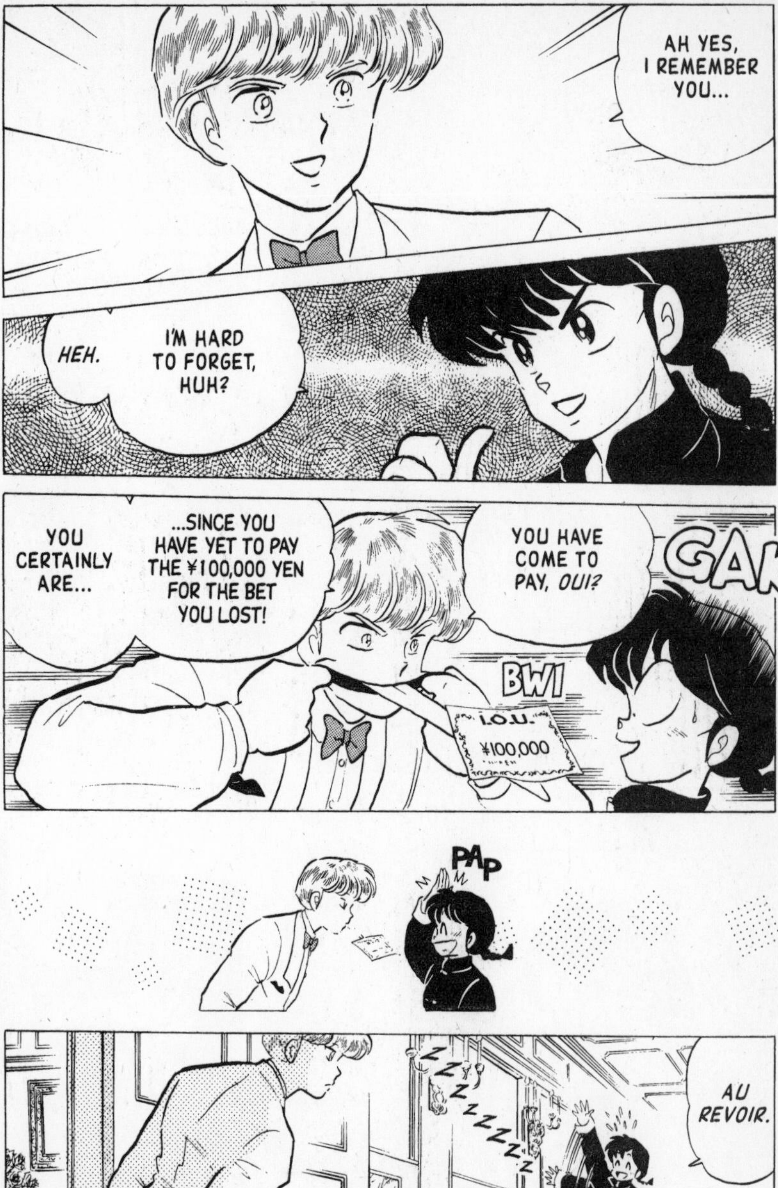
AH YES, I REMEMBER YOU...
HEH.
I'M HARD TO FORGET, HUH?
YOU CERTAINLY ARE...
...SINCE YOU HAVE YET TO PAY THE ¥100,000 YEN FOR THE BET YOU LOST!
YOU HAVE COME TO PAY, *OUI?*
GAK
BWI
I.O.U.
¥100,000
PAP
ZZZZZZZZZ
AU REVOIR.

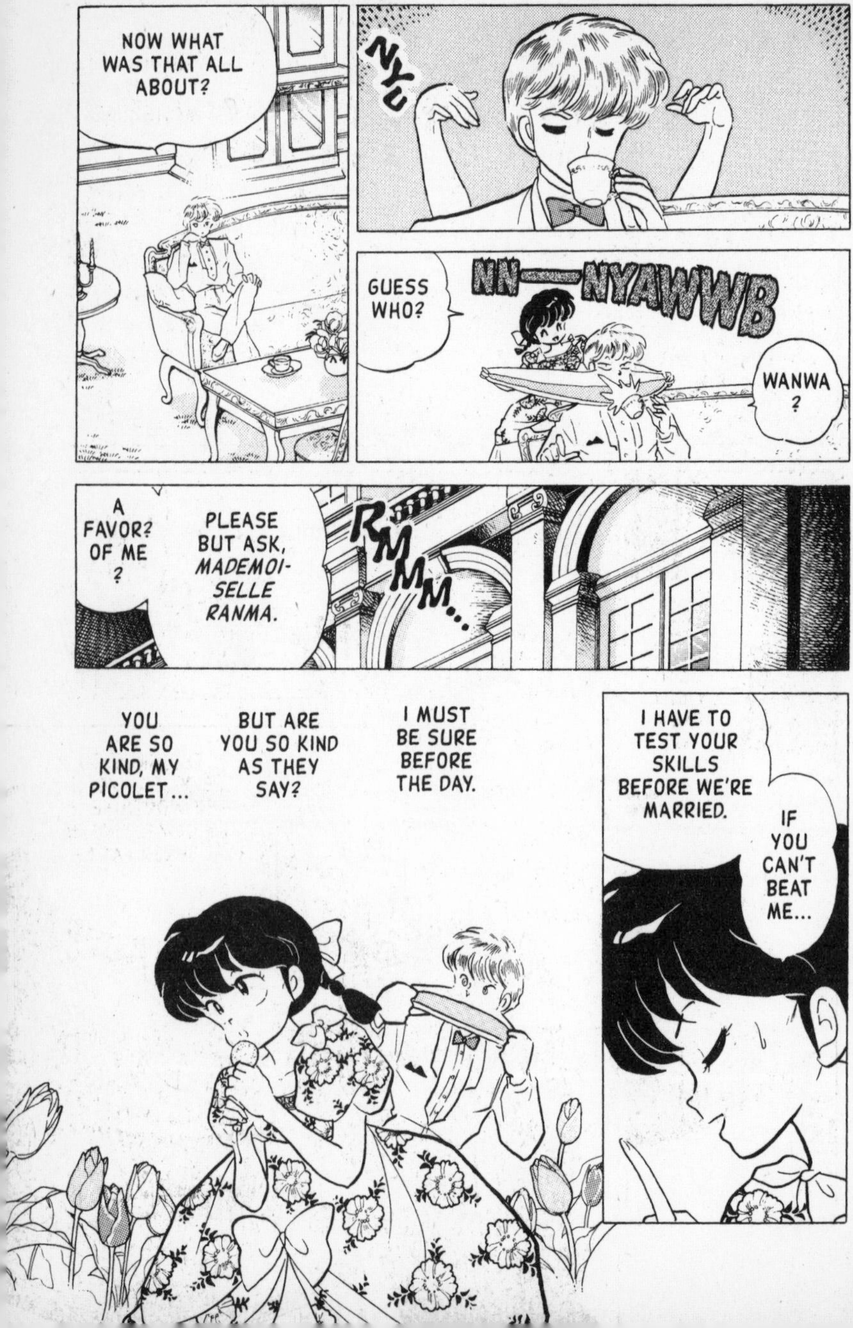
NOW WHAT WAS THAT ALL ABOUT?
NYU
GUESS WHO?
NN—NYAWWB
WANWA ?
A FAVOR? OF ME ?
PLEASE BUT ASK, *MADEMOISELLE RANMA.*
RMMM...
YOU ARE SO KIND, MY PICOLET...
BUT ARE YOU SO KIND AS THEY SAY?
I MUST BE SURE BEFORE THE DAY.
I HAVE TO TEST YOUR SKILLS BEFORE WE'RE MARRIED.
IF YOU CAN'T BEAT ME...

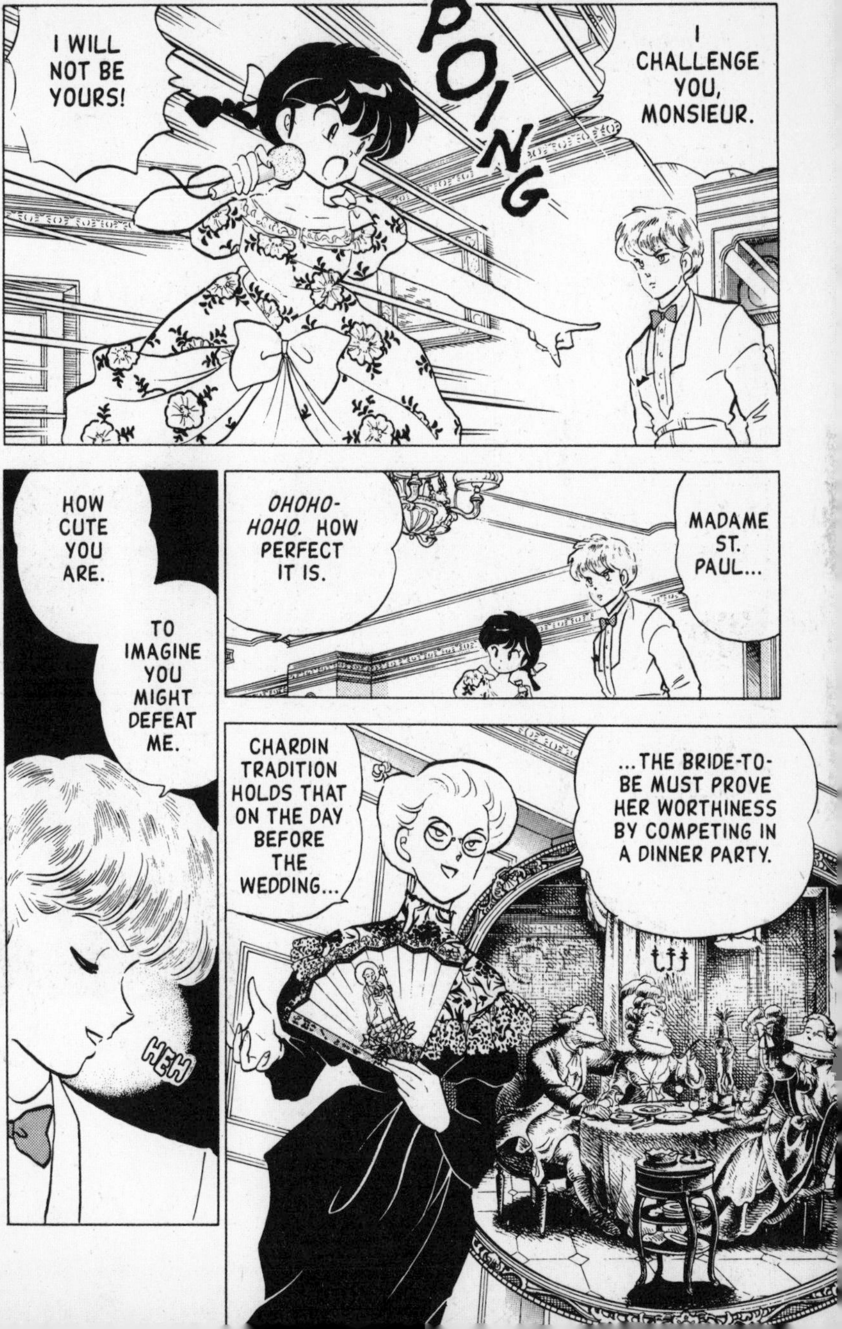
I WILL NOT BE YOURS!
POING
I CHALLENGE YOU, MONSIEUR.
HOW CUTE YOU ARE.
TO IMAGINE YOU MIGHT DEFEAT ME.
HEH
OHOHO-HOHO. HOW PERFECT IT IS.
MADAME ST. PAUL...
CHARDIN TRADITION HOLDS THAT ON THE DAY BEFORE THE WEDDING...
...THE BRIDE-TO-BE MUST PROVE HER WORTHINESS BY COMPETING IN A DINNER PARTY.

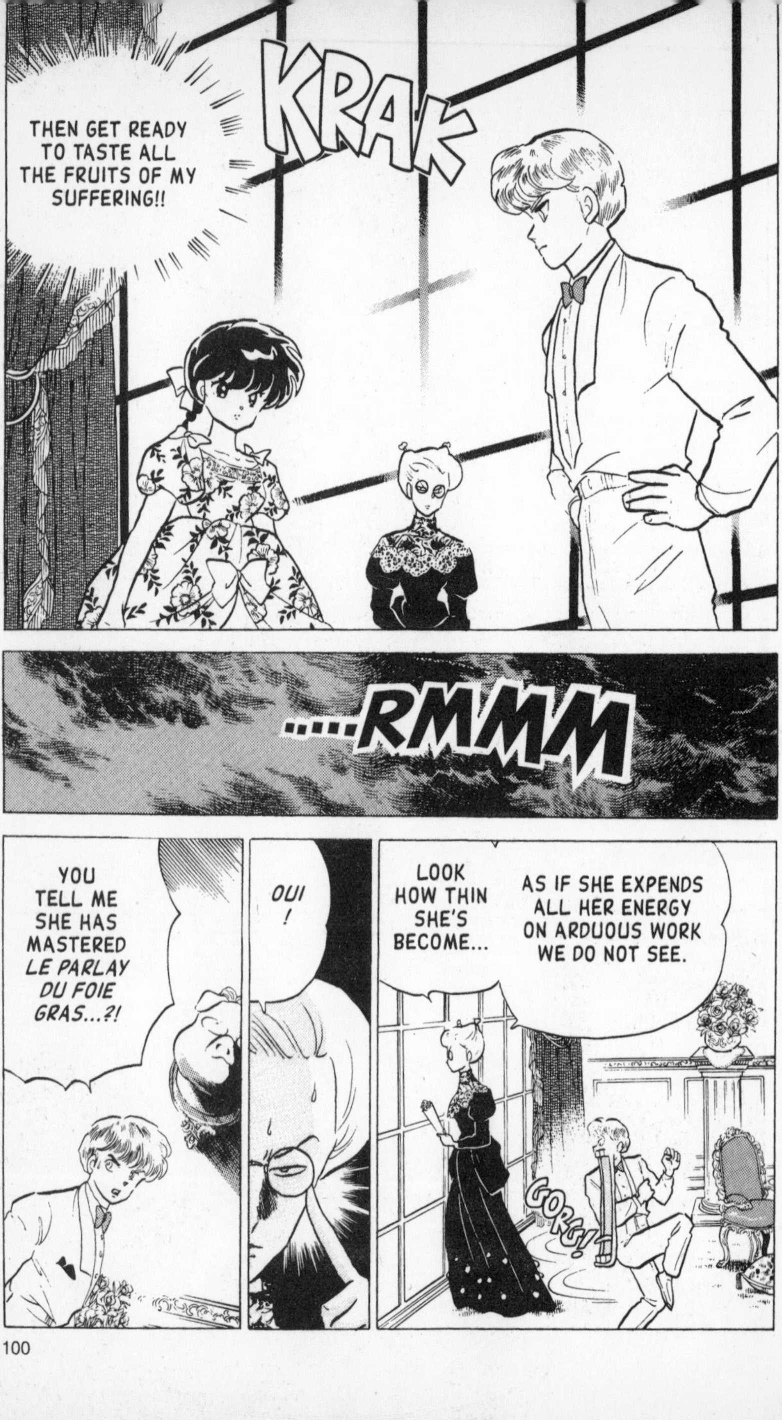
THEN GET READY TO TASTE ALL THE FRUITS OF MY SUFFERING!!
KRAK
.....RMMM
YOU TELL ME SHE HAS MASTERED *LE PARLAY DU FOIE GRAS*...?!
OUI!
LOOK HOW THIN SHE'S BECOME...
AS IF SHE EXPENDS ALL HER ENERGY ON ARDUOUS WORK WE DO NOT SEE.
GORG!

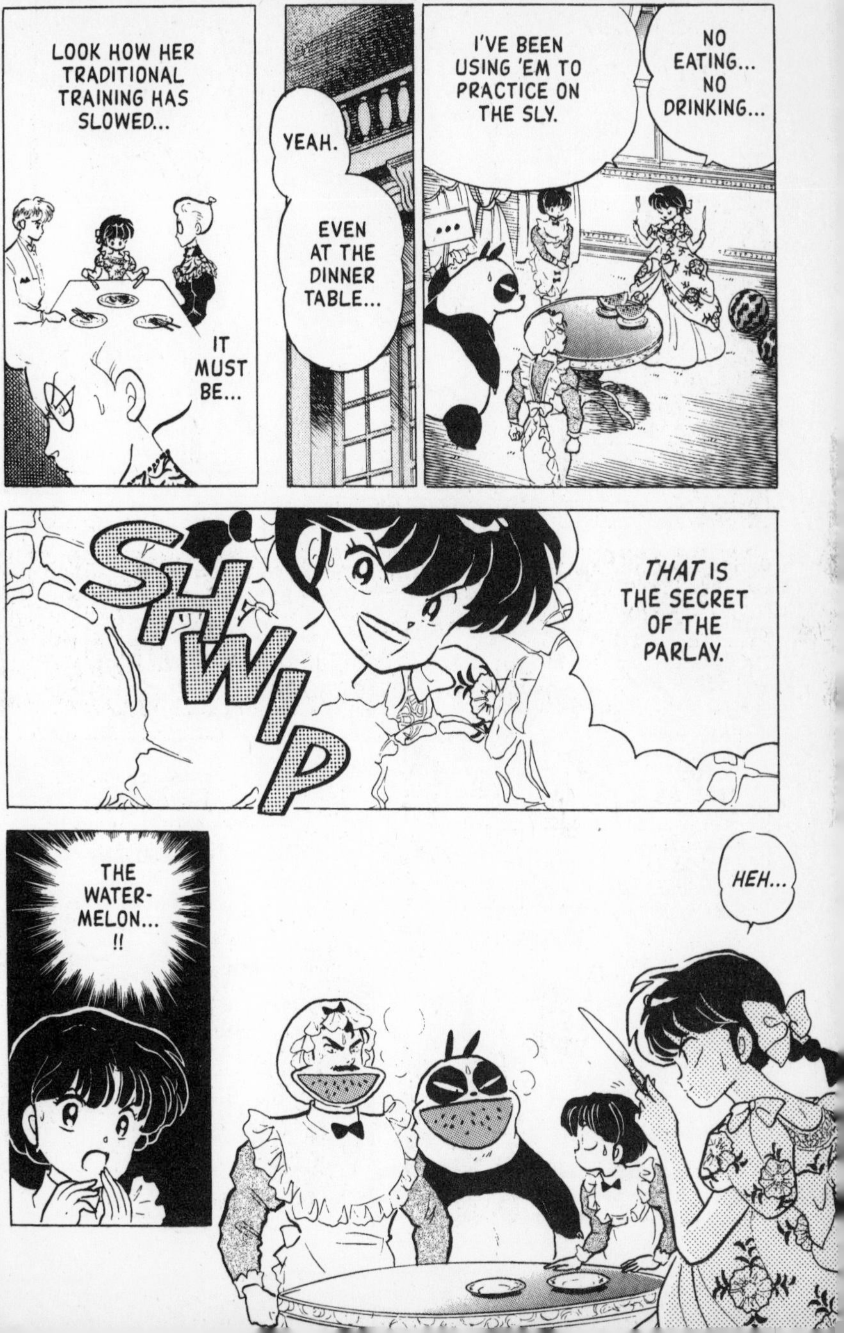
LOOK HOW HER TRADITIONAL TRAINING HAS SLOWED...
IT MUST BE...
YEAH.
EVEN AT THE DINNER TABLE...
I'VE BEEN USING 'EM TO PRACTICE ON THE SLY.
NO EATING... NO DRINKING...
...
SHWIP
THAT IS THE SECRET OF THE PARLAY.
THE WATER-MELON... !!
HEH...

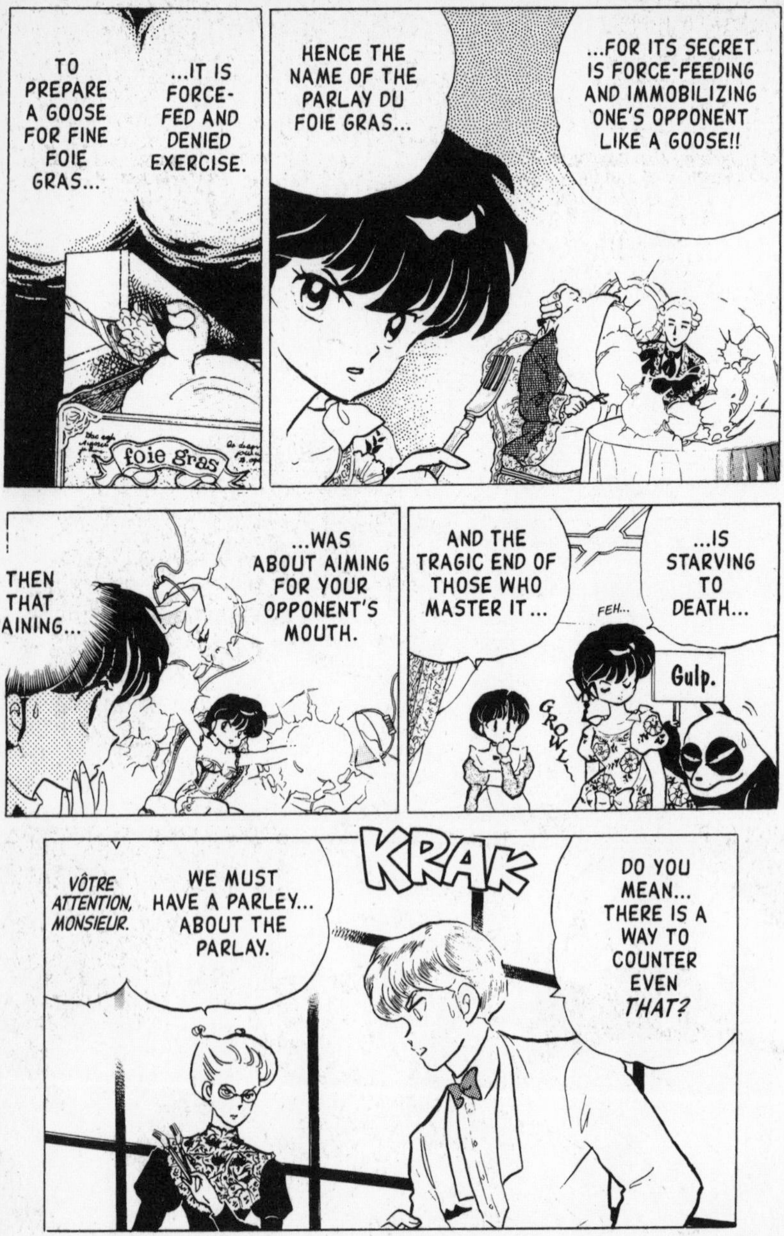
TO PREPARE A GOOSE FOR FINE FOIE GRAS...
...IT IS FORCE-FED AND DENIED EXERCISE.
foie gras
HENCE THE NAME OF THE PARLAY DU FOIE GRAS...
...FOR ITS SECRET IS FORCE-FEEDING AND IMMOBILIZING ONE'S OPPONENT LIKE A GOOSE!!
THEN THAT TRAINING...
...WAS ABOUT AIMING FOR YOUR OPPONENT'S MOUTH.
AND THE TRAGIC END OF THOSE WHO MASTER IT...
FEH...
...IS STARVING TO DEATH...
GROWL
Gulp.
VÔTRE ATTENTION, MONSIEUR.
WE MUST HAVE A PARLEY... ABOUT THE PARLAY.
KRAK
DO YOU MEAN... THERE IS A WAY TO COUNTER EVEN THAT?

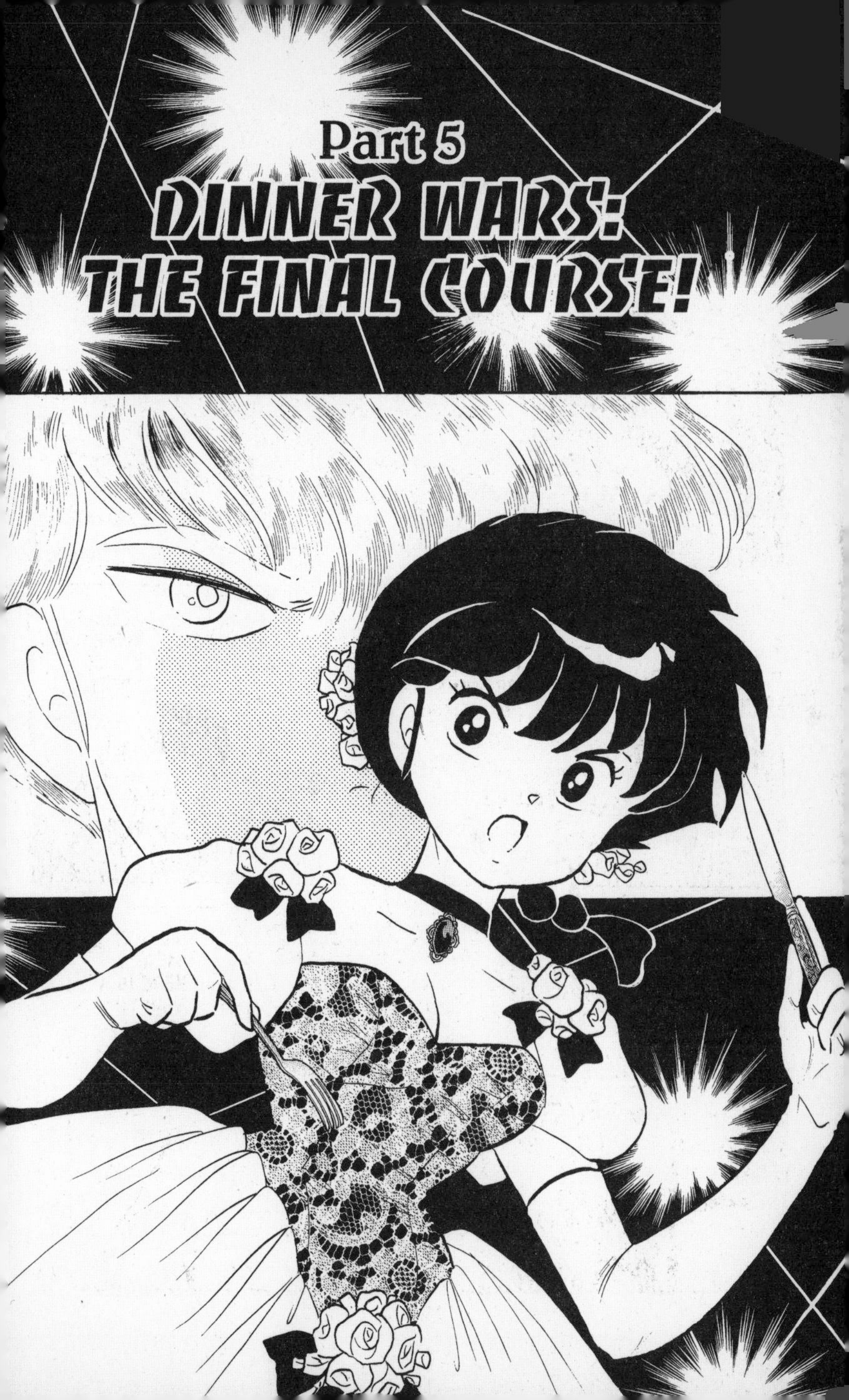
Part 5
DINNER WARS:
THE FINAL COURSE!

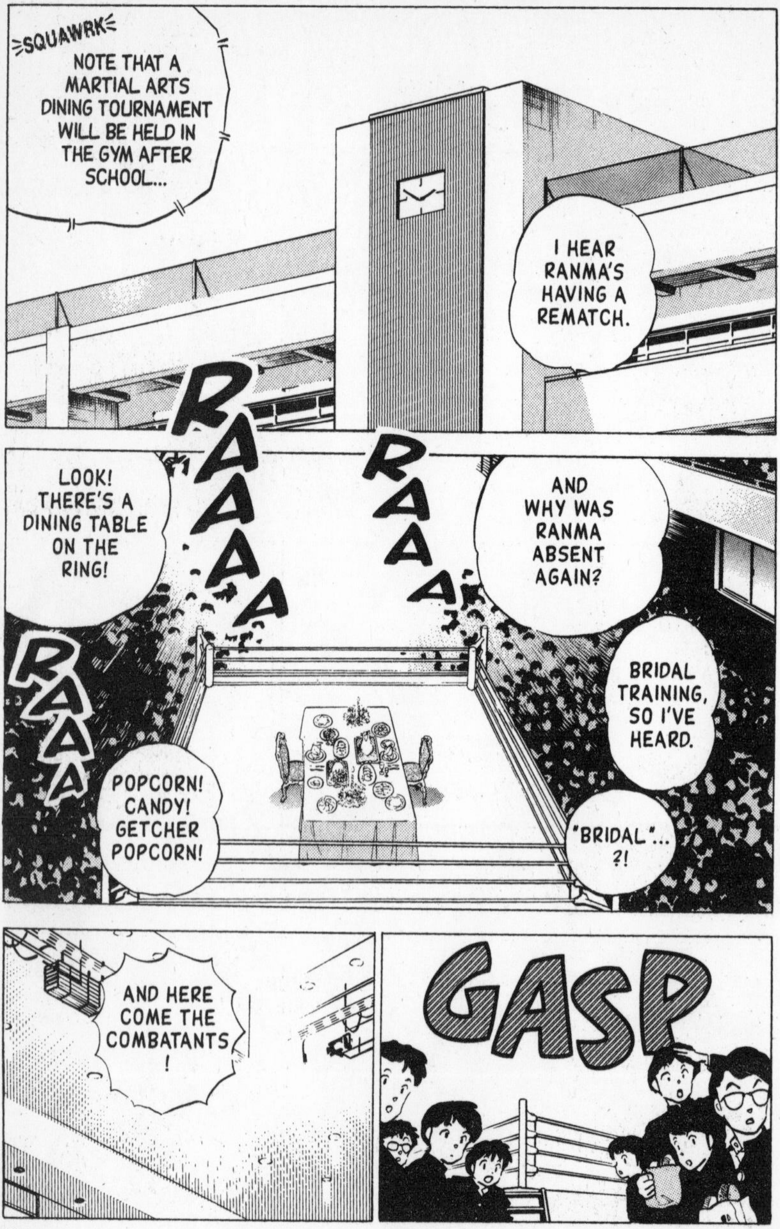
SQUAWRK
NOTE THAT A MARTIAL ARTS DINING TOURNAMENT WILL BE HELD IN THE GYM AFTER SCHOOL...
I HEAR RANMA'S HAVING A REMATCH.
RAAAAA
RAAA
LOOK! THERE'S A DINING TABLE ON THE RING!
AND WHY WAS RANMA ABSENT AGAIN?
BRIDAL TRAINING, SO I'VE HEARD.
RAAAA
POPCORN! CANDY! GETCHER POPCORN!
"BRIDAL"... ?!
AND HERE COME THE COMBATANTS!
GASP

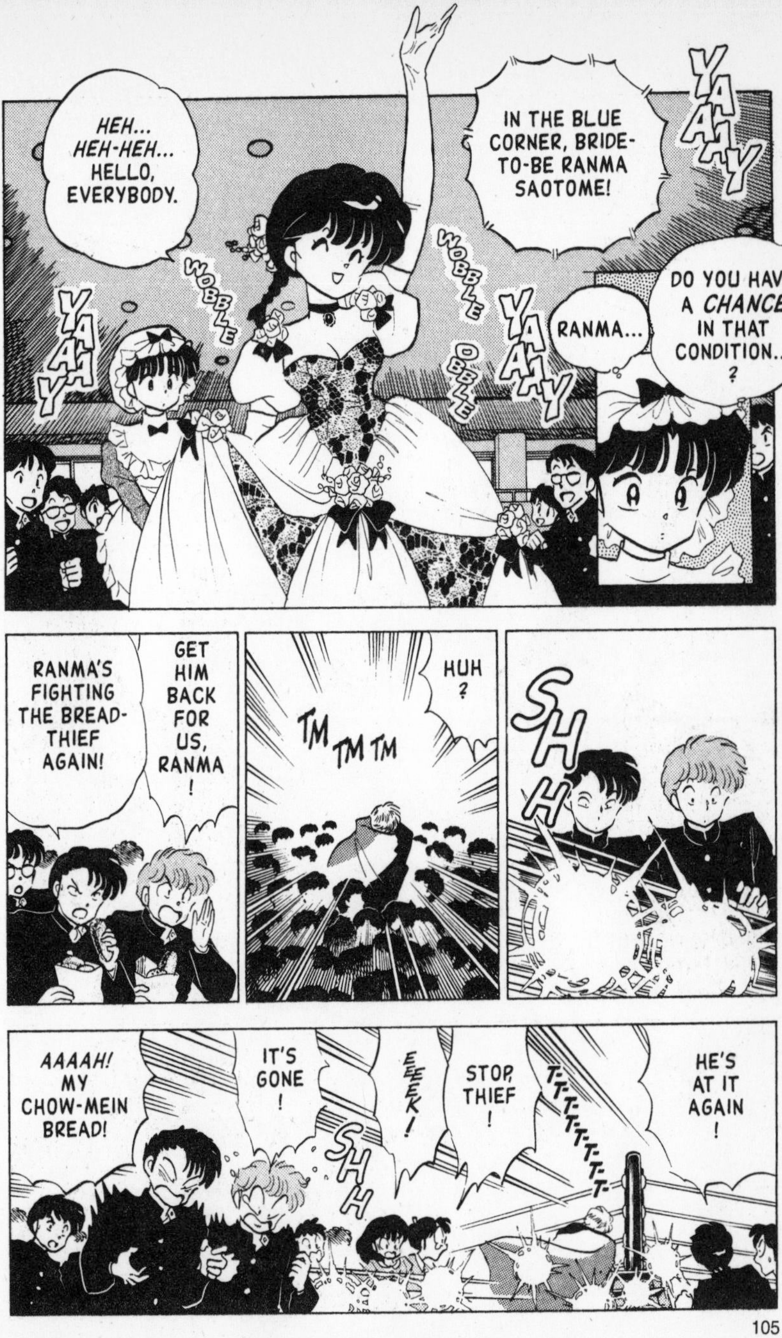
HEH... HEH-HEH... HELLO, EVERYBODY.
IN THE BLUE CORNER, BRIDE-TO-BE RANMA SAOTOME!
YAAAY
YAAAY
WOBBLE
WOBBLE
OBBLE
YAAAY
RANMA...
DO YOU HAVE A *CHANCE* IN THAT CONDITION...?
RANMA'S FIGHTING THE BREAD-THIEF AGAIN!
GET HIM BACK FOR US, RANMA!
HUH?
TM TM TM
SHH
AAAAH! MY CHOW-MEIN BREAD!
IT'S GONE!
EEEK!
SHH
STOP, THIEF!
T-T-T-T-T-T-T-T-T-
HE'S AT IT AGAIN!

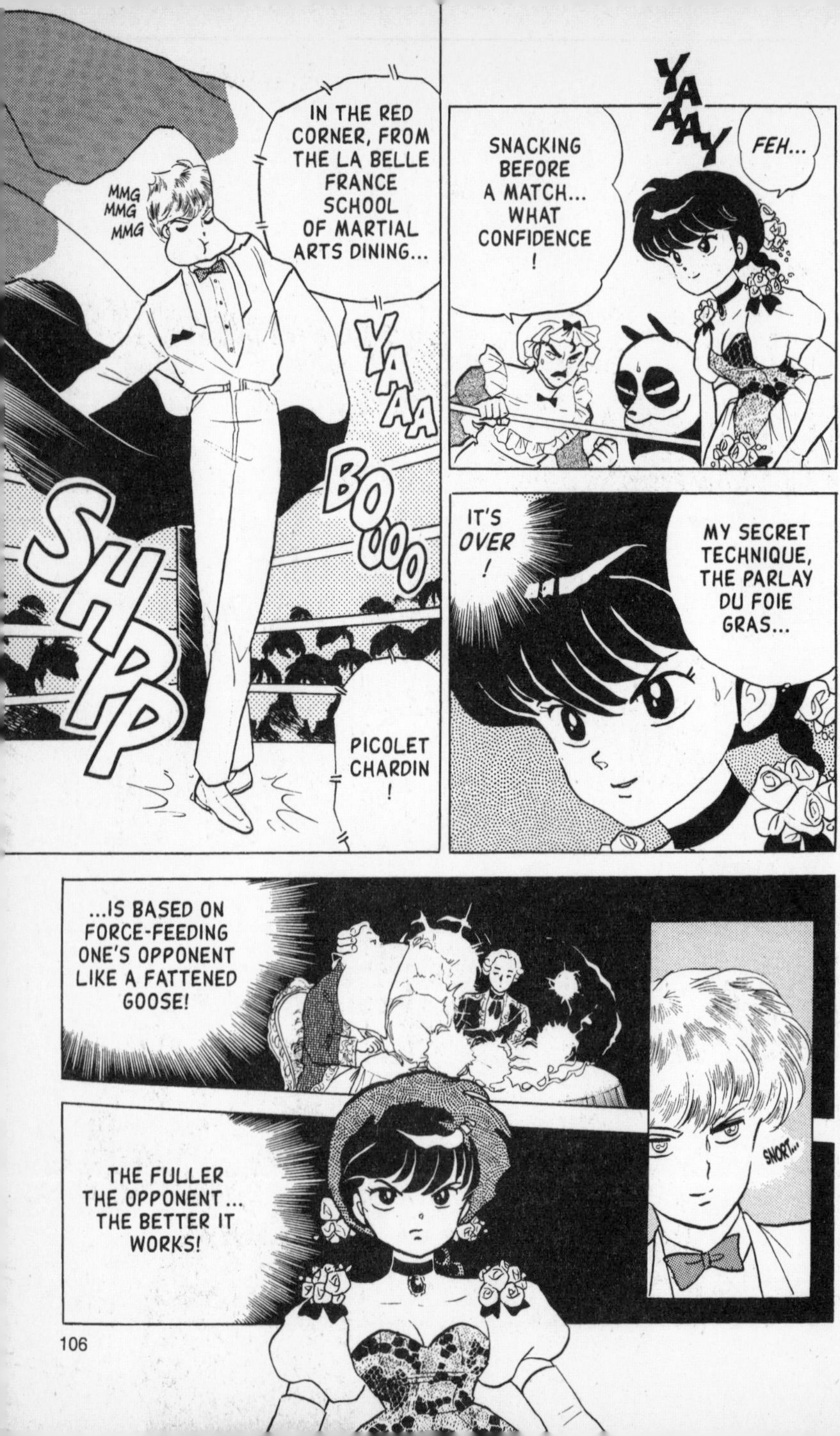
MMG MMG MMG
IN THE RED CORNER, FROM THE LA BELLE FRANCE SCHOOL OF MARTIAL ARTS DINING...
YAAAA
BOOOOO
SHPP
PICOLET CHARDIN!
YAAAY
SNACKING BEFORE A MATCH... WHAT CONFIDENCE!
FEH...
IT'S OVER!
MY SECRET TECHNIQUE, THE PARLAY DU FOIE GRAS...
...IS BASED ON FORCE-FEEDING ONE'S OPPONENT LIKE A FATTENED GOOSE!
THE FULLER THE OPPONENT... THE BETTER IT WORKS!
SNORT...

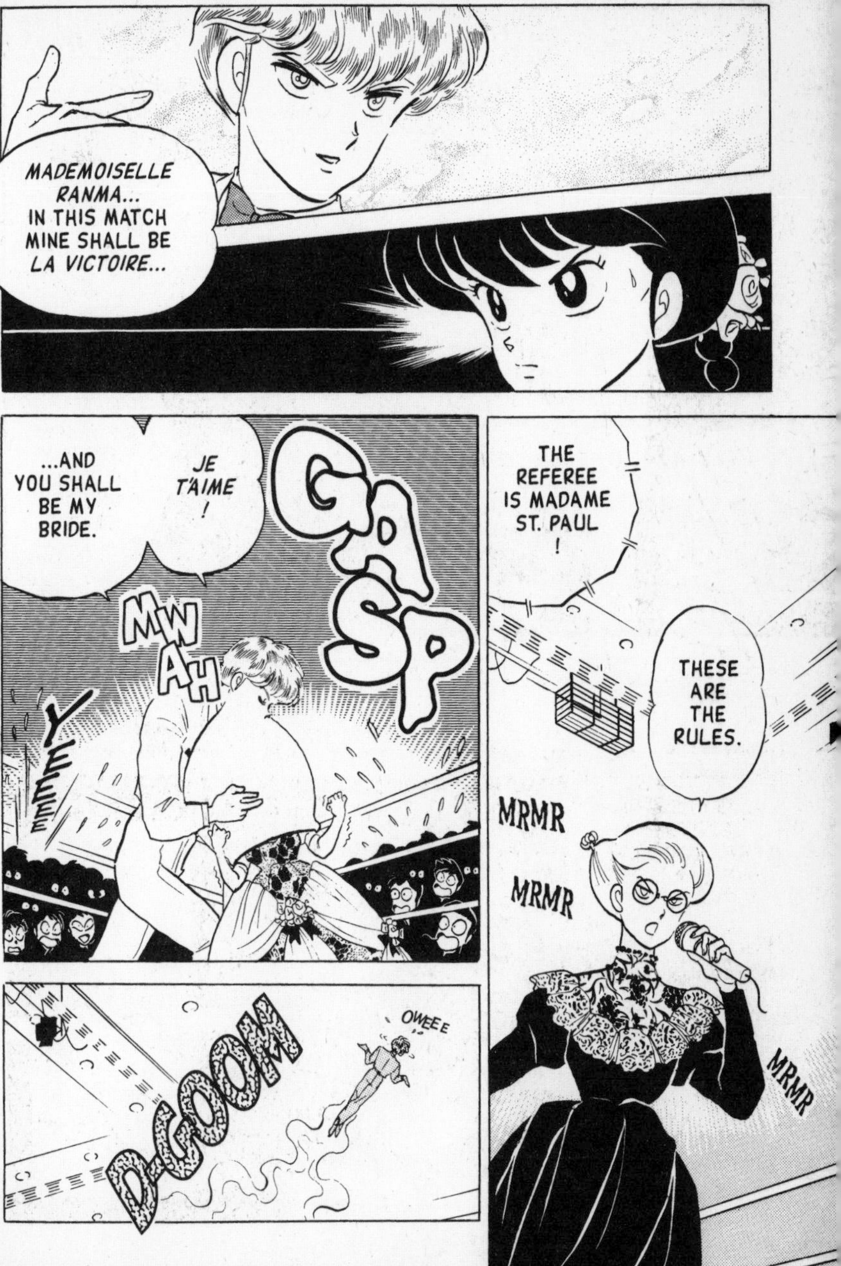
MADEMOISELLE RANMA... IN THIS MATCH MINE SHALL BE LA VICTOIRE...
...AND YOU SHALL BE MY BRIDE.
JE T'AIME !
GASP
MWAH
YEEEE
OWEEE
D-GOOM
THE REFEREE IS MADAME ST. PAUL !
THESE ARE THE RULES.
MRMR
MRMR
MRMR

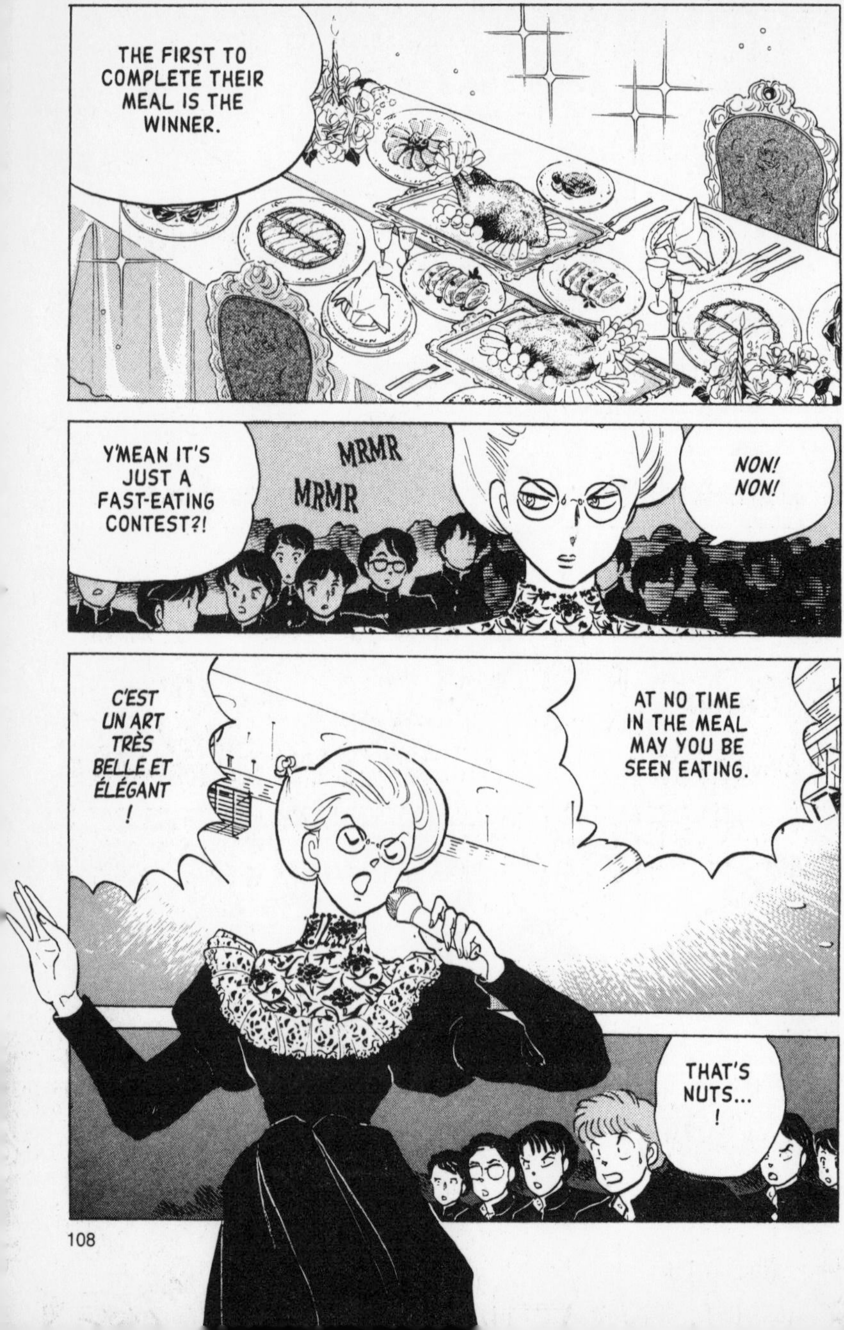
THE FIRST TO COMPLETE THEIR MEAL IS THE WINNER.
Y'MEAN IT'S JUST A FAST-EATING CONTEST?!
MRMR
MRMR
NON! NON!
C'EST UN ART TRÈS BELLE ET ÉLÉGANT!
AT NO TIME IN THE MEAL MAY YOU BE SEEN EATING.
THAT'S NUTS...!

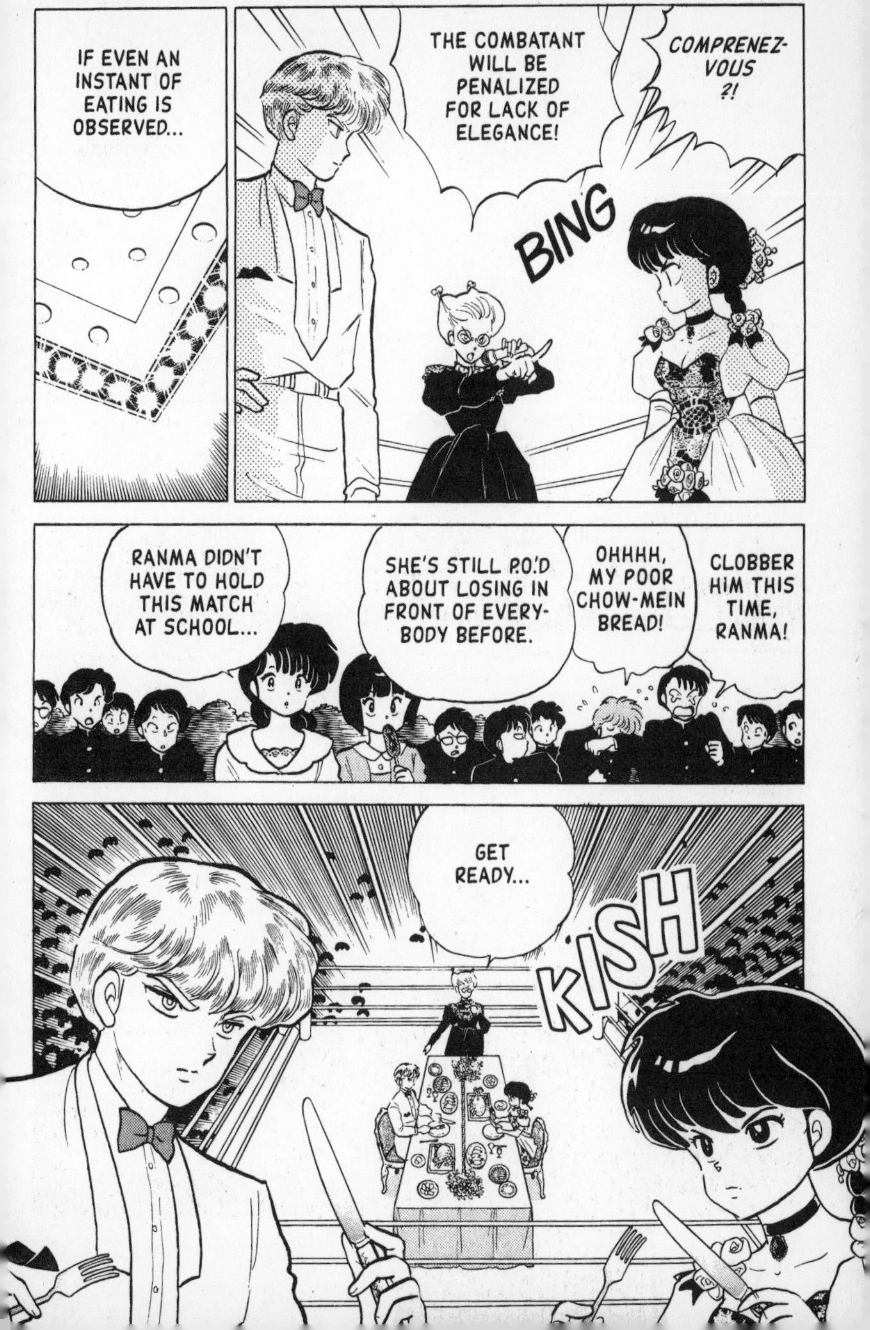
IF EVEN AN INSTANT OF EATING IS OBSERVED...
THE COMBATANT WILL BE PENALIZED FOR LACK OF ELEGANCE!
COMPRENEZ-VOUS ?!
BING
RANMA DIDN'T HAVE TO HOLD THIS MATCH AT SCHOOL...
SHE'S STILL P.O.'D ABOUT LOSING IN FRONT OF EVERY-BODY BEFORE.
OHHHH, MY POOR CHOW-MEIN BREAD!
CLOBBER HIM THIS TIME, RANMA!
GET READY...
KISH

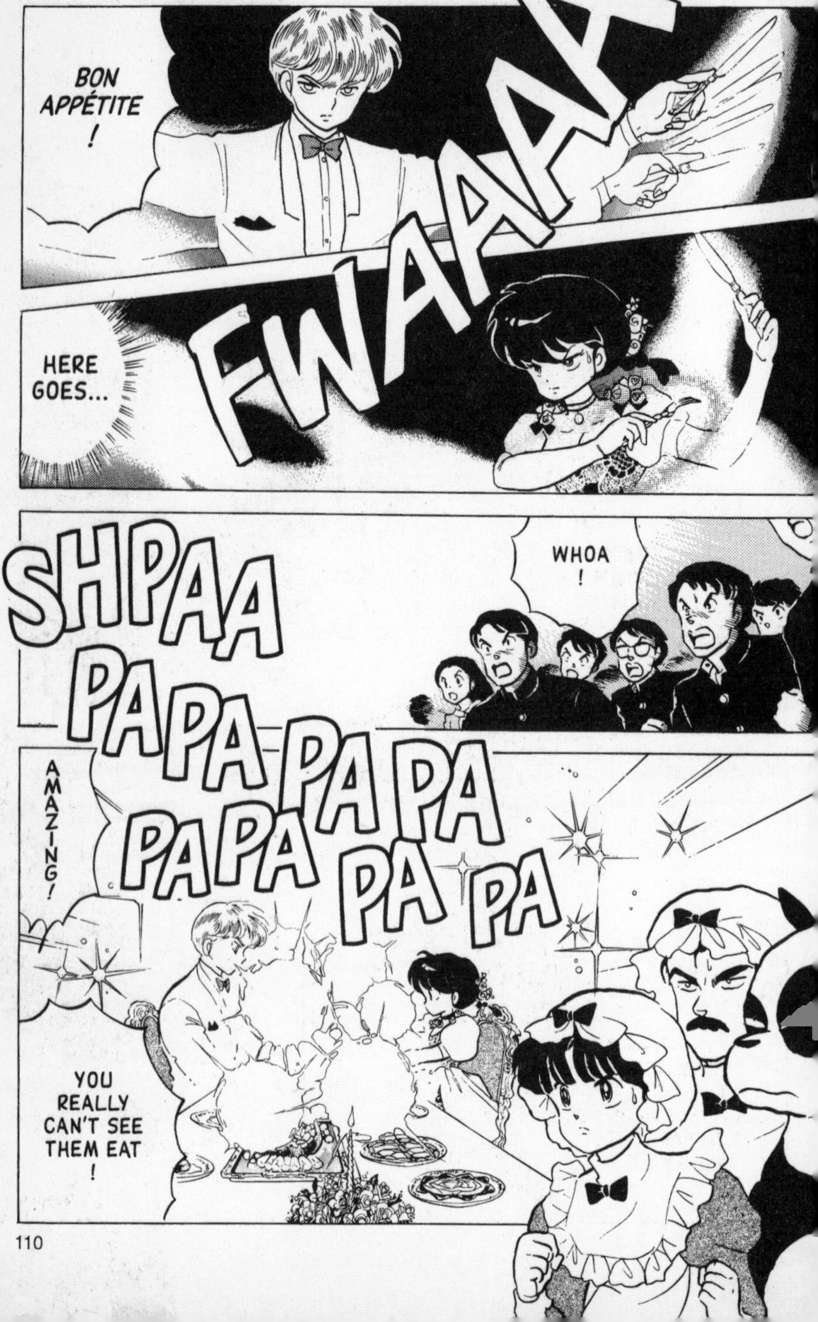
BON APPÉTITE !
FWAAAA
HERE GOES...
SHPAA PAPA PA PA PA PAPA PA PA
WHOA !
AMAZING !
YOU REALLY CAN'T SEE THEM EAT !

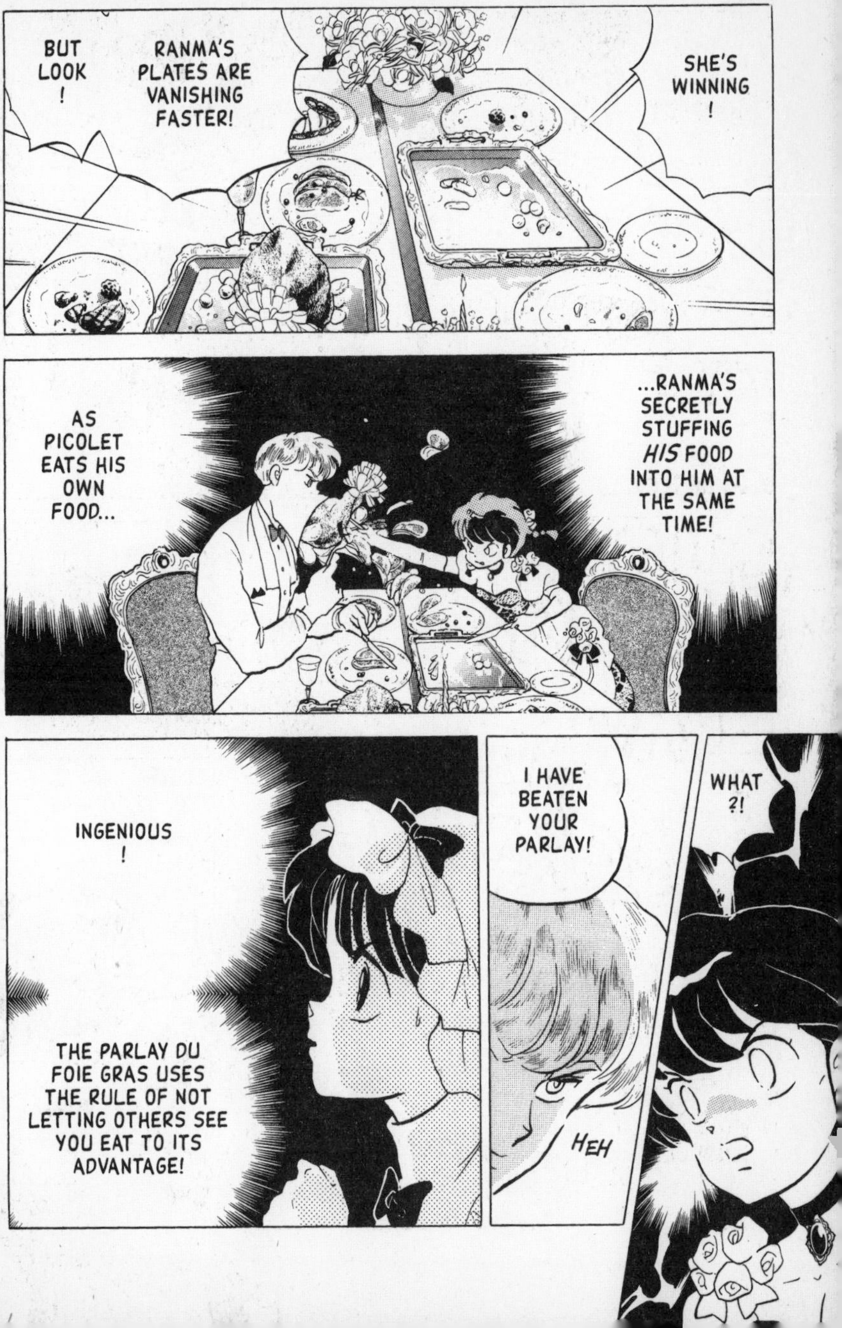
BUT LOOK !
RANMA'S PLATES ARE VANISHING FASTER!
SHE'S WINNING !
AS PICOLET EATS HIS OWN FOOD...
...RANMA'S SECRETLY STUFFING *HIS* FOOD INTO HIM AT THE SAME TIME!
INGENIOUS !
THE PARLAY DU FOIE GRAS USES THE RULE OF NOT LETTING OTHERS SEE YOU EAT TO ITS ADVANTAGE!
I HAVE BEATEN YOUR PARLAY!
HEH
WHAT ?!

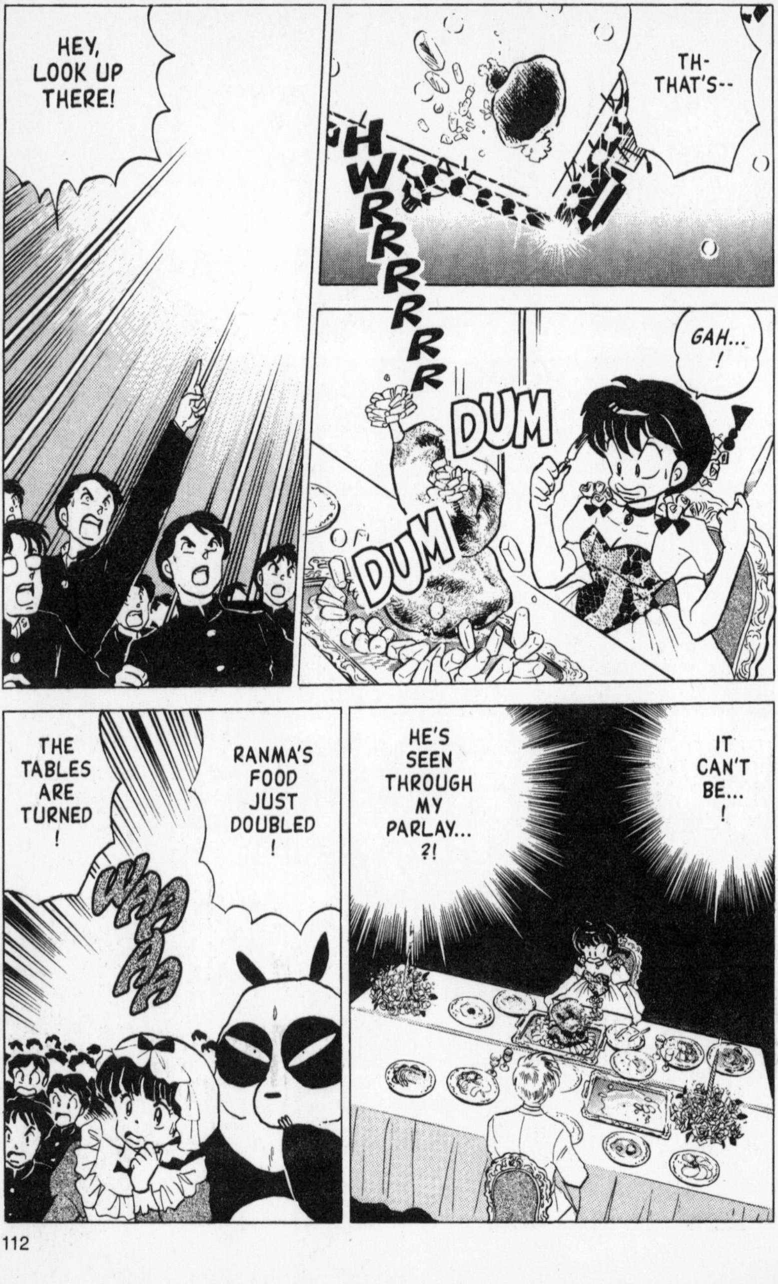
HEY, LOOK UP THERE!
TH- THAT'S--
HWRRRRRRR
GAH...!
DUM
DUM
THE TABLES ARE TURNED!
RANMA'S FOOD JUST DOUBLED!
HE'S SEEN THROUGH MY PARLAY...?!
IT CAN'T BE...!

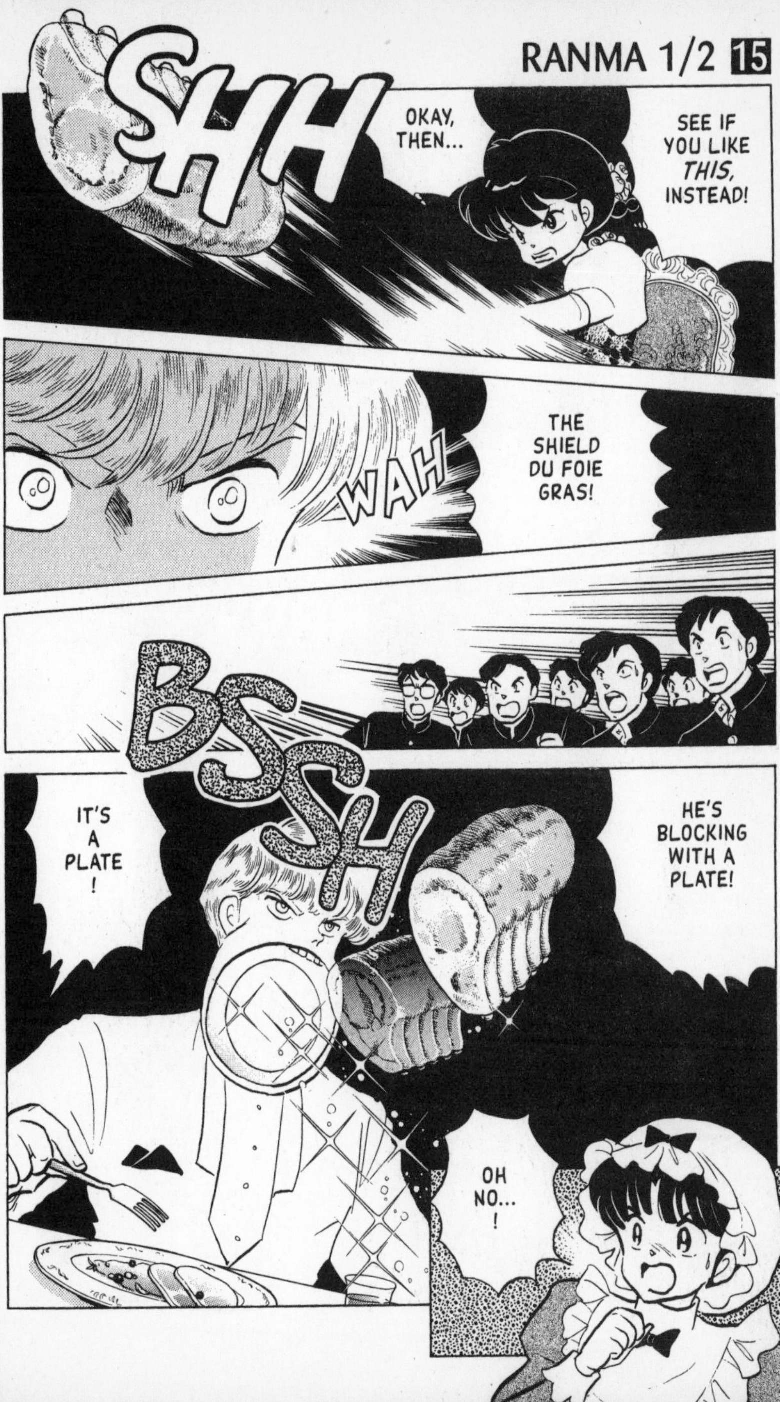
SHH
OKAY, THEN...
SEE IF YOU LIKE *THIS,* INSTEAD!
WAH
THE SHIELD DU FOIE GRAS!
BSSH
IT'S A PLATE!
HE'S BLOCKING WITH A PLATE!
OH NO...!

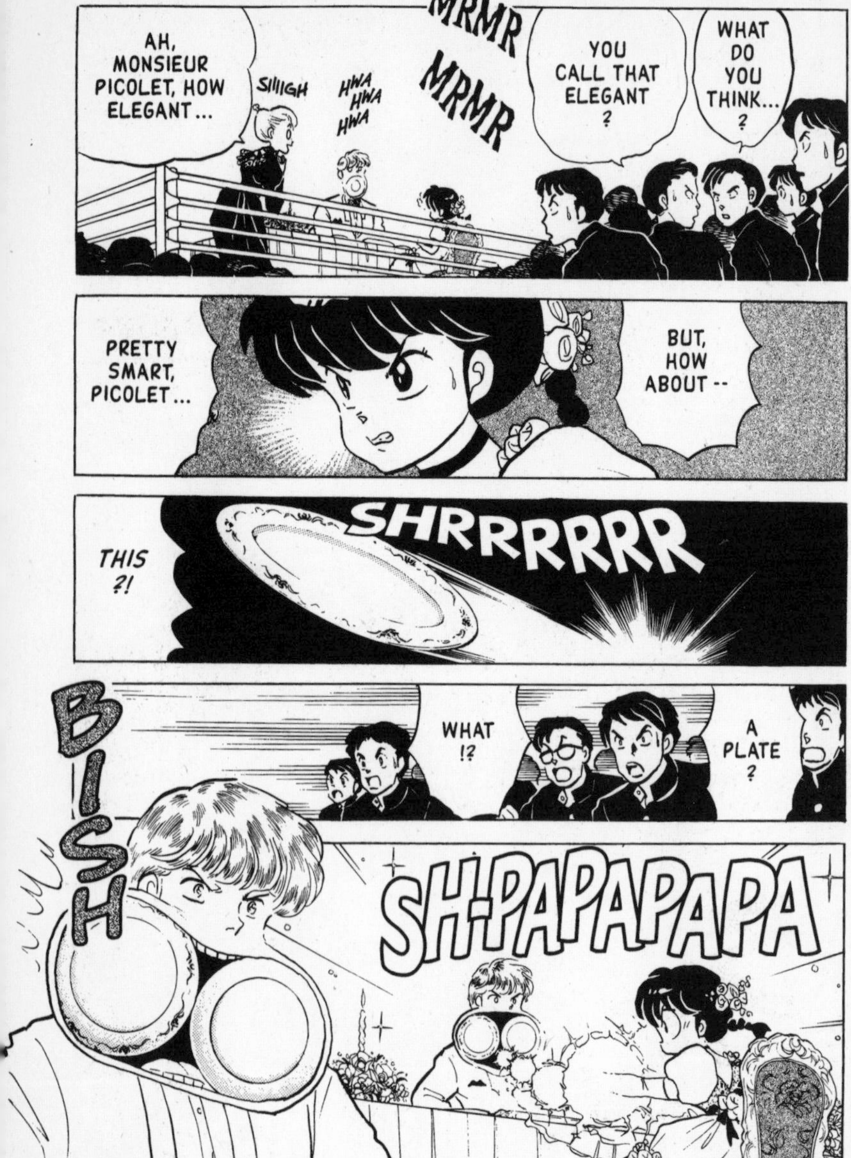
AH, MONSIEUR PICOLET, HOW ELEGANT...
SIIIGH
HWA HWA HWA
MRMR MRMR
YOU CALL THAT ELEGANT ?
WHAT DO YOU THINK... ?
PRETTY SMART, PICOLET...
BUT, HOW ABOUT --
THIS ?!
SHRRRRRR
BISH
WHAT !?
A PLATE ?
SH-PAPAPAPA

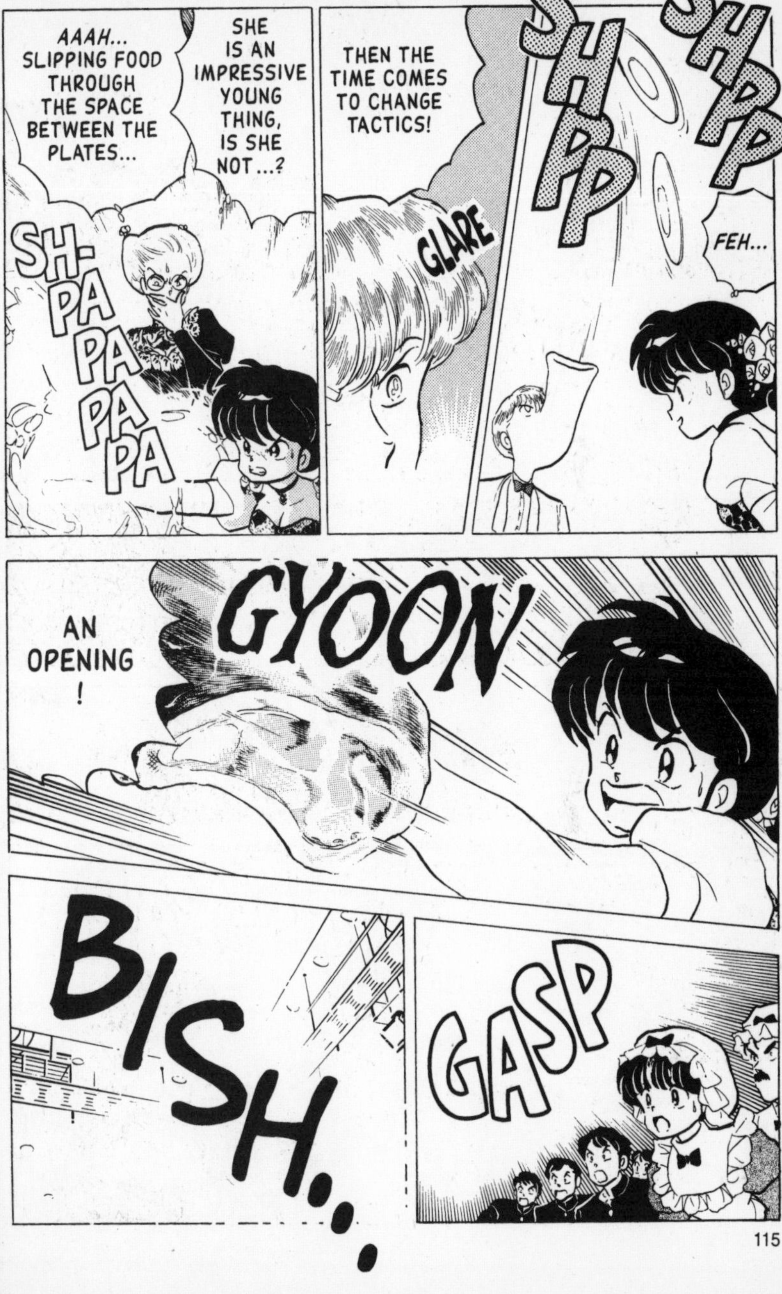
AAAH... SLIPPING FOOD THROUGH THE SPACE BETWEEN THE PLATES...
SHE IS AN IMPRESSIVE YOUNG THING, IS SHE NOT...?
SH-PA PA PA PA
THEN THE TIME COMES TO CHANGE TACTICS!
GLARE
SHPP
SHPP
FEH...
AN OPENING !
GYOON
BISH...
GASP

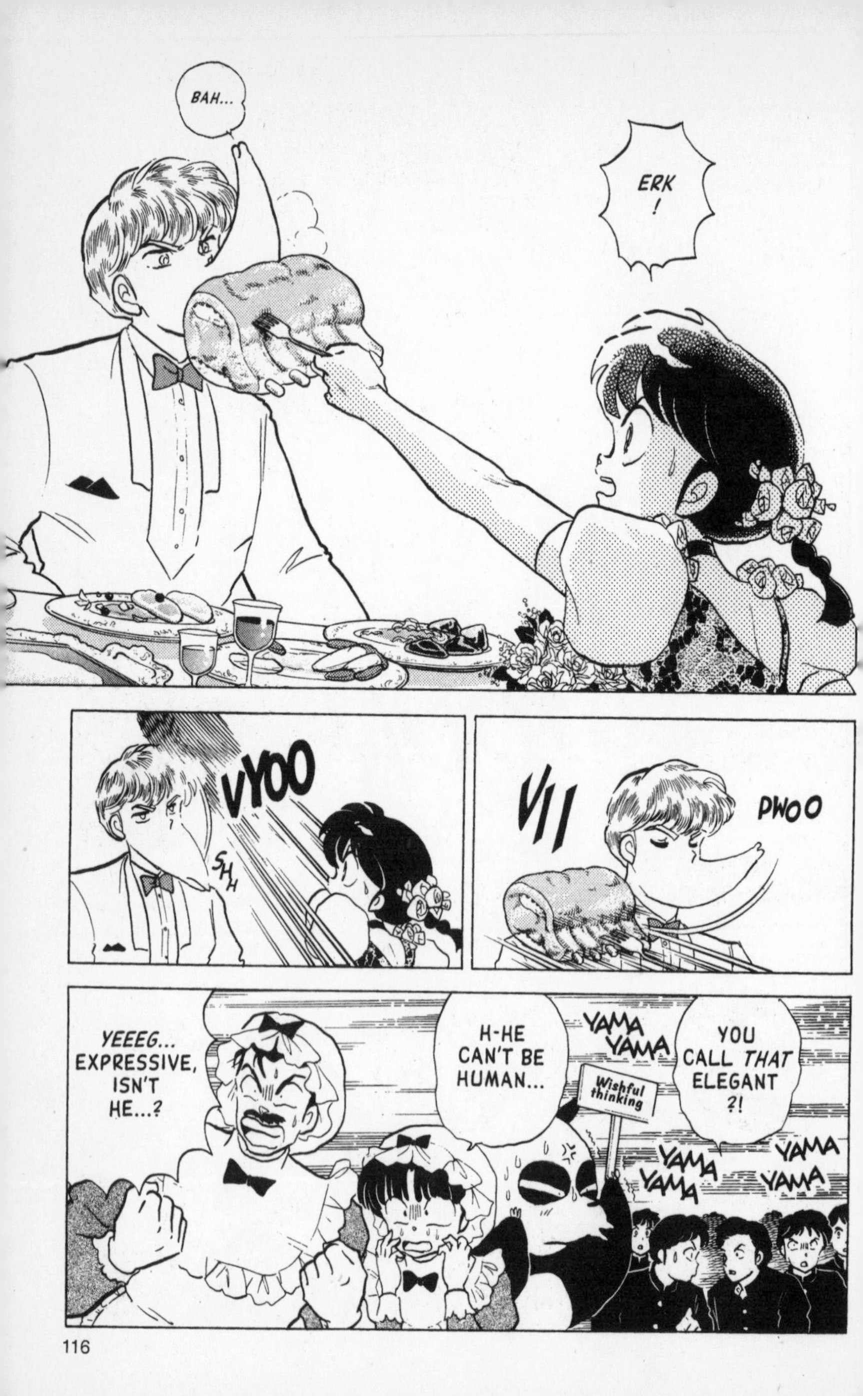

BAH...
ERK !
VYOO
SHH
VII
PWOO
YEEEG... EXPRESSIVE, ISN'T HE...?
H-HE CAN'T BE HUMAN...
YAMA YAMA
Wishful thinking
YOU CALL THAT ELEGANT ?!
YAMA YAMA
YAMA YAMA

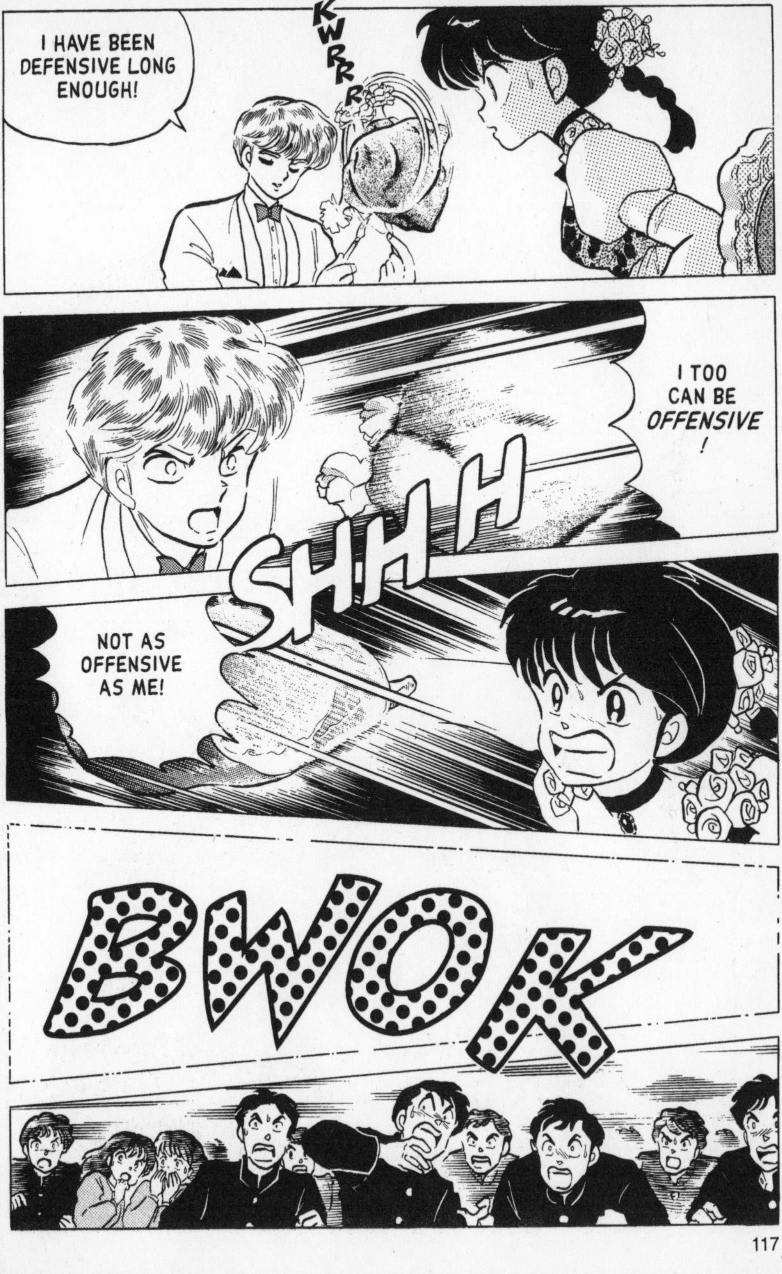
I HAVE BEEN DEFENSIVE LONG ENOUGH!
KWRRR
I TOO CAN BE OFFENSIVE !
SHHH
NOT AS OFFENSIVE AS ME!
BWOK

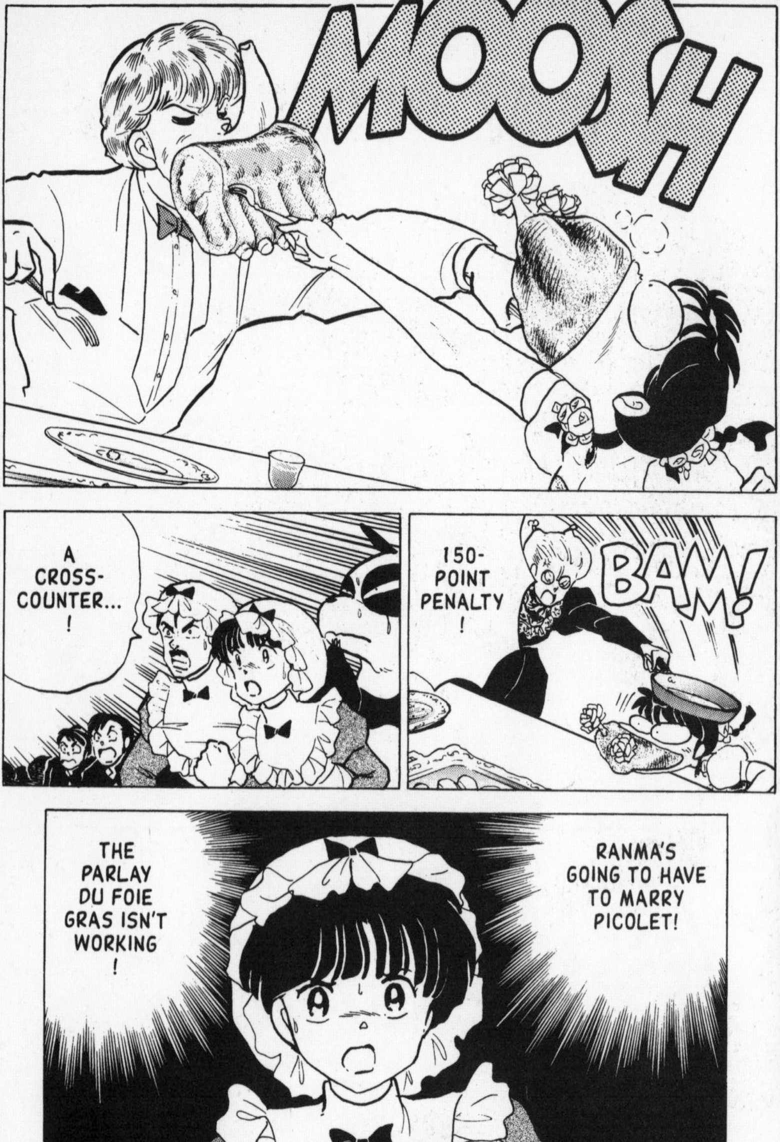
MOOSH
A CROSS-COUNTER...!
150-POINT PENALTY!
BAM!
THE PARLAY DU FOIE GRAS ISN'T WORKING!
RANMA'S GOING TO HAVE TO MARRY PICOLET!

Part 6
DO NOT DESSERT ME

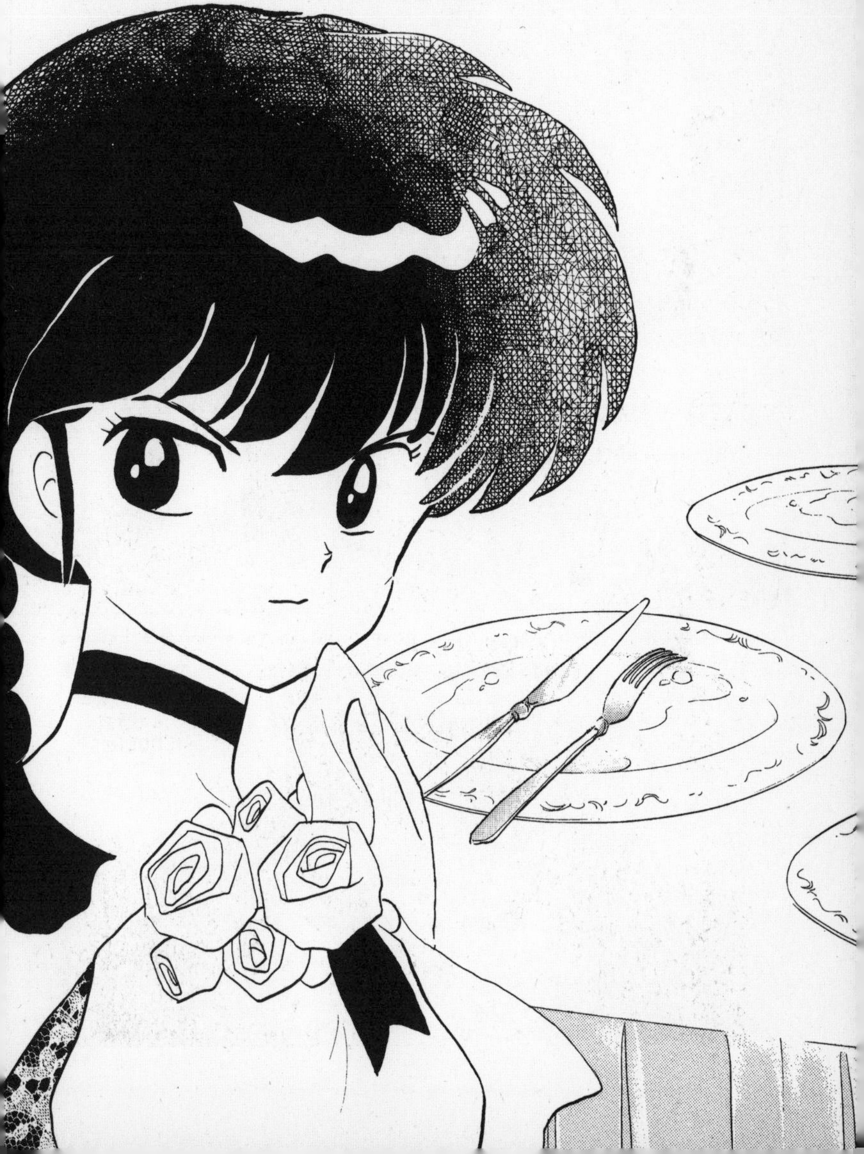

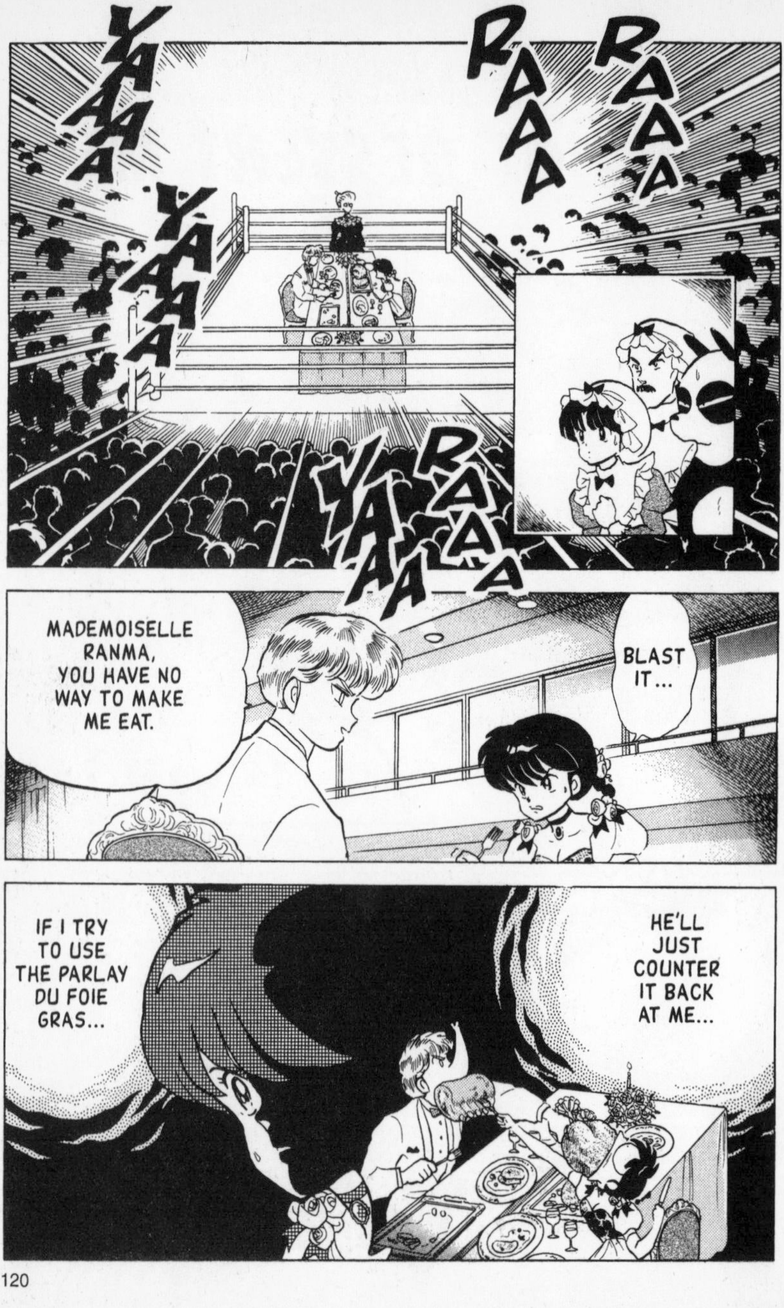
YAAAA
RAAAA
YAAAA
RAAAA
YAAAA
RAAAA
MADEMOISELLE RANMA, YOU HAVE NO WAY TO MAKE ME EAT.
BLAST IT...
IF I TRY TO USE THE PARLAY DU FOIE GRAS...
HE'LL JUST COUNTER IT BACK AT ME...

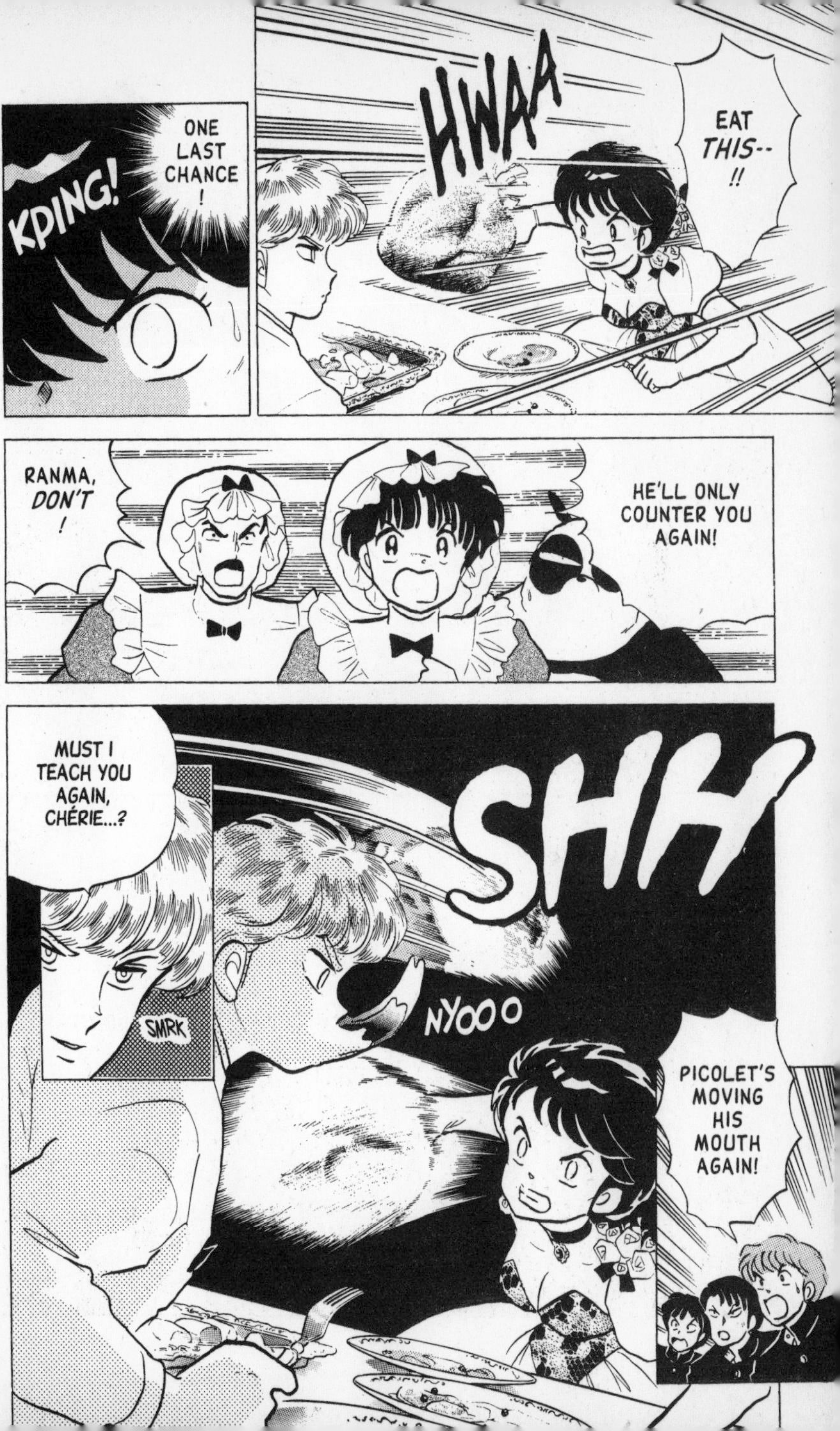
KPING!
ONE LAST CHANCE!
HWAA
EAT *THIS*--!!
RANMA, *DON'T*!
HE'LL ONLY COUNTER YOU AGAIN!
MUST I TEACH YOU AGAIN, CHÉRIE...?
SHH
SMRK
NYOOO
PICOLET'S MOVING HIS MOUTH AGAIN!

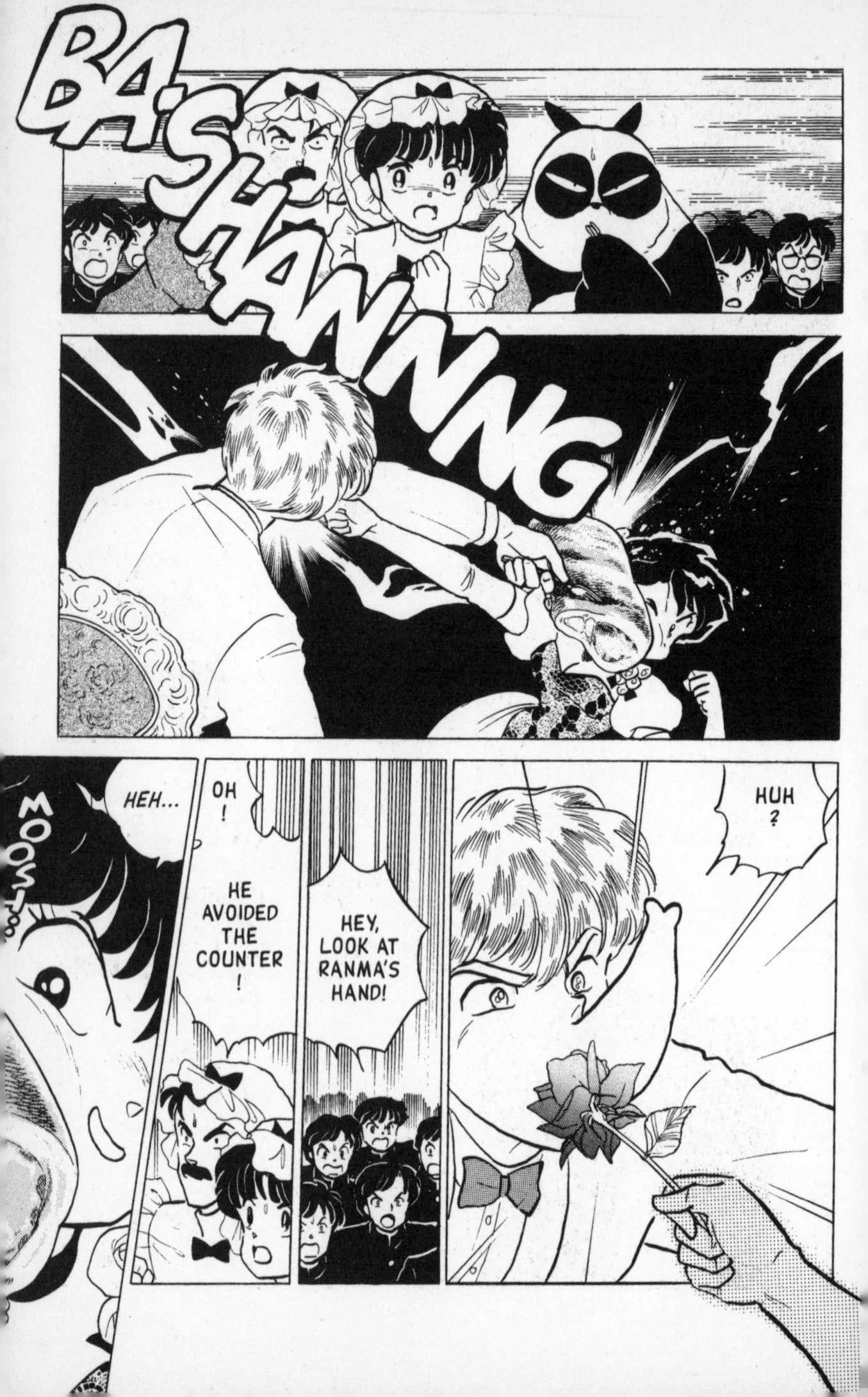
BA-SHANNNG
HEH...
OH!
HE AVOIDED THE COUNTER!
HEY, LOOK AT RANMA'S HAND!
HUH?

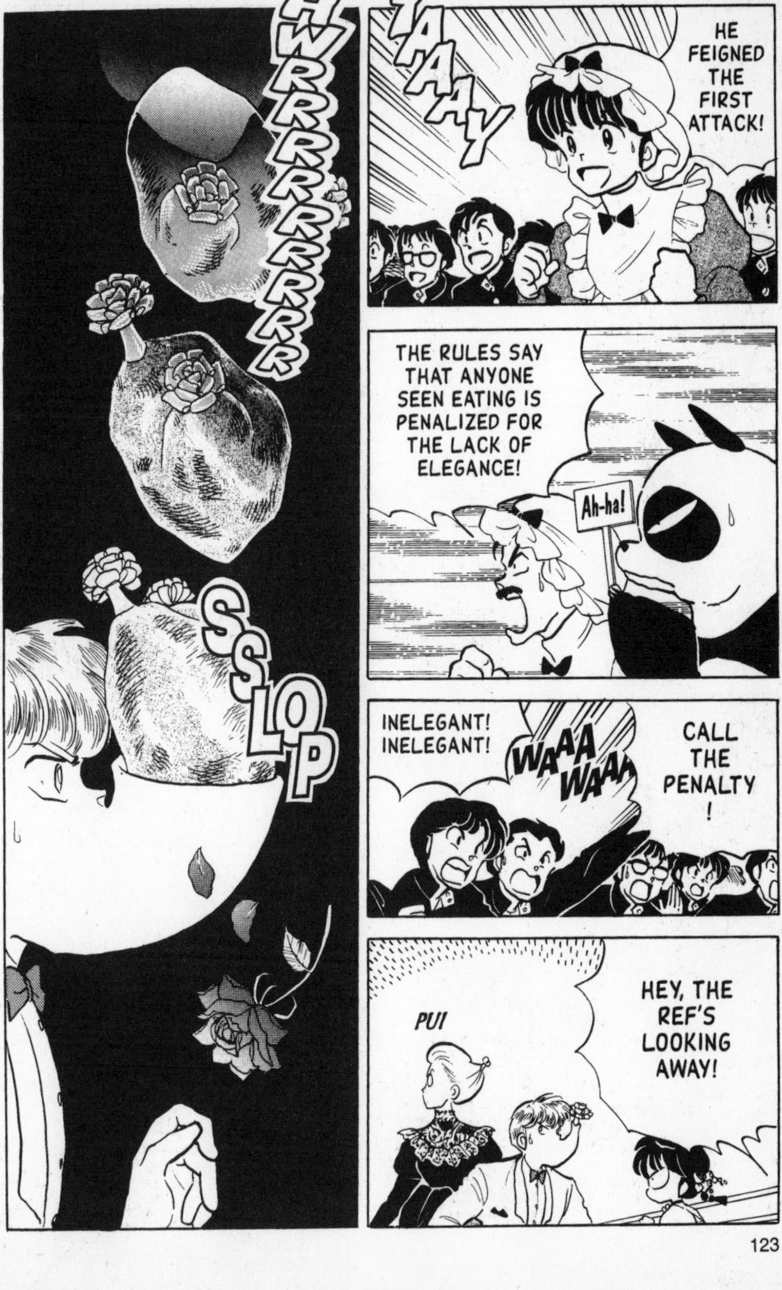
HWRRRRRRRRRR
SSLOP
YAAAY
HE FEIGNED THE FIRST ATTACK!
THE RULES SAY THAT ANYONE SEEN EATING IS PENALIZED FOR THE LACK OF ELEGANCE!
Ah-ha!
INELEGANT! INELEGANT!
WAAA WAAA
CALL THE PENALTY!
PUI
HEY, THE REF'S LOOKING AWAY!

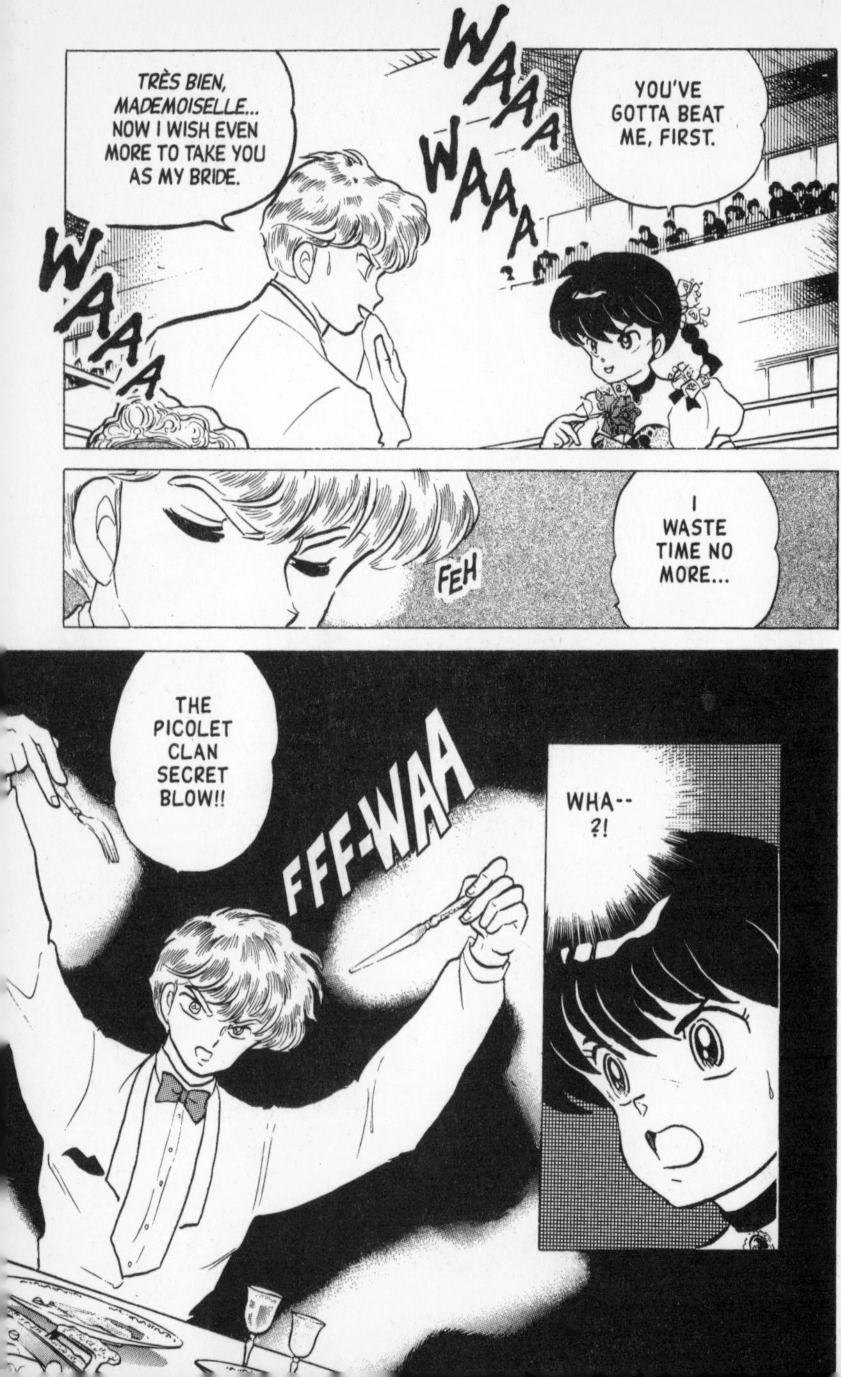
TRÈS BIEN, MADEMOISELLE... NOW I WISH EVEN MORE TO TAKE YOU AS MY BRIDE.
WAAAA
WAAAA
WAAAAA
YOU'VE GOTTA BEAT ME, FIRST.
FEH
I WASTE TIME NO MORE...
THE PICOLET CLAN SECRET BLOW!!
FFF-WAA
WHA-- ?!

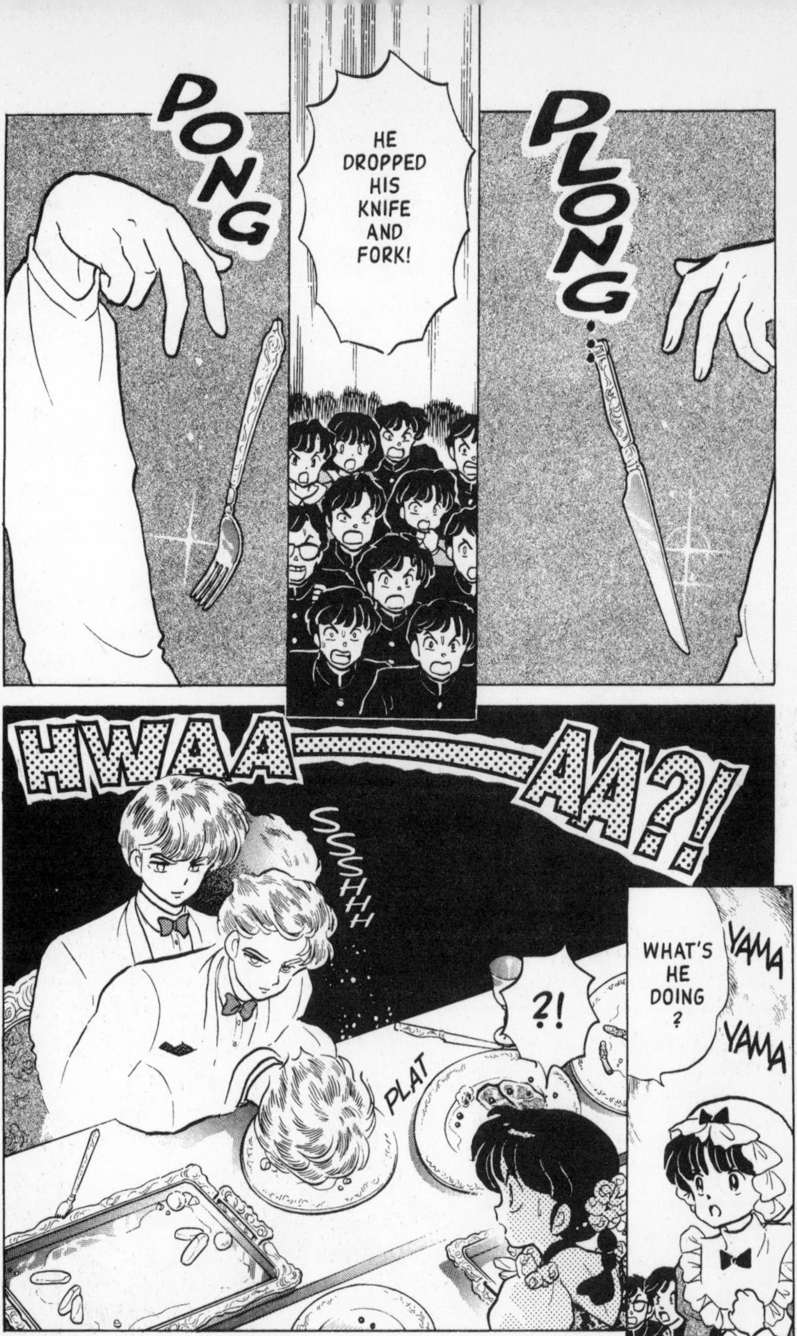
PONG
HE DROPPED HIS KNIFE AND FORK!
PLONG...
HWAA—AA?!
SSSHHH
PLAT
?!
WHAT'S HE DOING?
YAMA
YAMA

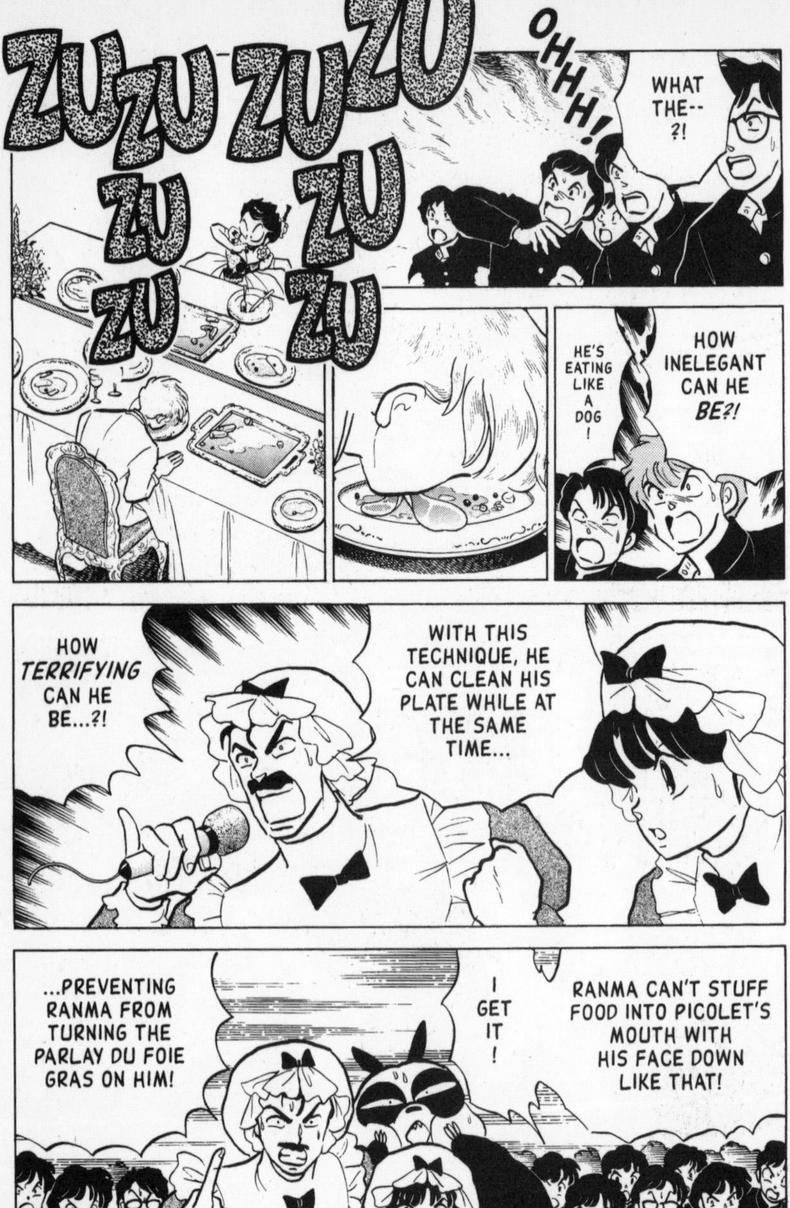

ZUZU ZUZUZU ZU ZU ZU ZU
OHHHH!
WHAT THE--?!
HE'S EATING LIKE A DOG!
HOW INELEGANT CAN HE BE?!
HOW TERRIFYING CAN HE BE...?!
WITH THIS TECHNIQUE, HE CAN CLEAN HIS PLATE WHILE AT THE SAME TIME...
...PREVENTING RANMA FROM TURNING THE PARLAY DU FOIE GRAS ON HIM!
I GET IT!
RANMA CAN'T STUFF FOOD INTO PICOLET'S MOUTH WITH HIS FACE DOWN LIKE THAT!

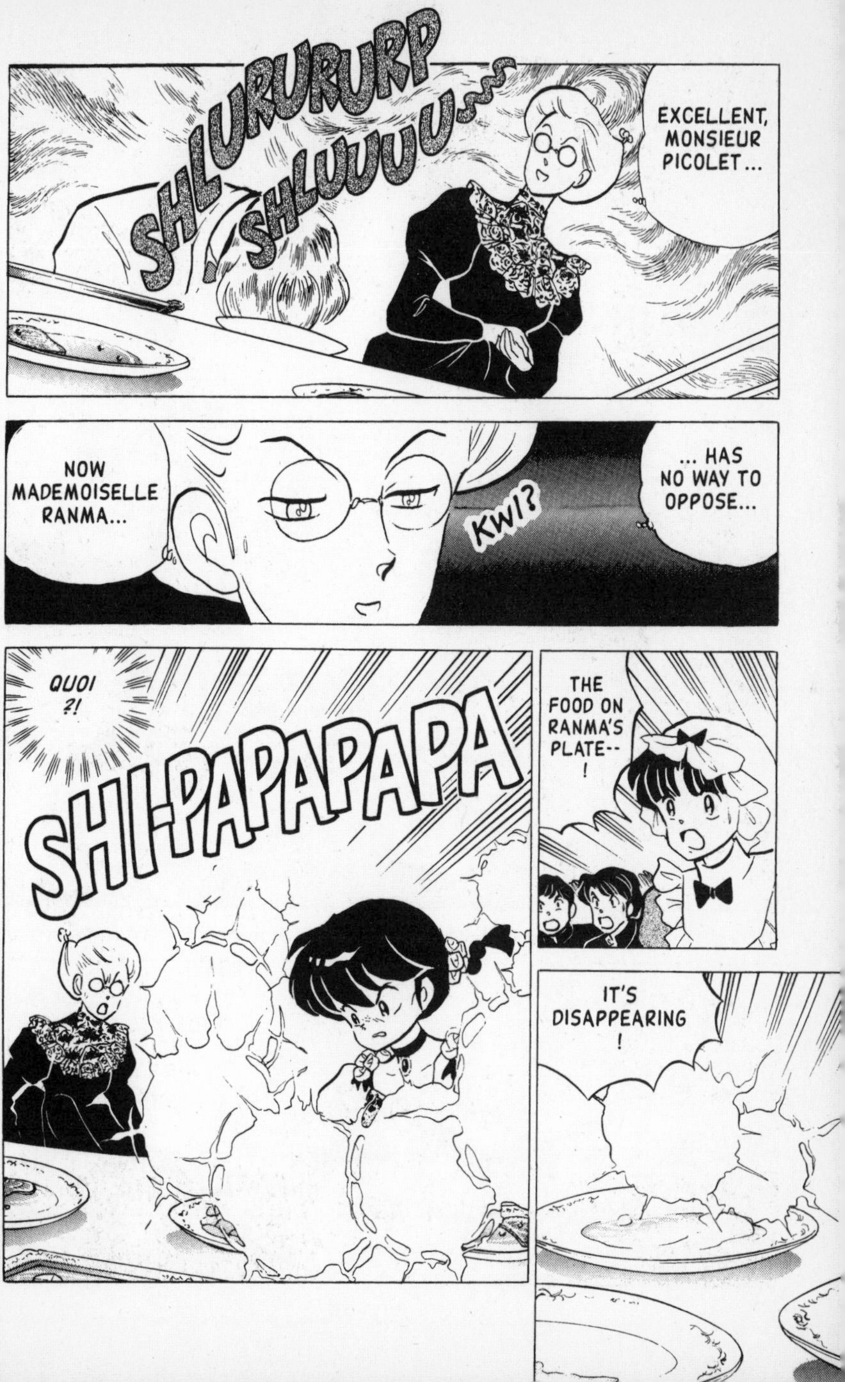
SHLURURURP SHLUUUU
EXCELLENT, MONSIEUR PICOLET...
NOW MADEMOISELLE RANMA...
KWI?
... HAS NO WAY TO OPPOSE...
QUOI ?!
SHI-PAPAPAPA
THE FOOD ON RANMA'S PLATE-- !
IT'S DISAPPEARING !

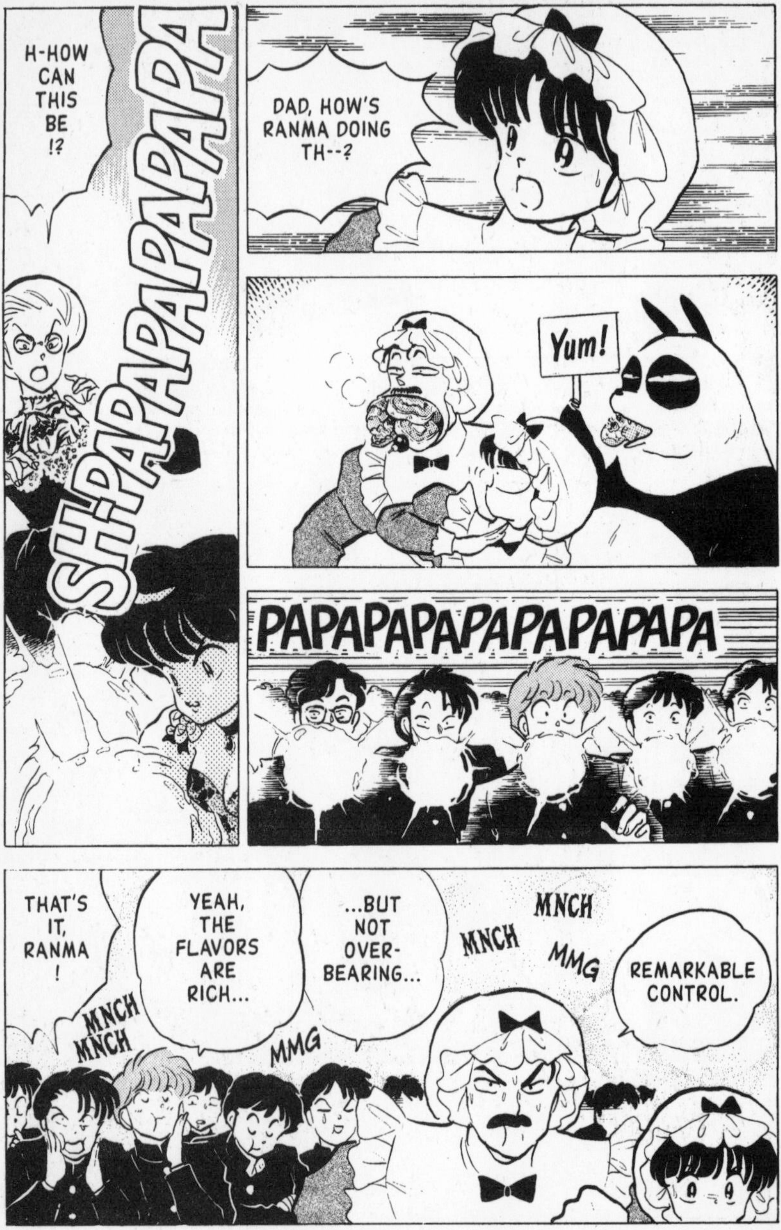
H-HOW CAN THIS BE !?
SH-PAPAPAPAPAPA
DAD, HOW'S RANMA DOING TH--?
Yum!
PAPAPAPAPAPAPAPAPA
THAT'S IT, RANMA !
YEAH, THE FLAVORS ARE RICH...
...BUT NOT OVER-BEARING...
MNCH MNCH
MMG
MNCH
MNCH
MMG
REMARKABLE CONTROL.

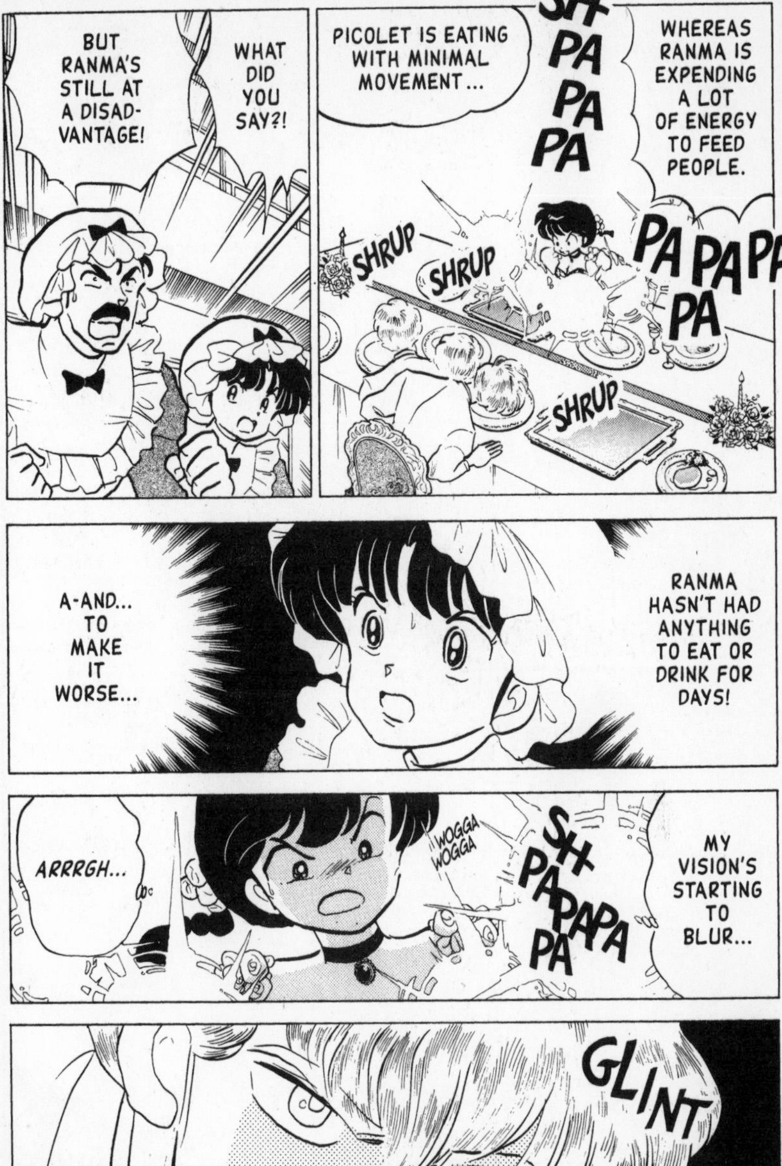
BUT RANMA'S STILL AT A DISAD-VANTAGE!
WHAT DID YOU SAY?!
PICOLET IS EATING WITH MINIMAL MOVEMENT...
SH PA PA PA
WHEREAS RANMA IS EXPENDING A LOT OF ENERGY TO FEED PEOPLE.
SHRUP
SHRUP
PA PA PA PA
SHRUP
A-AND... TO MAKE IT WORSE...
RANMA HASN'T HAD ANYTHING TO EAT OR DRINK FOR DAYS!
ARRRGH...
WOGGA WOGGA
SH PA PA PA PA
MY VISION'S STARTING TO BLUR...
GLINT

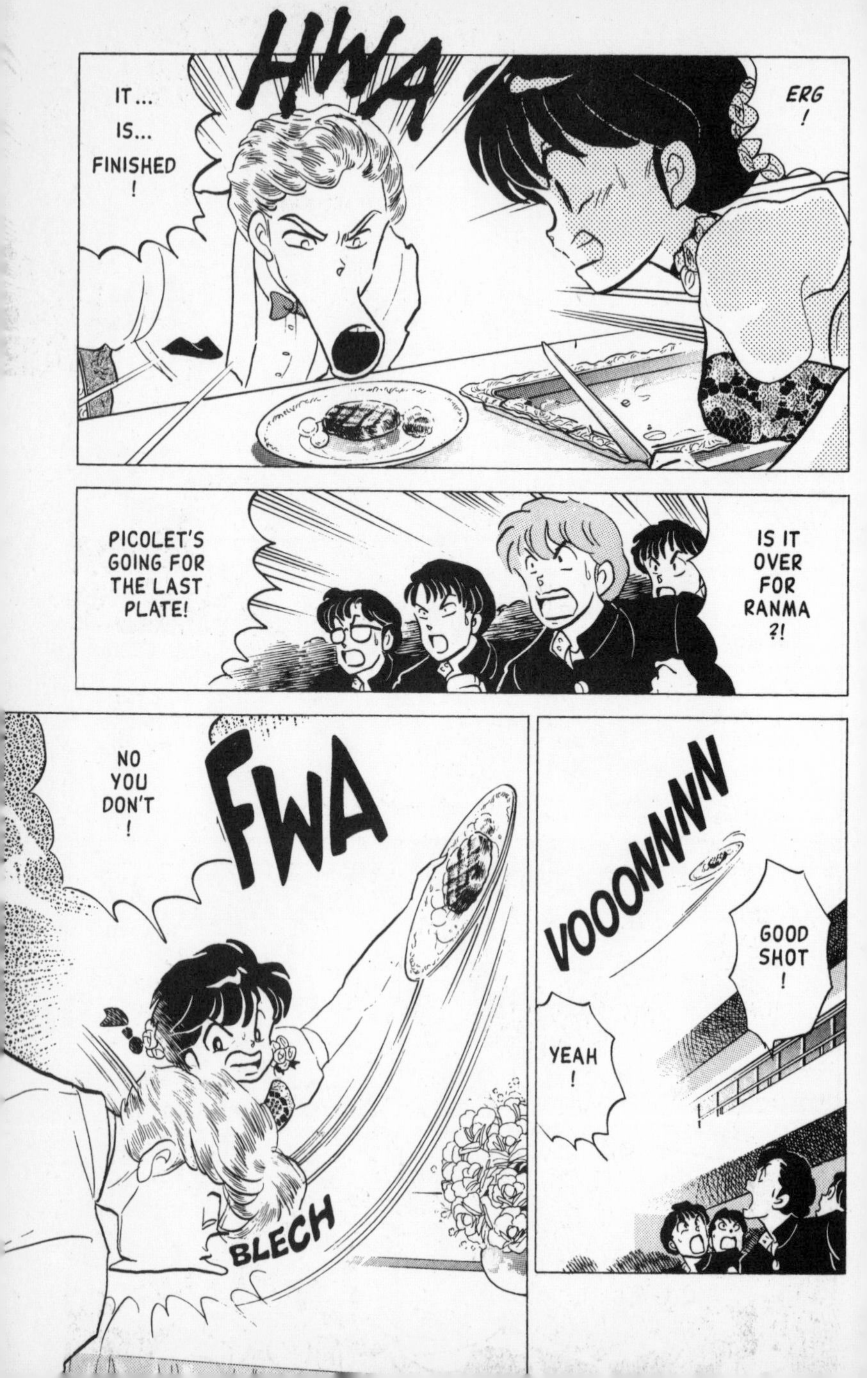
HWA
IT... IS... FINISHED!
ERG!
PICOLET'S GOING FOR THE LAST PLATE!
IS IT OVER FOR RANMA?!
NO YOU DON'T!
FWA
BLECH
VOOONNNN
GOOD SHOT!
YEAH!

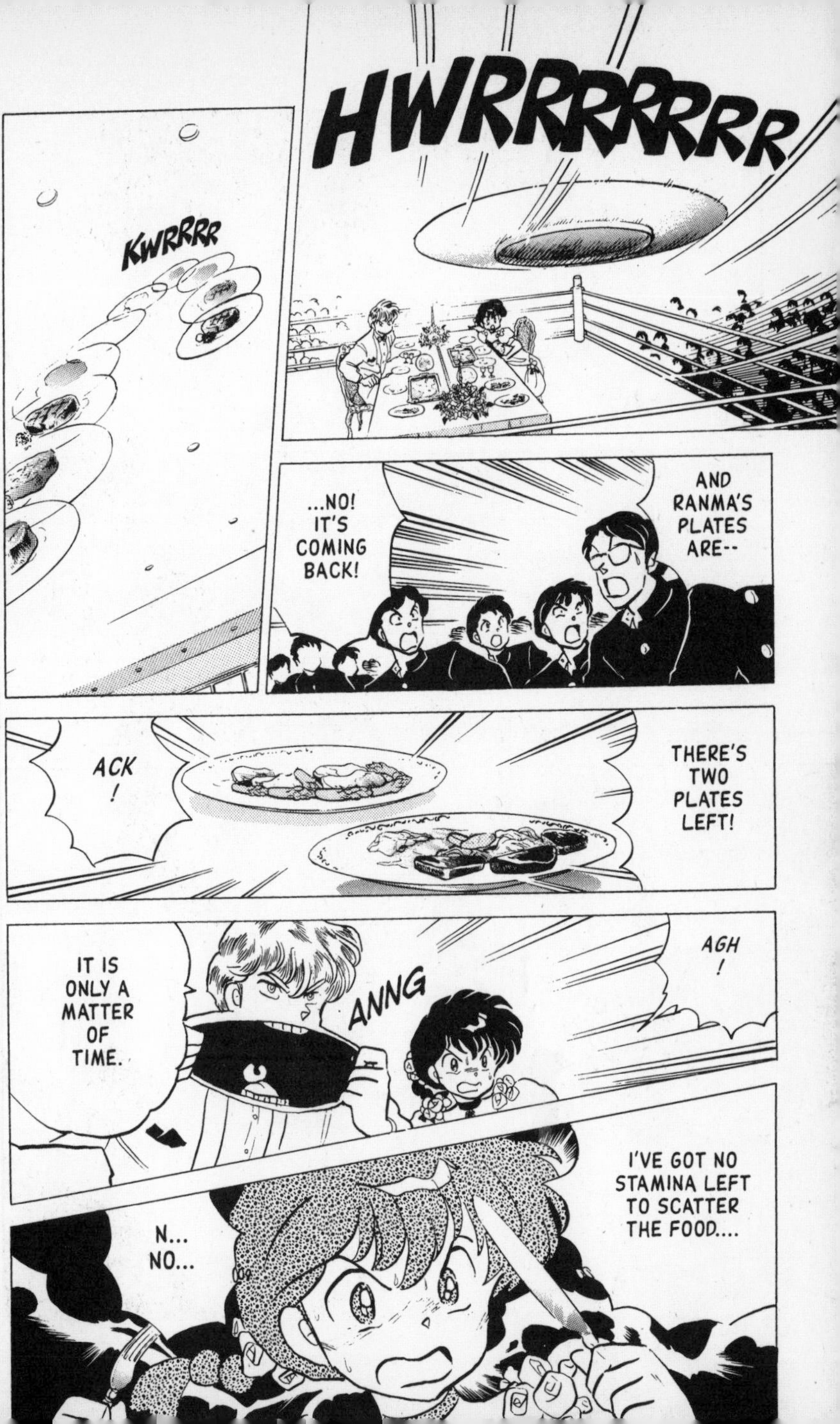

KWRRRR
HWRRRRRRRR
...NO! IT'S COMING BACK!
AND RANMA'S PLATES ARE--
ACK!
THERE'S TWO PLATES LEFT!
IT IS ONLY A MATTER OF TIME.
ANNG
AGH!
N... NO...
I'VE GOT NO STAMINA LEFT TO SCATTER THE FOOD....

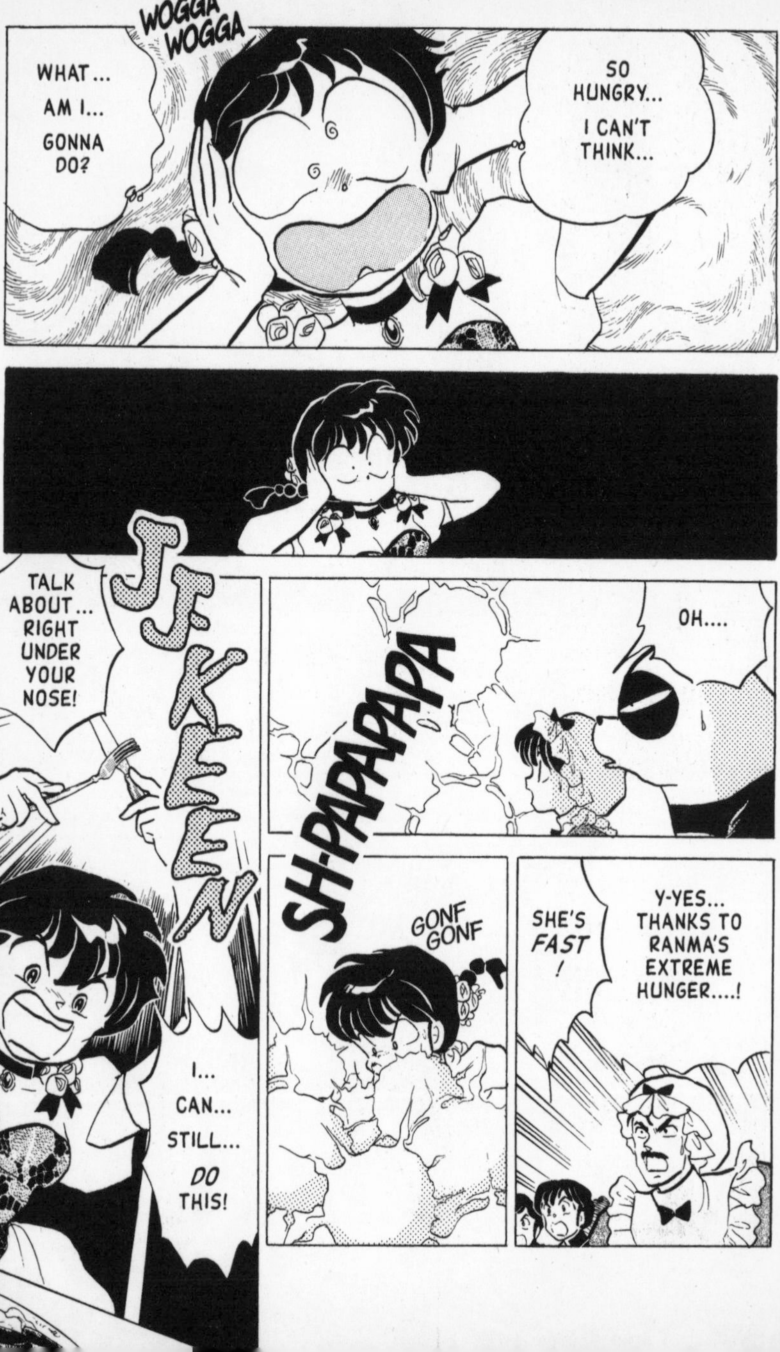
WOGGA WOGGA
WHAT... AM I... GONNA DO?
SO HUNGRY... I CAN'T THINK...
TALK ABOUT... RIGHT UNDER YOUR NOSE!
JJKEEN
I... CAN... STILL... DO THIS!
OH....
SH-PAPAPAPA
GONF GONF
SHE'S FAST!
Y-YES... THANKS TO RANMA'S EXTREME HUNGER....!

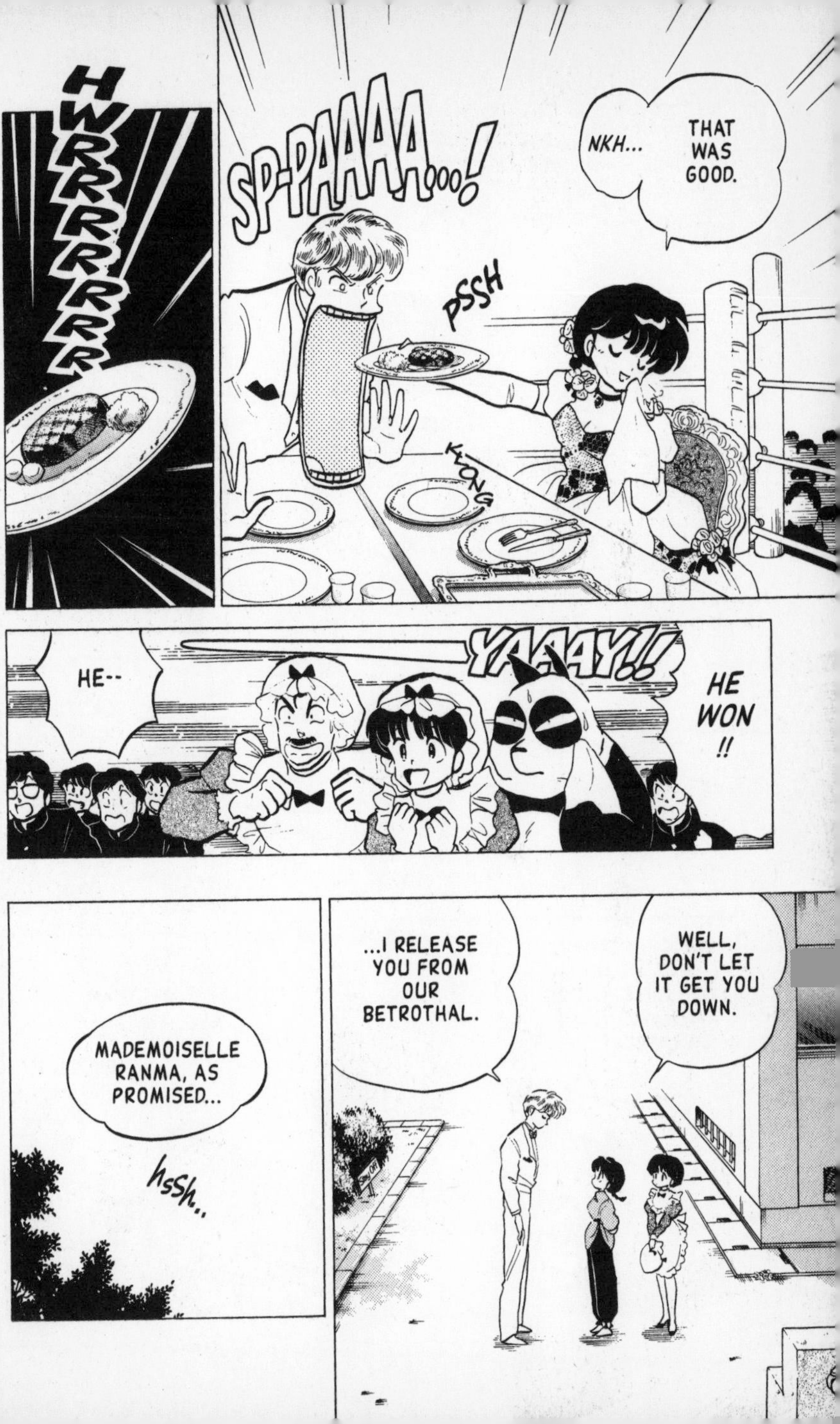
HWRRRRRRR
SP-PAAAA...!
PSSH
KLONG
NKH...
THAT WAS GOOD.
HE--
YAAAY!!
HE WON !!
MADEMOISELLE RANMA, AS PROMISED...
hsSh..
...I RELEASE YOU FROM OUR BETROTHAL.
WELL, DON'T LET IT GET YOU DOWN.

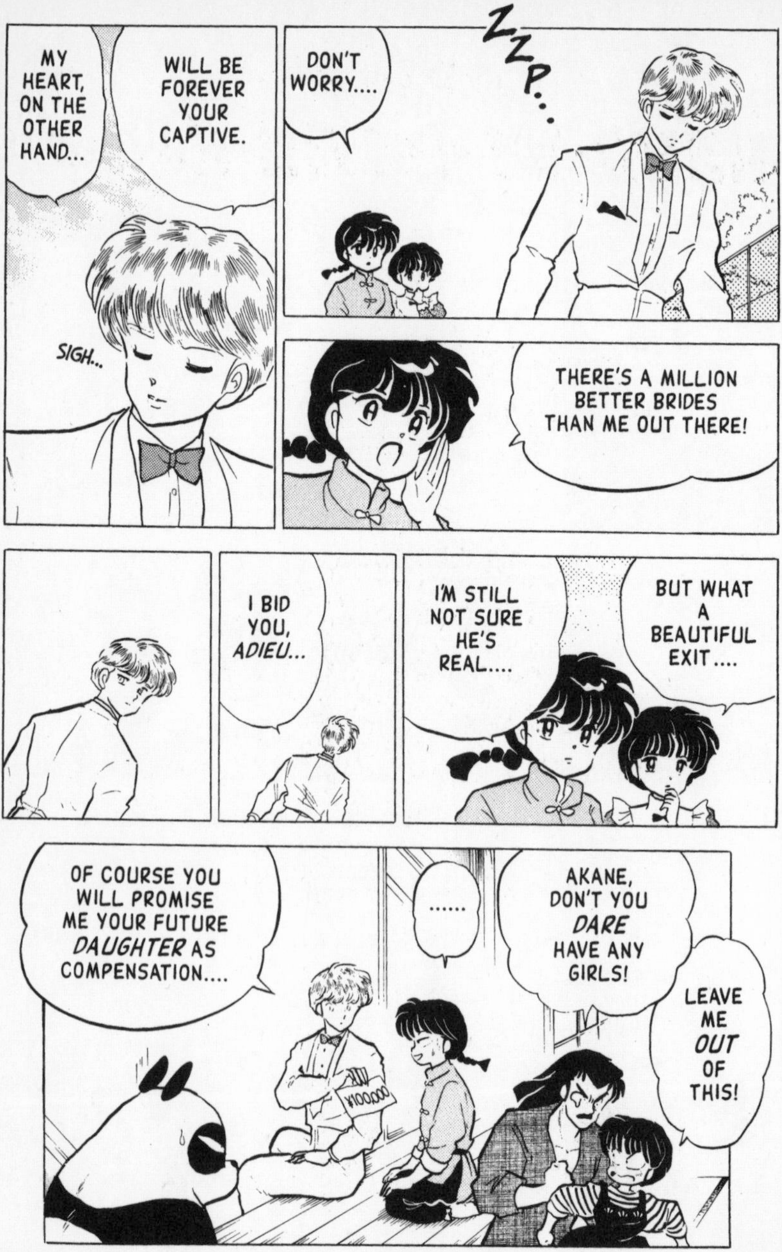
MY HEART, ON THE OTHER HAND...
WILL BE FOREVER YOUR CAPTIVE.
SIGH...
DON'T WORRY....
ZZZP...
THERE'S A MILLION BETTER BRIDES THAN ME OUT THERE!
I BID YOU, *ADIEU*...
I'M STILL NOT SURE HE'S REAL....
BUT WHAT A BEAUTIFUL EXIT....
OF COURSE YOU WILL PROMISE ME YOUR FUTURE *DAUGHTER* AS COMPENSATION....
......
¥100,000
AKANE, DON'T YOU *DARE* HAVE ANY GIRLS!
LEAVE ME *OUT* OF THIS!

Part 9
HAND-ME-DOWN RANMA

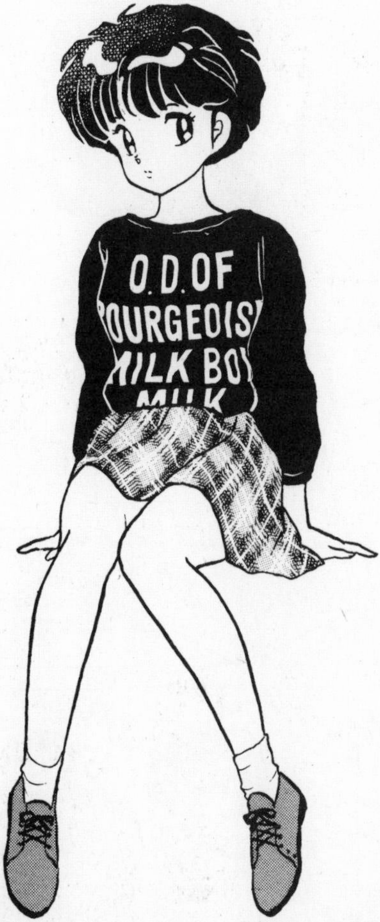
O.D.OF

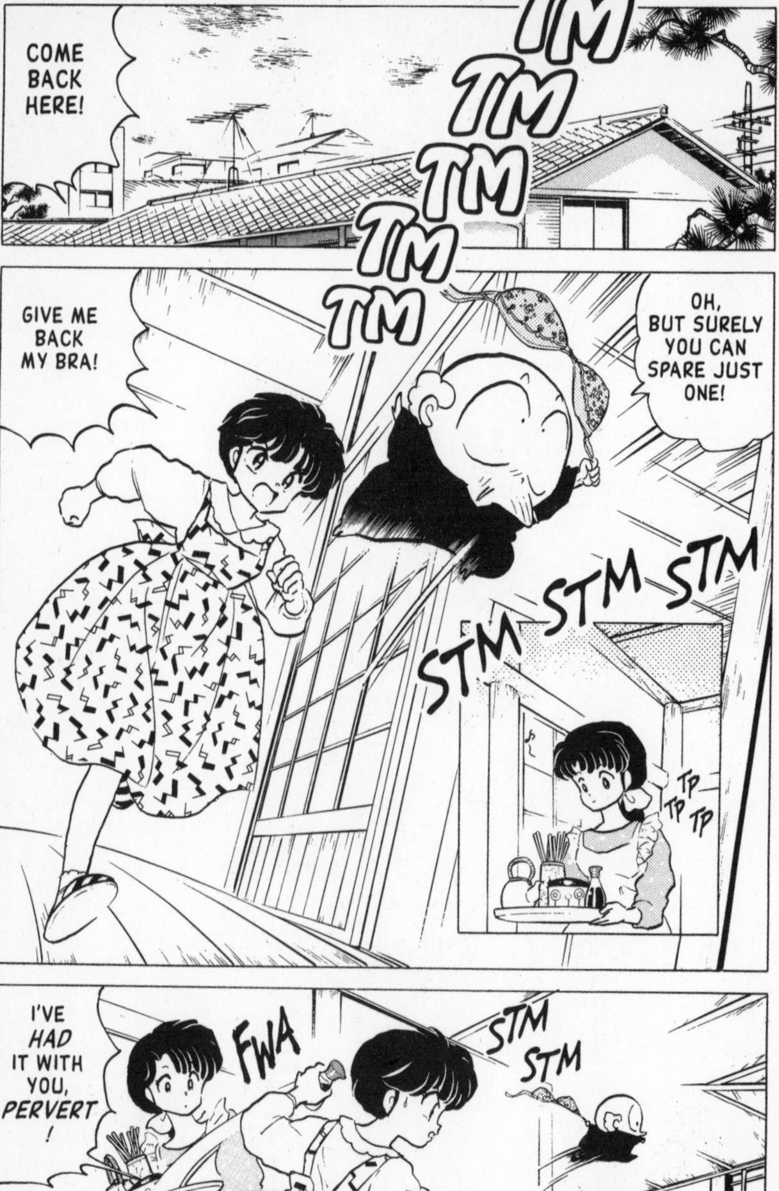
COME BACK HERE!
TM TM TM TM TM
GIVE ME BACK MY BRA!
OH, BUT SURELY YOU CAN SPARE JUST ONE!
STM STM STM
TP TP TP TP
I'VE *HAD* IT WITH YOU, *PERVERT*!
FWA
STM STM

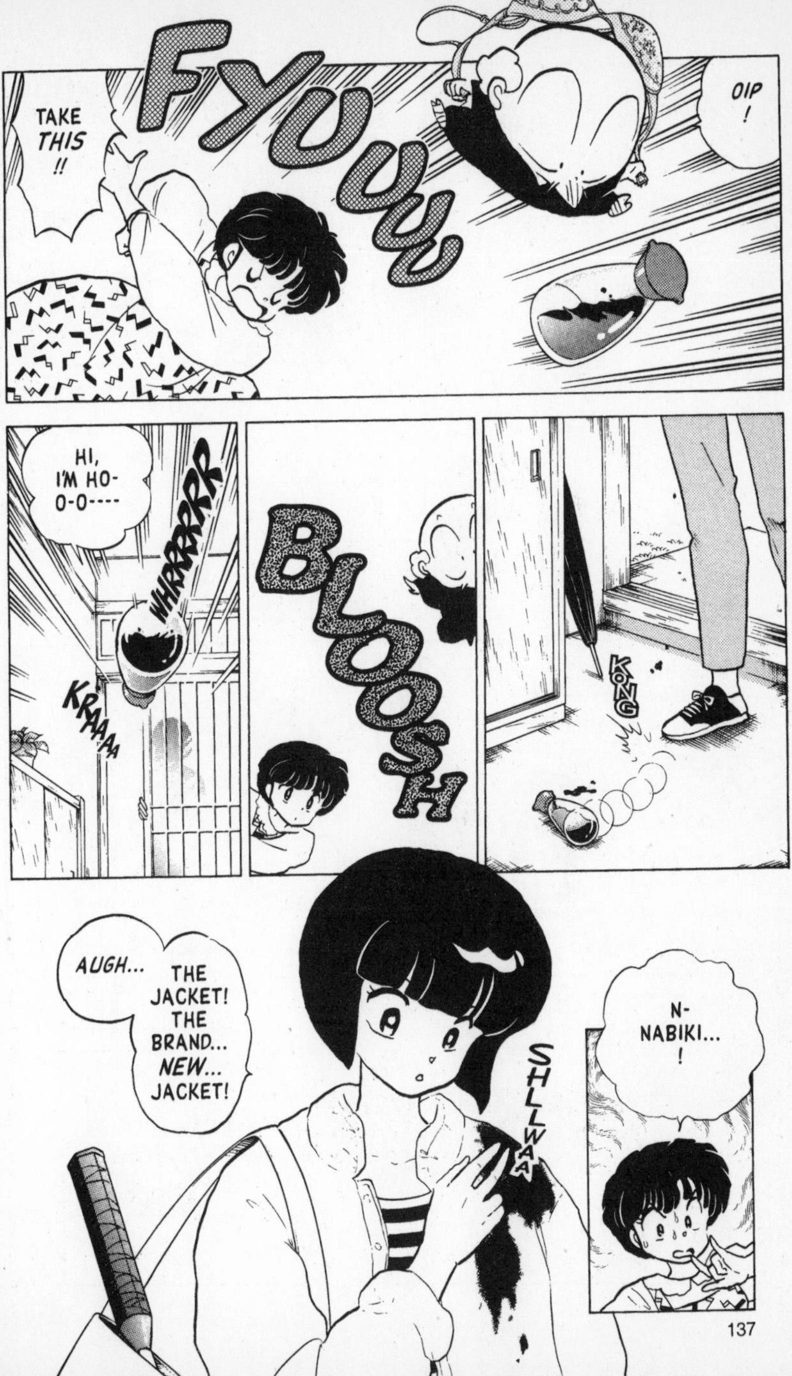
TAKE THIS !!
FYUUUU
OIP !
HI, I'M HO-O-O----
WHRRRRRR
KRAAAAA
BLOOSH
KONG
AUGH... THE JACKET! THE BRAND... NEW... JACKET!
SHLLWAA
N-NABIKI... !

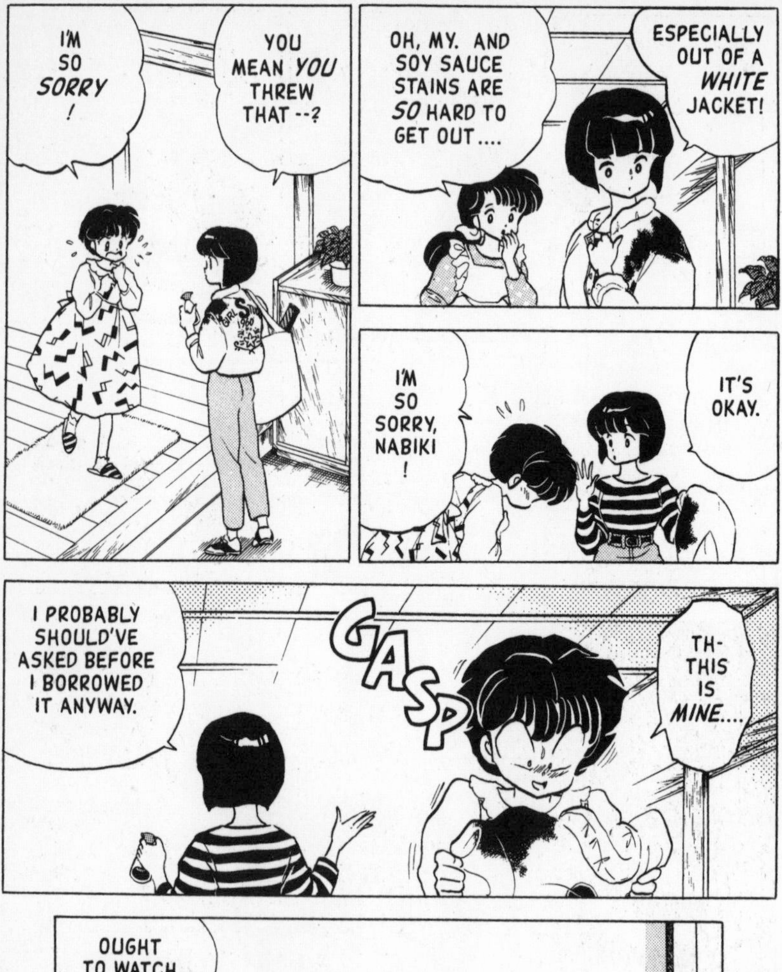
I'M SO *SORRY* !
YOU MEAN *YOU* THREW THAT --?
OH, MY. AND SOY SAUCE STAINS ARE *SO* HARD TO GET OUT....
ESPECIALLY OUT OF A *WHITE* JACKET!
I'M SO SORRY, NABIKI !
IT'S OKAY.
I PROBABLY SHOULD'VE ASKED BEFORE I BORROWED IT ANYWAY.
GASP
TH- THIS IS *MINE*....
OUGHT TO WATCH WHERE YOU THROW THINGS.
NABIKI
THAT WAS MY *FAVORITE* JACKET!

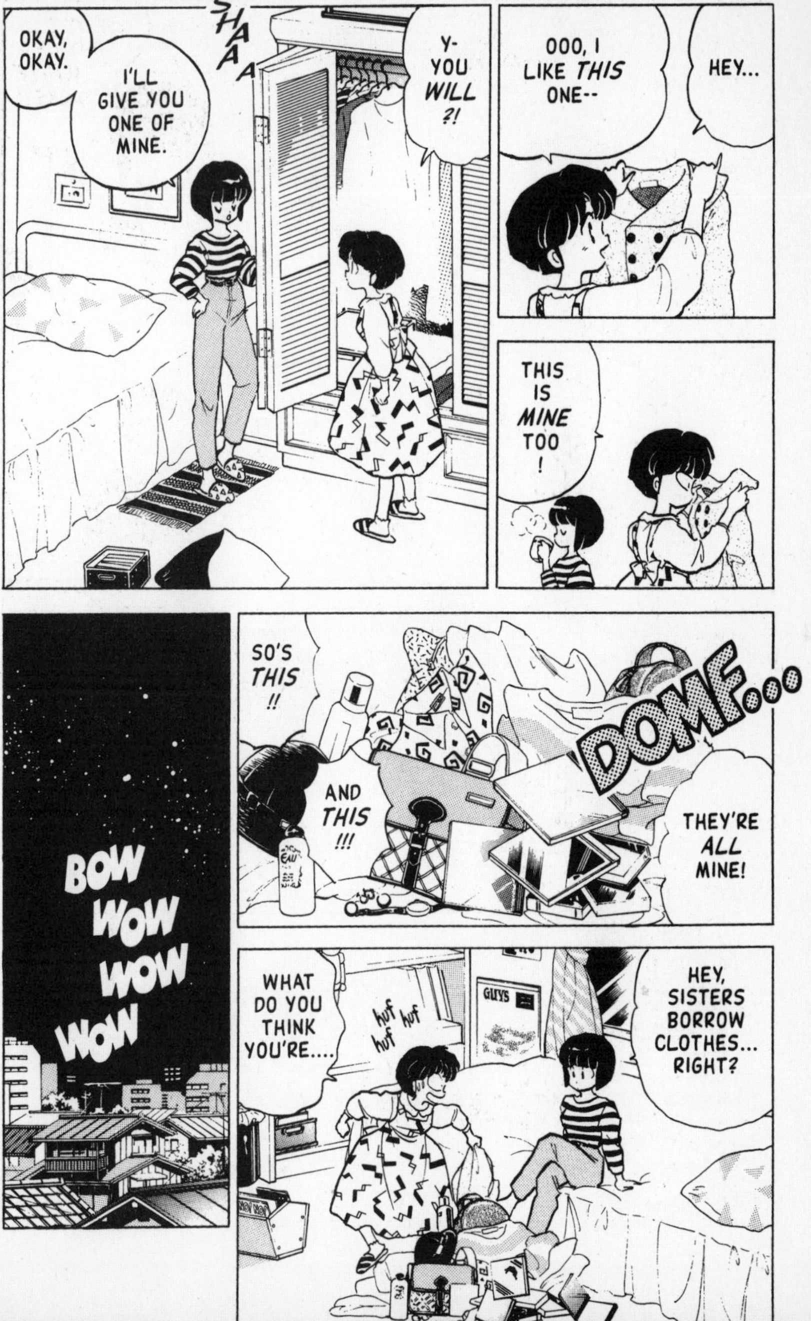
OKAY, OKAY.
I'LL GIVE YOU ONE OF MINE.
SHAAA
Y- YOU *WILL* ?!
OOO, I LIKE *THIS* ONE--
HEY...
THIS IS *MINE* TOO !
BOW WOW WOW WOW
SO'S *THIS* !!
DOMF...
AND *THIS* !!!
THEY'RE *ALL* MINE!
WHAT DO YOU THINK YOU'RE....
huf huf huf
HEY, SISTERS BORROW CLOTHES... RIGHT?

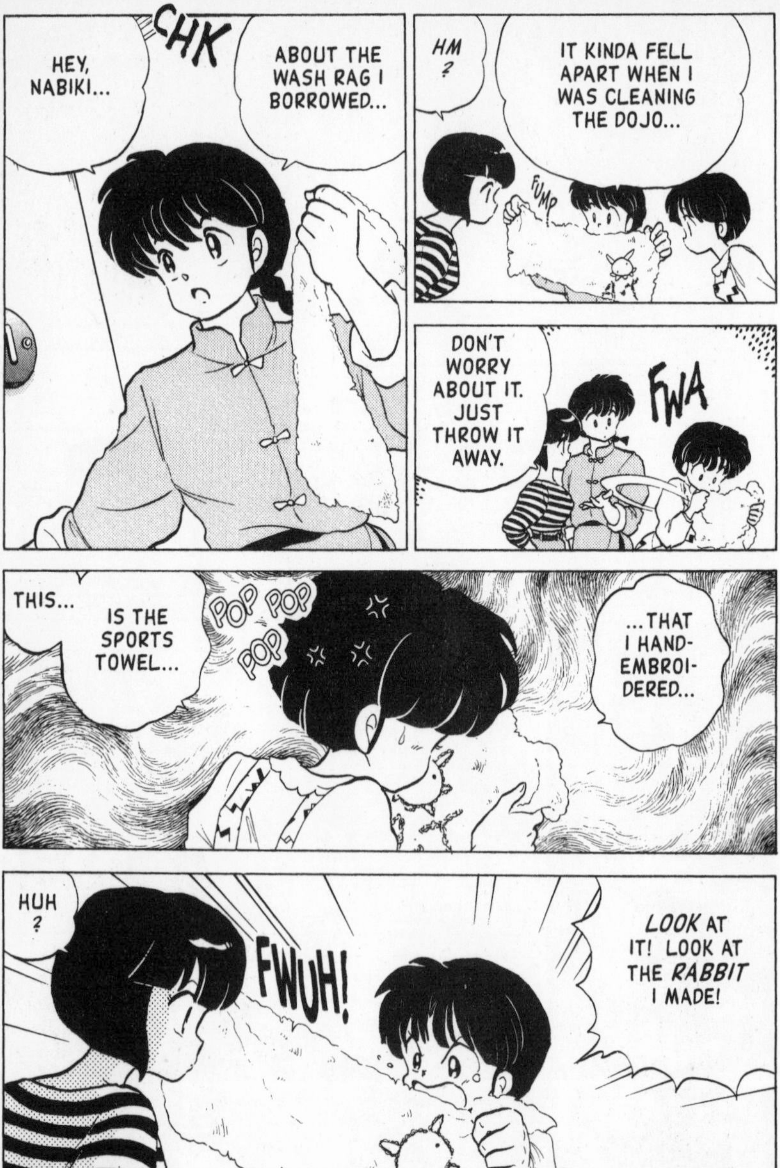
HEY, NABIKI...
CHK
ABOUT THE WASH RAG I BORROWED...
HM?
IT KINDA FELL APART WHEN I WAS CLEANING THE DOJO...
FUMP
DON'T WORRY ABOUT IT. JUST THROW IT AWAY.
FWA
THIS...
IS THE SPORTS TOWEL...
POP POP POP
...THAT I HAND-EMBROIDERED...
HUH?
FWUH!
LOOK AT IT! LOOK AT THE *RABBIT* I MADE!

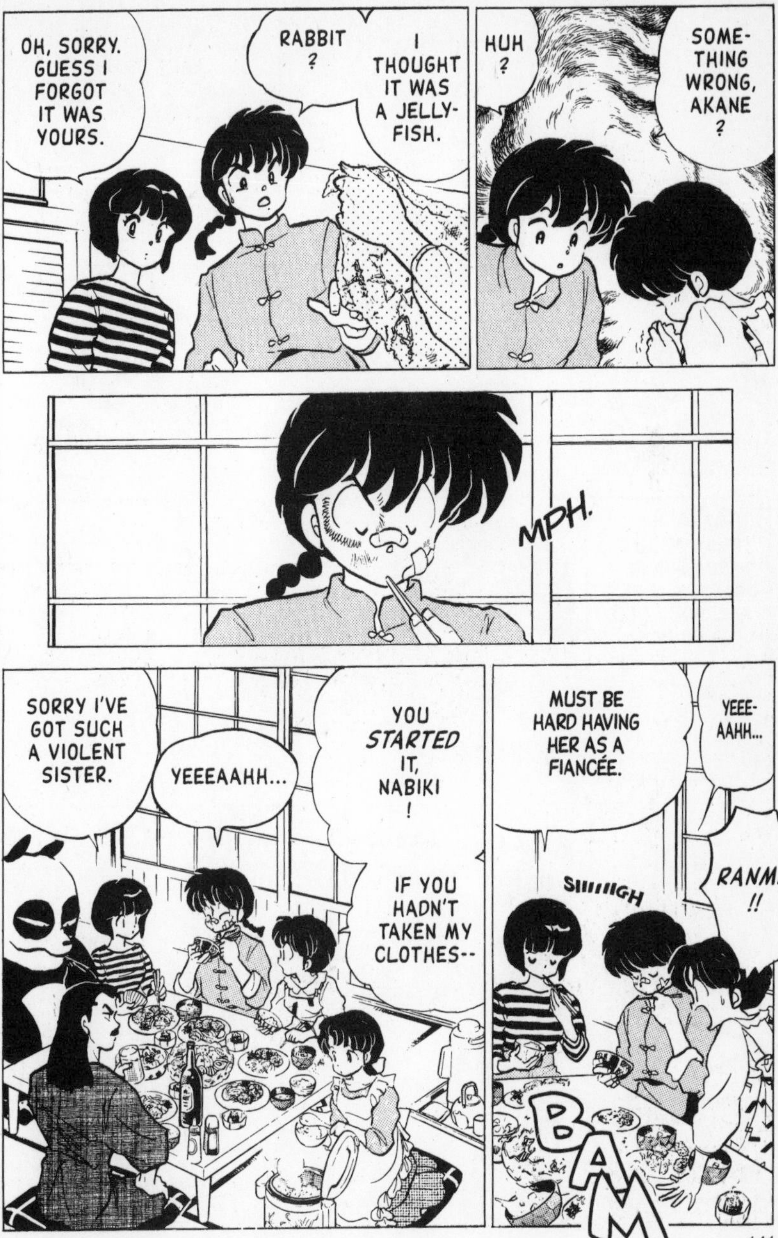
OH, SORRY. GUESS I FORGOT IT WAS YOURS.
RABBIT?
I THOUGHT IT WAS A JELLY-FISH.
HUH?
SOME-THING WRONG, AKANE?
MPH.
SORRY I'VE GOT SUCH A VIOLENT SISTER.
YEEEAAHH...
YOU *STARTED* IT, NABIKI!
IF YOU HADN'T TAKEN MY CLOTHES--
MUST BE HARD HAVING HER AS A FIANCÉE.
YEEE-AAHH...
SIIIIIGH
RANMA!!
BAM

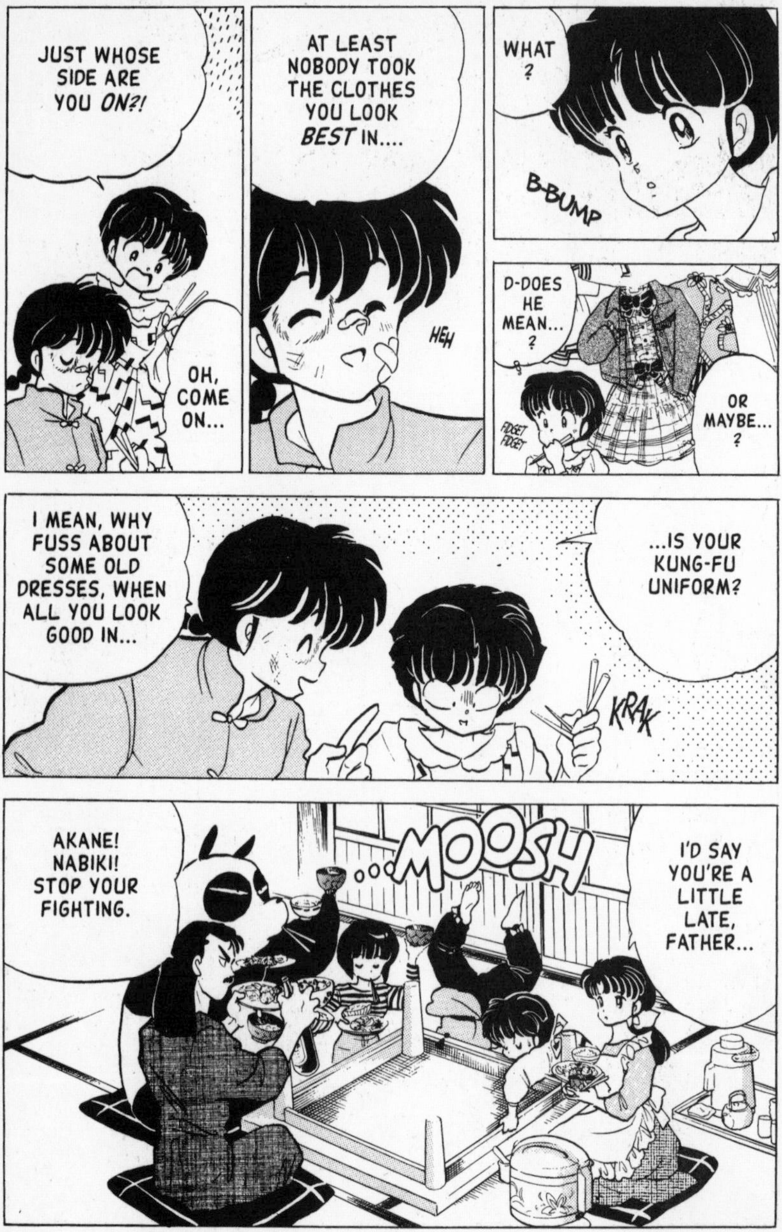
JUST WHOSE SIDE ARE YOU ON?!
OH, COME ON...
AT LEAST NOBODY TOOK THE CLOTHES YOU LOOK BEST IN....
HEH
WHAT?
B-BUMP
D-DOES HE MEAN...?
FIDGET FIDGET
OR MAYBE...?
I MEAN, WHY FUSS ABOUT SOME OLD DRESSES, WHEN ALL YOU LOOK GOOD IN...
...IS YOUR KUNG-FU UNIFORM?
KRAK
AKANE! NABIKI! STOP YOUR FIGHTING.
...MOOSH
I'D SAY YOU'RE A LITTLE LATE, FATHER...

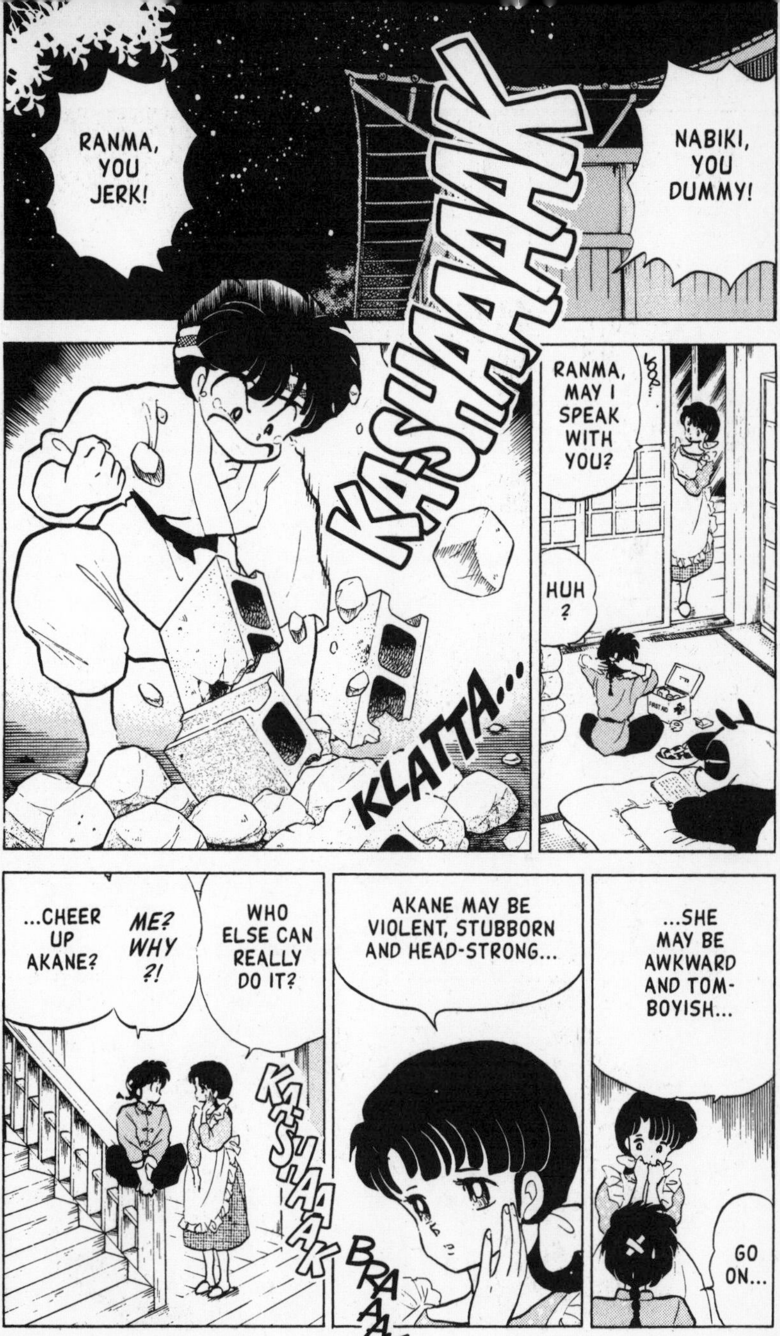
RANMA, YOU JERK!
KASHAAAK
NABIKI, YOU DUMMY!
KLATTA...
RANMA, MAY I SPEAK WITH YOU?
HUH?
...CHEER UP AKANE?
ME? WHY?!
WHO ELSE CAN REALLY DO IT?
KASHAAAK
BRAAAK
AKANE MAY BE VIOLENT, STUBBORN AND HEAD-STRONG...
...SHE MAY BE AWKWARD AND TOM-BOYISH...
GO ON...

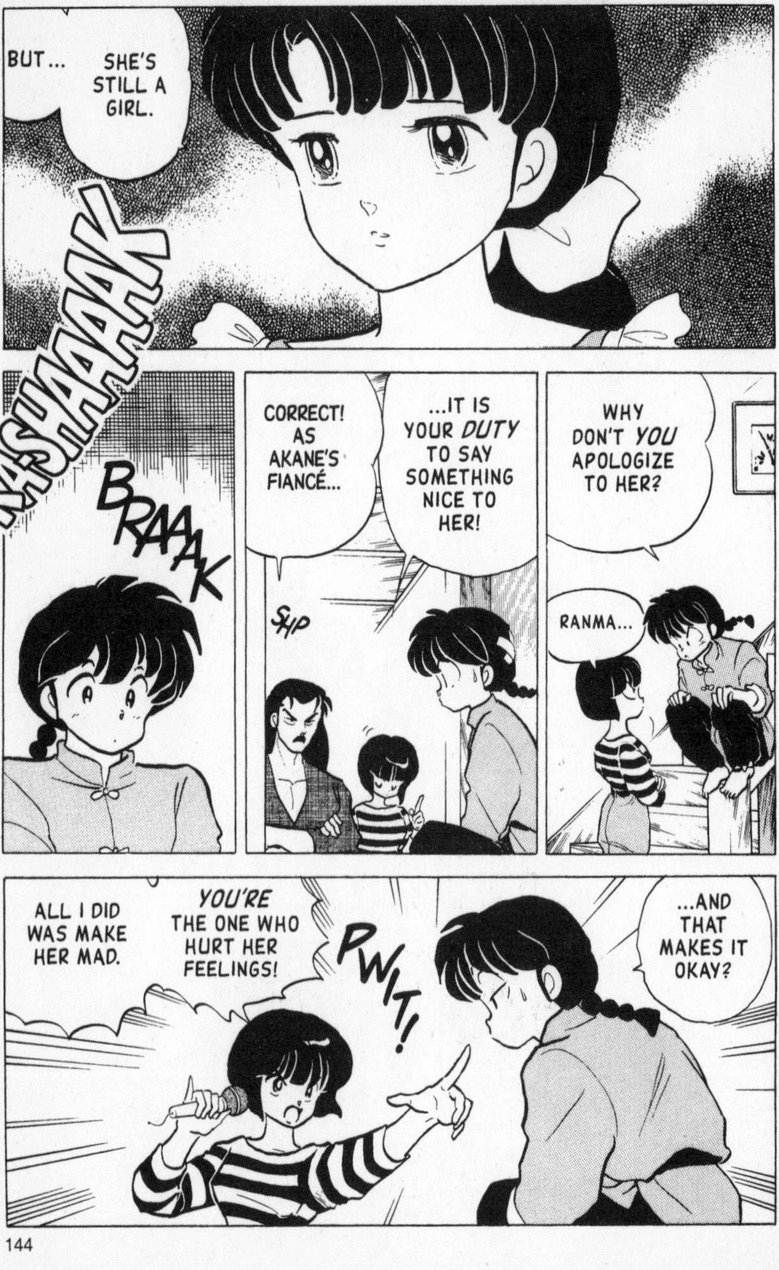
BUT...
SHE'S STILL A GIRL.
KASHAAAK
BRAAAAK
CORRECT! AS AKANE'S FIANCÉ...
...IT IS YOUR *DUTY* TO SAY SOMETHING NICE TO HER!
SHP
WHY DON'T *YOU* APOLOGIZE TO HER?
RANMA...
ALL I DID WAS MAKE HER MAD.
YOU'RE THE ONE WHO HURT HER FEELINGS!
PWIT!
...AND THAT MAKES IT OKAY?

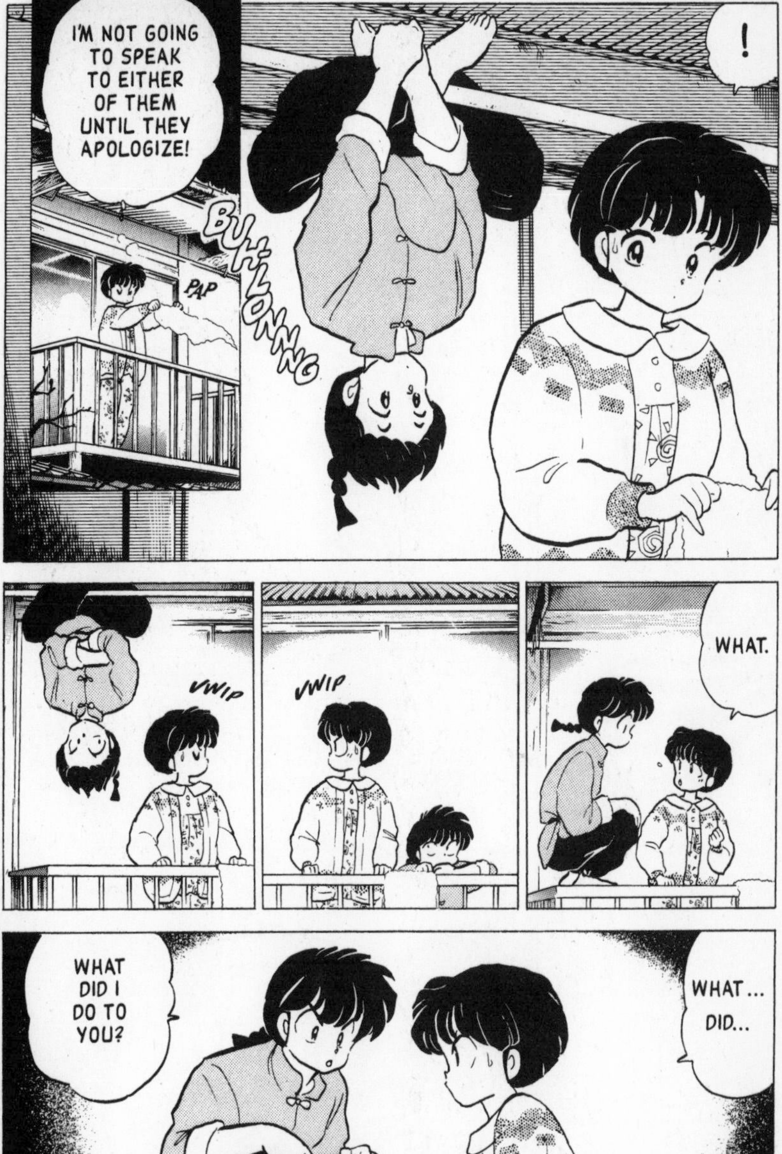
I'M NOT GOING TO SPEAK TO EITHER OF THEM UNTIL THEY APOLOGIZE!
PAP
BUHLONNG
!
VWIP
VWIP
WHAT.
WHAT DID I DO TO YOU?
WHAT... DID...

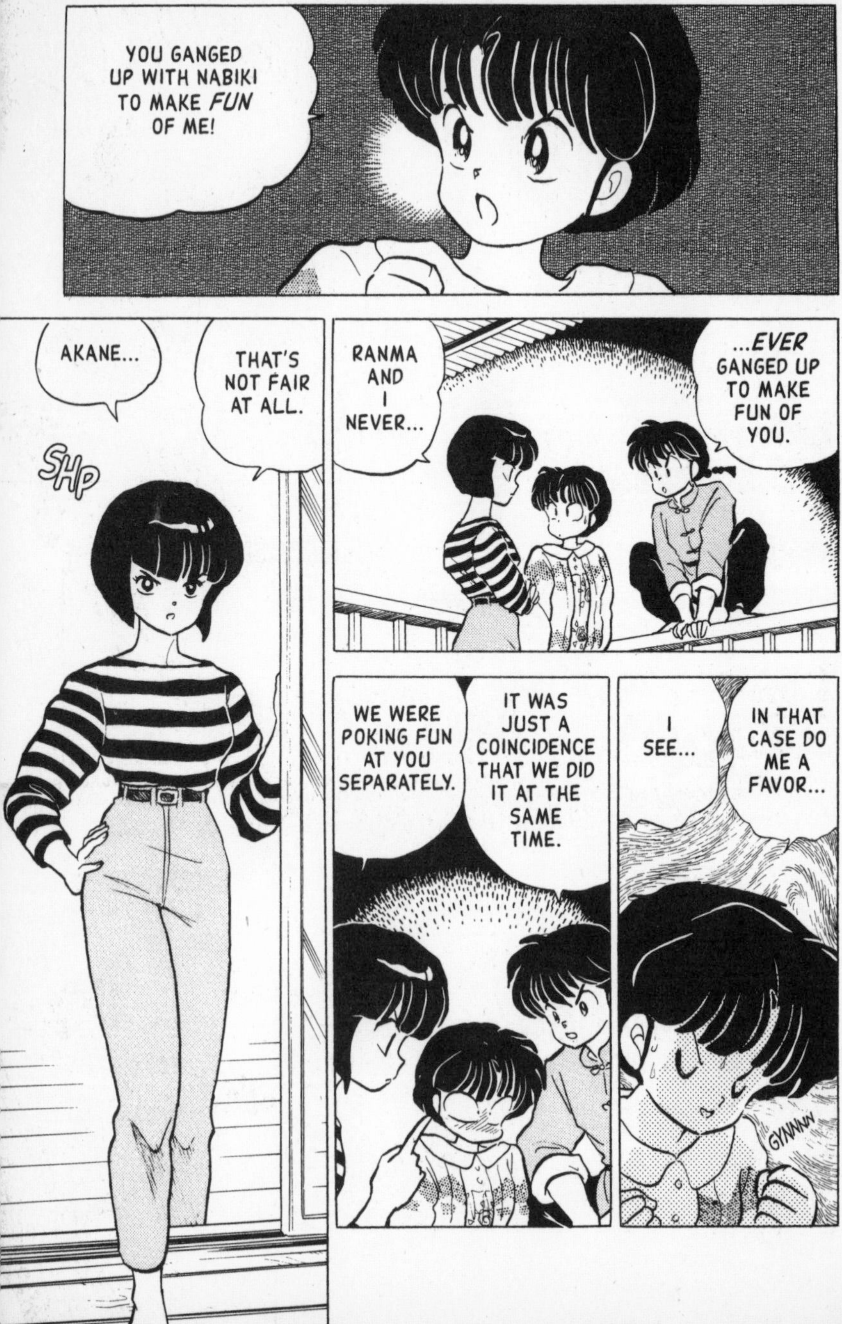
YOU GANGED UP WITH NABIKI TO MAKE FUN OF ME!
AKANE...
THAT'S NOT FAIR AT ALL.
SHP
RANMA AND I NEVER...
...EVER GANGED UP TO MAKE FUN OF YOU.
WE WERE POKING FUN AT YOU SEPARATELY.
IT WAS JUST A COINCIDENCE THAT WE DID IT AT THE SAME TIME.
I SEE...
IN THAT CASE DO ME A FAVOR...
GYNNNN

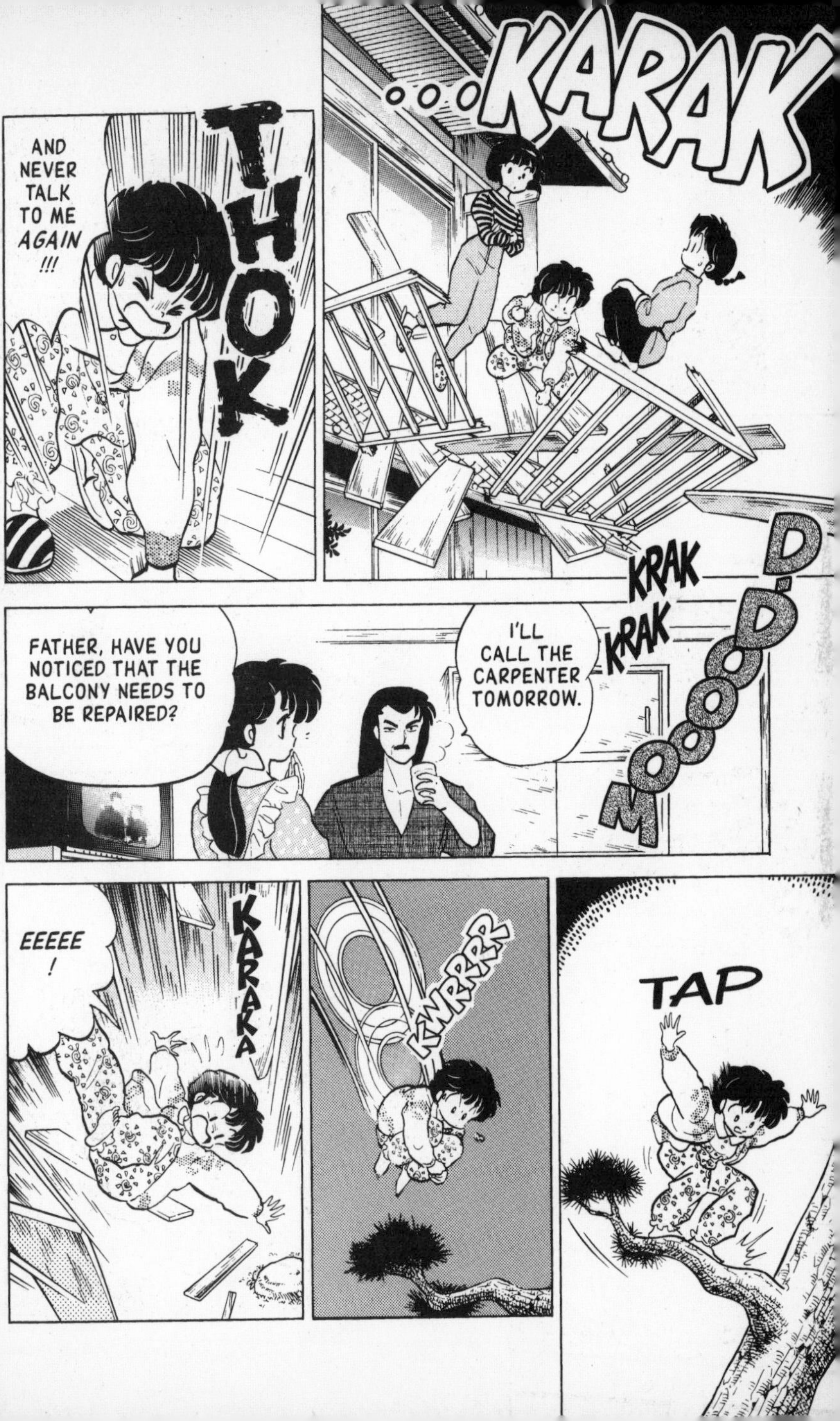
AND NEVER TALK TO ME AGAIN !!!
THOK
...KARAK
FATHER, HAVE YOU NOTICED THAT THE BALCONY NEEDS TO BE REPAIRED?
I'LL CALL THE CARPENTER TOMORROW.
KRAK KRAK
MOOOOOD'D
EEEEE !
KARAKA
KWRRRR
TAP

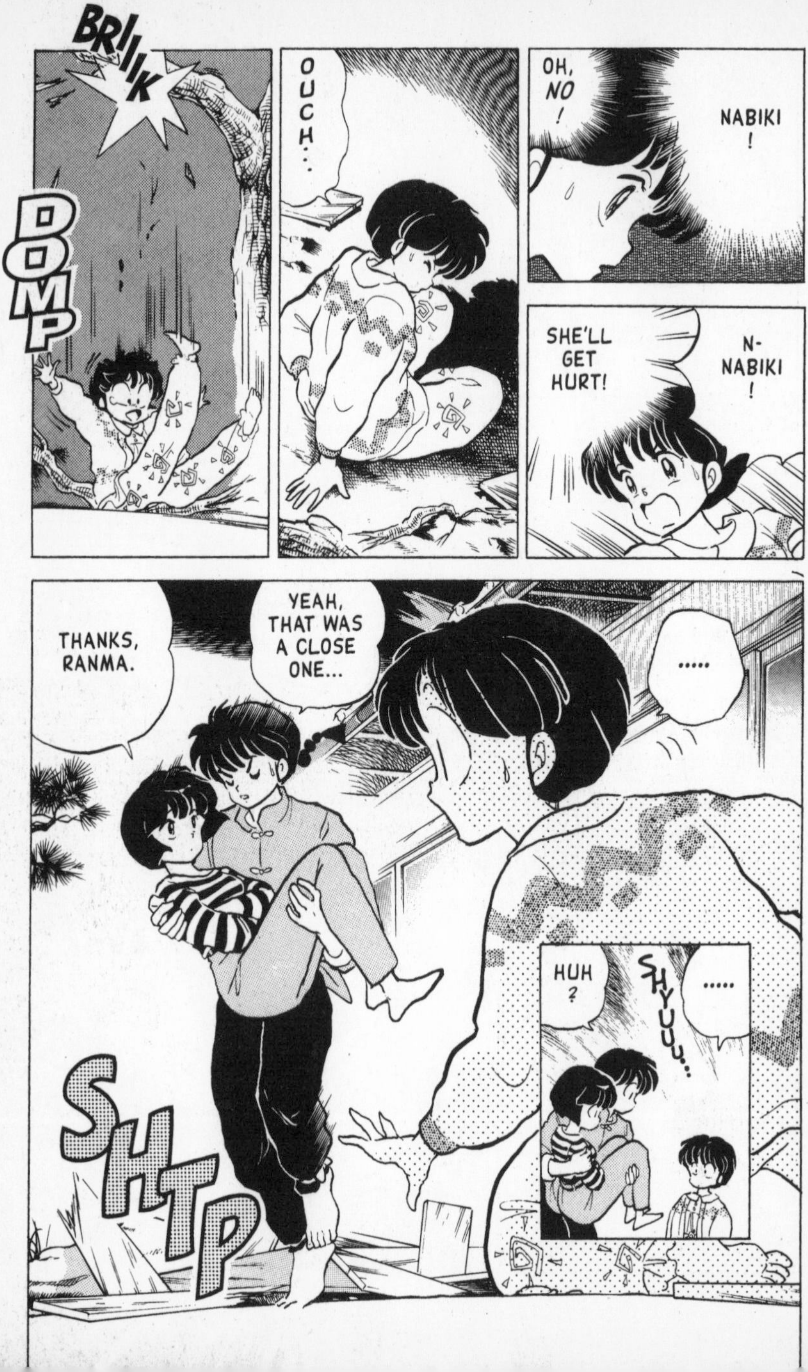
BRIIIK
DOMP
OUCH...
OH, NO!
NABIKI!
SHE'LL GET HURT!
N-NABIKI!
THANKS, RANMA.
YEAH, THAT WAS A CLOSE ONE...
.....
SHTP
HUH?
SHYUUU...
.....

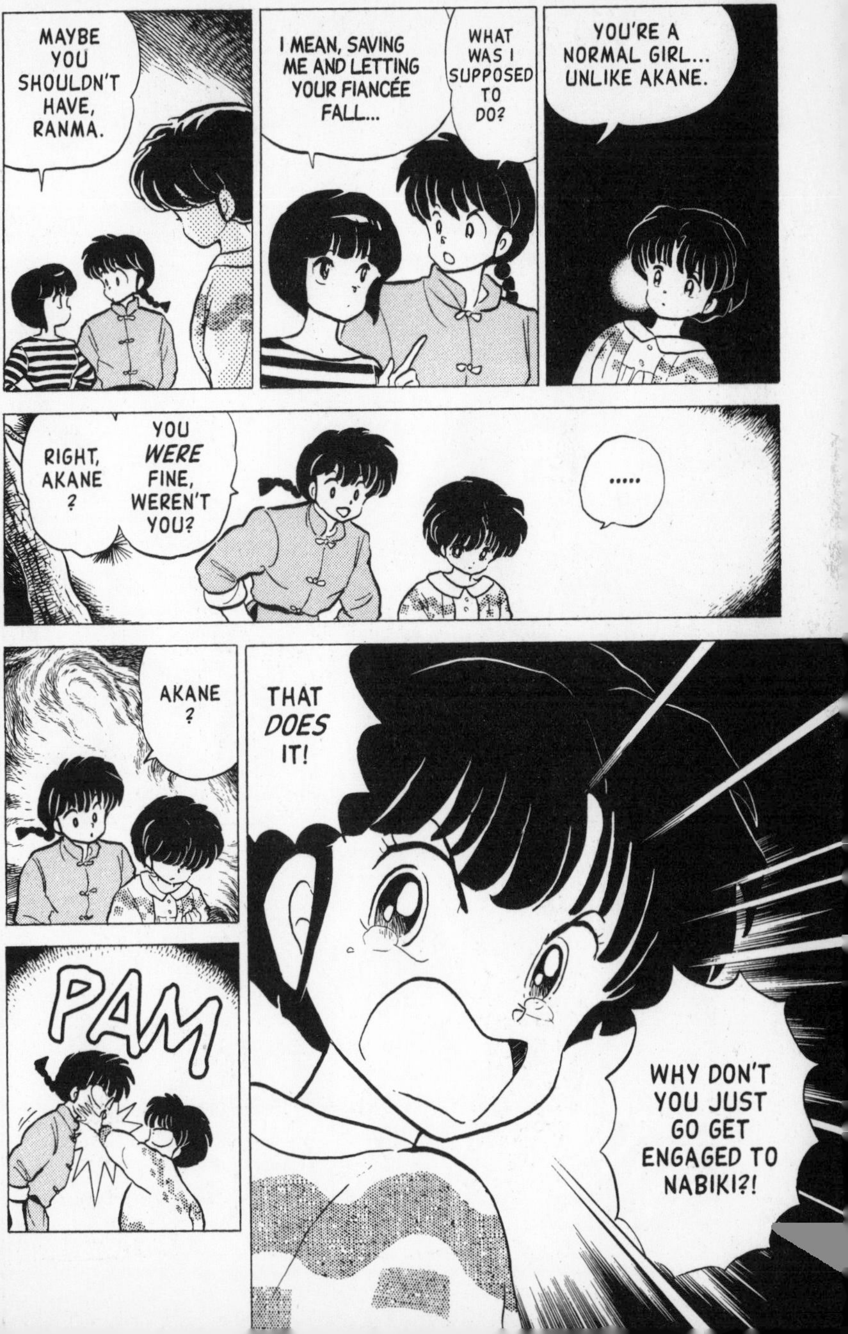
MAYBE YOU SHOULDN'T HAVE, RANMA.
I MEAN, SAVING ME AND LETTING YOUR FIANCÉE FALL...
WHAT WAS I SUPPOSED TO DO?
YOU'RE A NORMAL GIRL... UNLIKE AKANE.
YOU *WERE* FINE, WEREN'T YOU? RIGHT, AKANE?
.....
AKANE?
THAT *DOES* IT!
PAM
WHY DON'T YOU JUST GO GET ENGAGED TO NABIKI?!

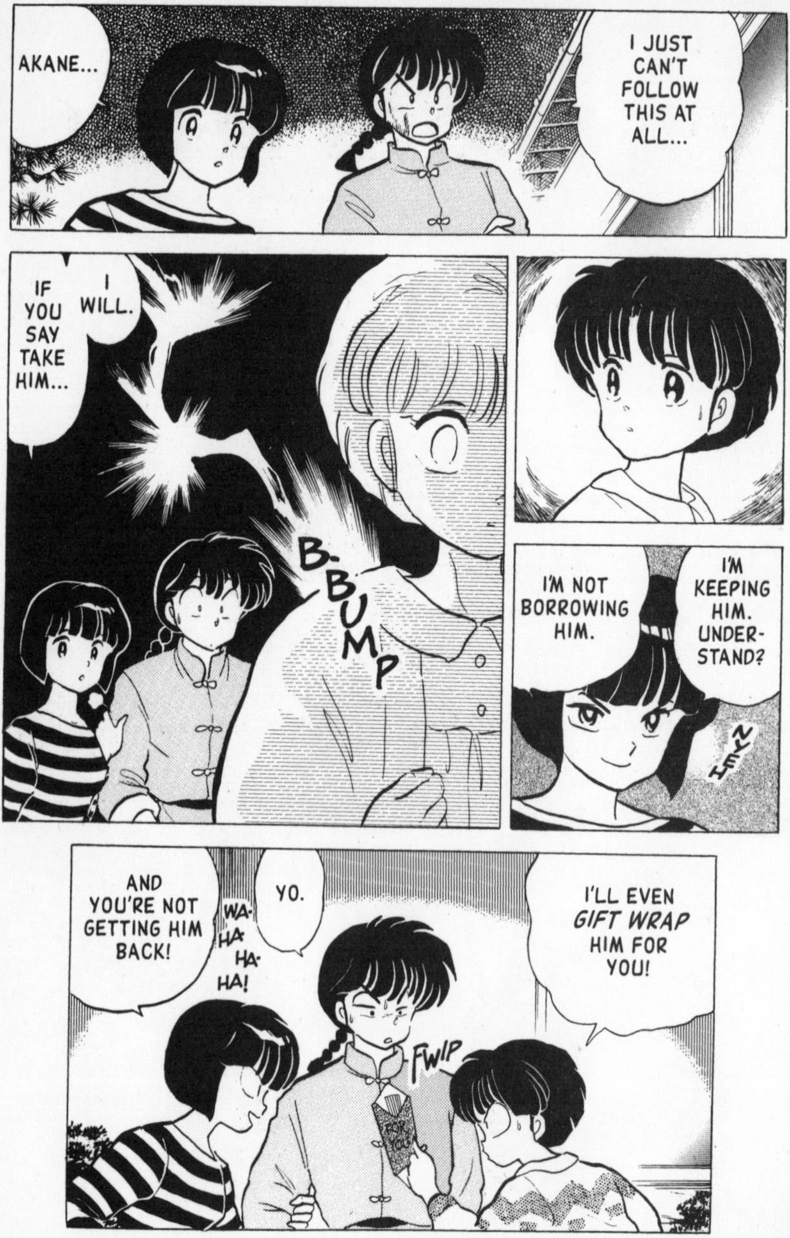
AKANE...
I JUST CAN'T FOLLOW THIS AT ALL...
IF YOU SAY TAKE HIM...
I WILL.
B-BUMP
I'M NOT BORROWING HIM.
I'M KEEPING HIM. UNDER-STAND?
NYEH
AND YOU'RE NOT GETTING HIM BACK!
WA-HA-HA-HA!
YO.
I'LL EVEN *GIFT WRAP* HIM FOR YOU!
FWIP
FOR YOU

Part 10
THE TERRIBLE TRUTH!

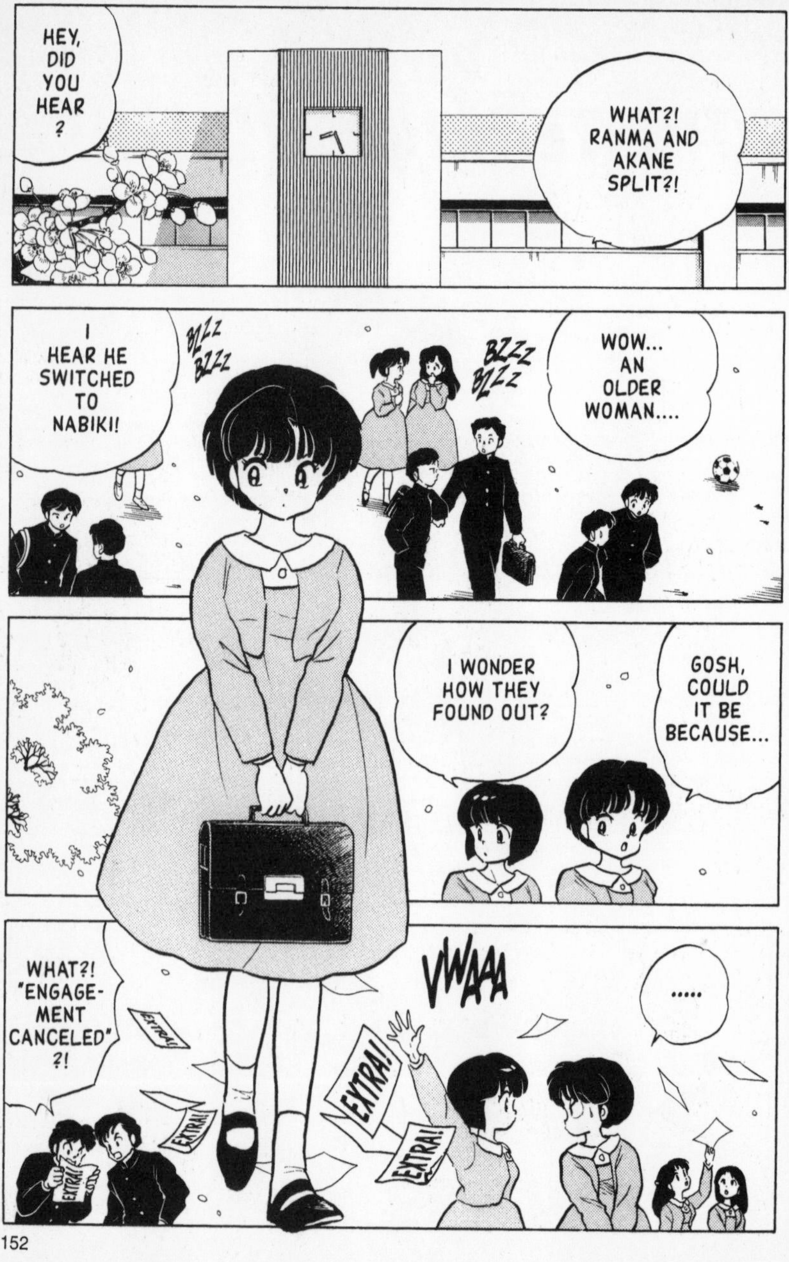

HEY, DID YOU HEAR?
WHAT?! RANMA AND AKANE SPLIT?!
I HEAR HE SWITCHED TO NABIKI!
BZZZ BZZZ
BZZZ BZZZ
WOW... AN OLDER WOMAN....
I WONDER HOW THEY FOUND OUT?
GOSH, COULD IT BE BECAUSE...
WHAT?! "ENGAGE-MENT CANCELED"?!
EXTRA!
EXTRA!
EXTRA!
EXTRA!
VWAAA
EXTRA!
EXTRA!
.....

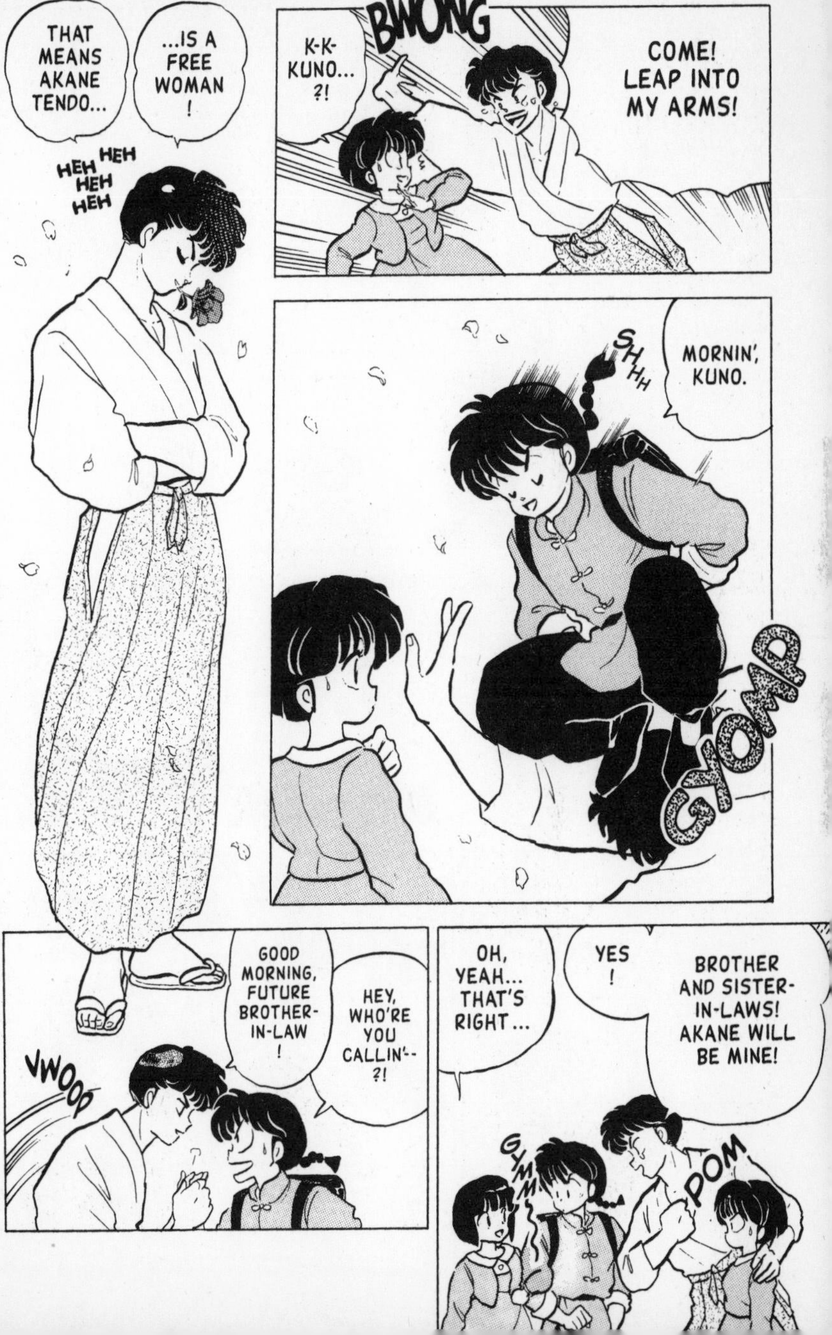
THAT MEANS AKANE TENDO...
...IS A FREE WOMAN !
HEH HEH HEH HEH
BWONG
K-K-KUNO... ?!
COME! LEAP INTO MY ARMS!
SHHH
MORNIN', KUNO.
GYOMP
VWOOP
GOOD MORNING, FUTURE BROTHER-IN-LAW !
HEY, WHO'RE YOU CALLIN'-- ?!
OH, YEAH... THAT'S RIGHT...
YES !
BROTHER AND SISTER-IN-LAWS! AKANE WILL BE MINE!
POM

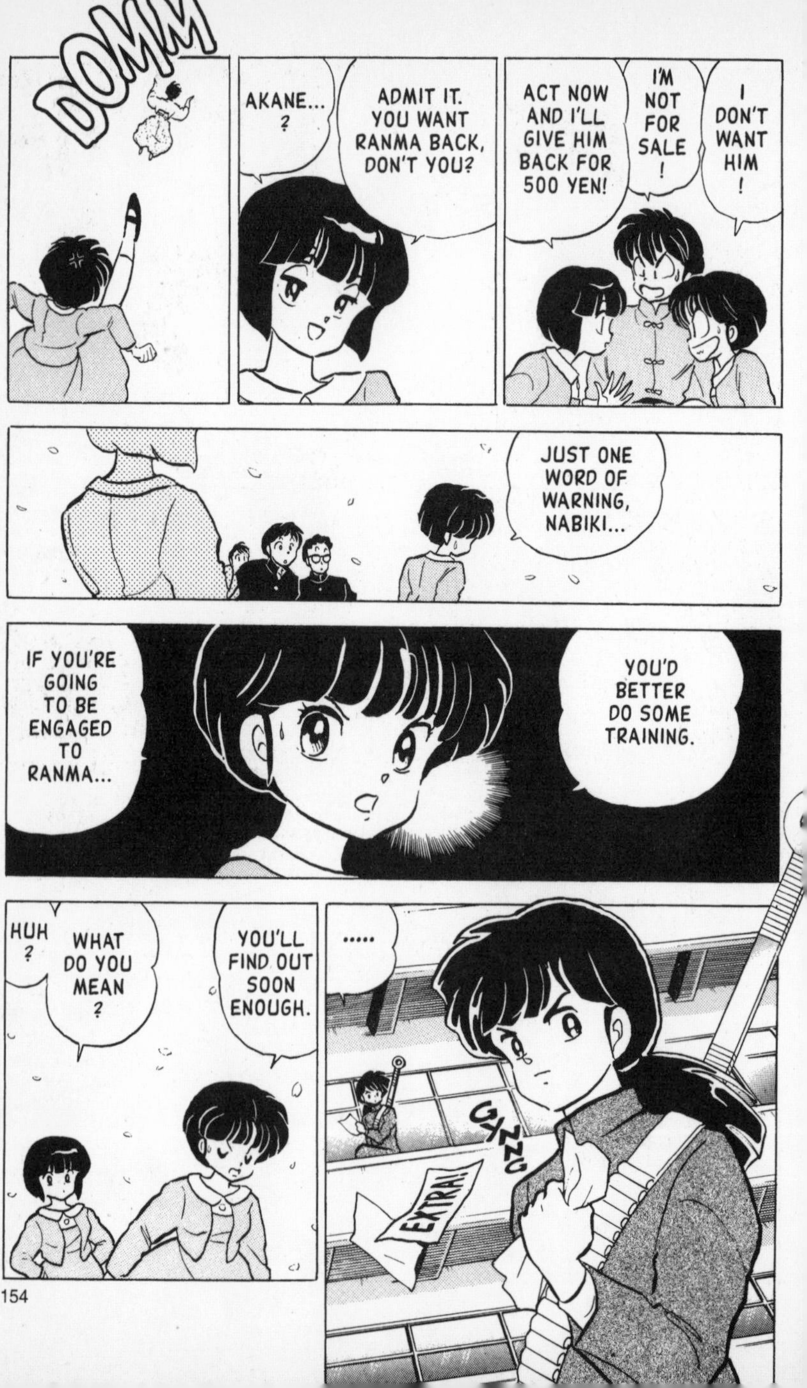
DOMM
AKANE... ?
ADMIT IT. YOU WANT RANMA BACK, DON'T YOU?
ACT NOW AND I'LL GIVE HIM BACK FOR 500 YEN!
I'M NOT FOR SALE!
I DON'T WANT HIM!
JUST ONE WORD OF WARNING, NABIKI...
IF YOU'RE GOING TO BE ENGAGED TO RANMA...
YOU'D BETTER DO SOME TRAINING.
HUH?
WHAT DO YOU MEAN?
YOU'LL FIND OUT SOON ENOUGH.
.....
EXTRA!

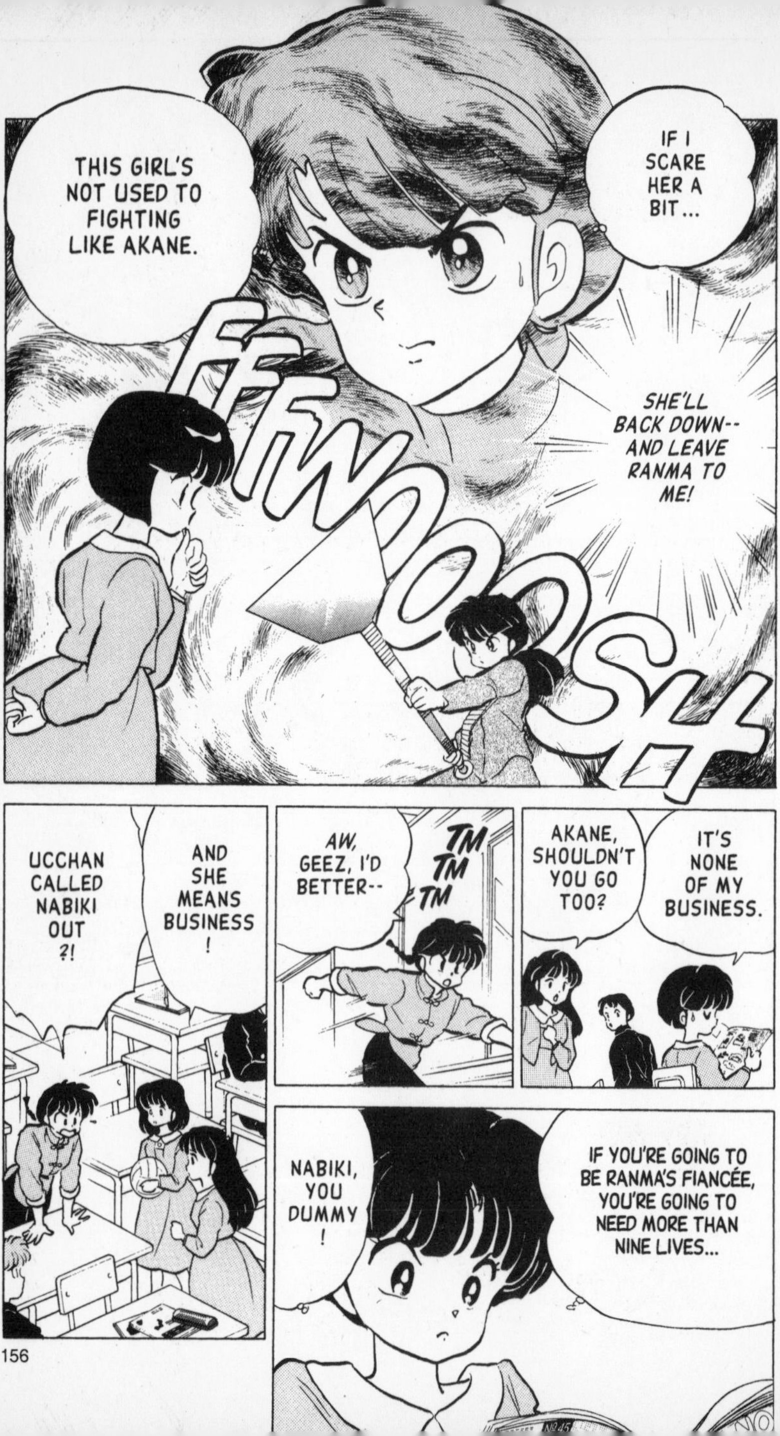
THIS GIRL'S NOT USED TO FIGHTING LIKE AKANE.
IF I SCARE HER A BIT...
FFWOOOSH
SHE'LL BACK DOWN-- AND LEAVE RANMA TO ME!
UCCHAN CALLED NABIKI OUT ?!
AND SHE MEANS BUSINESS !
AW, GEEZ, I'D BETTER--
TM TM TM
AKANE, SHOULDN'T YOU GO TOO?
IT'S NONE OF MY BUSINESS.
NABIKI, YOU DUMMY !
IF YOU'RE GOING TO BE RANMA'S FIANCÉE, YOU'RE GOING TO NEED MORE THAN NINE LIVES...

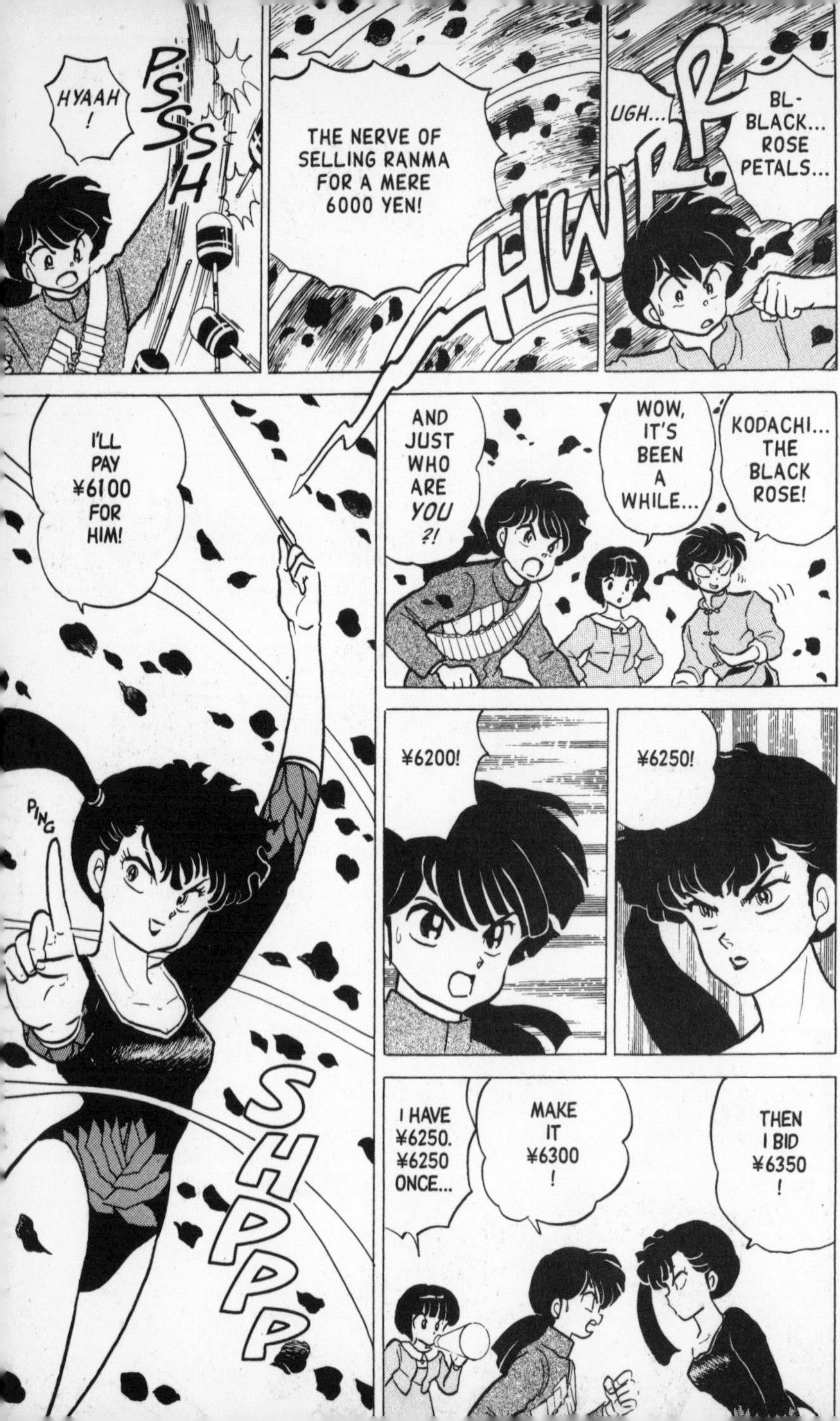
HYAAH!
PSSSH
THE NERVE OF SELLING RANMA FOR A MERE 6000 YEN!
UGH...
HWRP
BL-BLACK... ROSE PETALS...
I'LL PAY ¥6100 FOR HIM!
PING
SHPPP
AND JUST WHO ARE *YOU* ?!
WOW, IT'S BEEN A WHILE...
KODACHI... THE BLACK ROSE!
¥6200!
¥6250!
I HAVE ¥6250. ¥6250 ONCE...
MAKE IT ¥6300!
THEN I BID ¥6350!

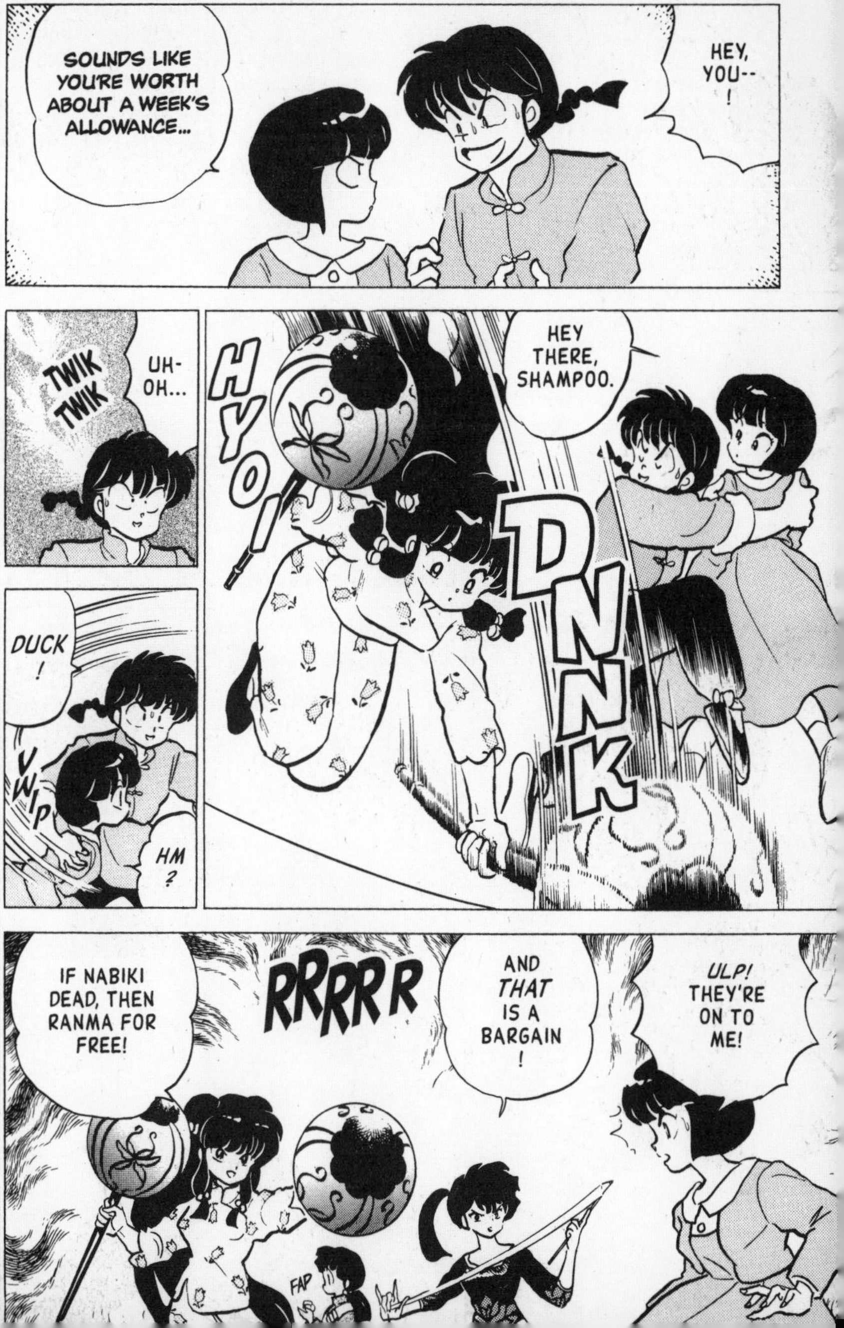
SOUNDS LIKE YOU'RE WORTH ABOUT A WEEK'S ALLOWANCE...
HEY, YOU-- !
TWIK TWIK
UH-OH...
DUCK!
VWIP
HM?
HYO!
HEY THERE, SHAMPOO.
DNNK
IF NABIKI DEAD, THEN RANMA FOR FREE!
RRRRR
AND *THAT* IS A BARGAIN!
ULP! THEY'RE ON TO ME!
FAP

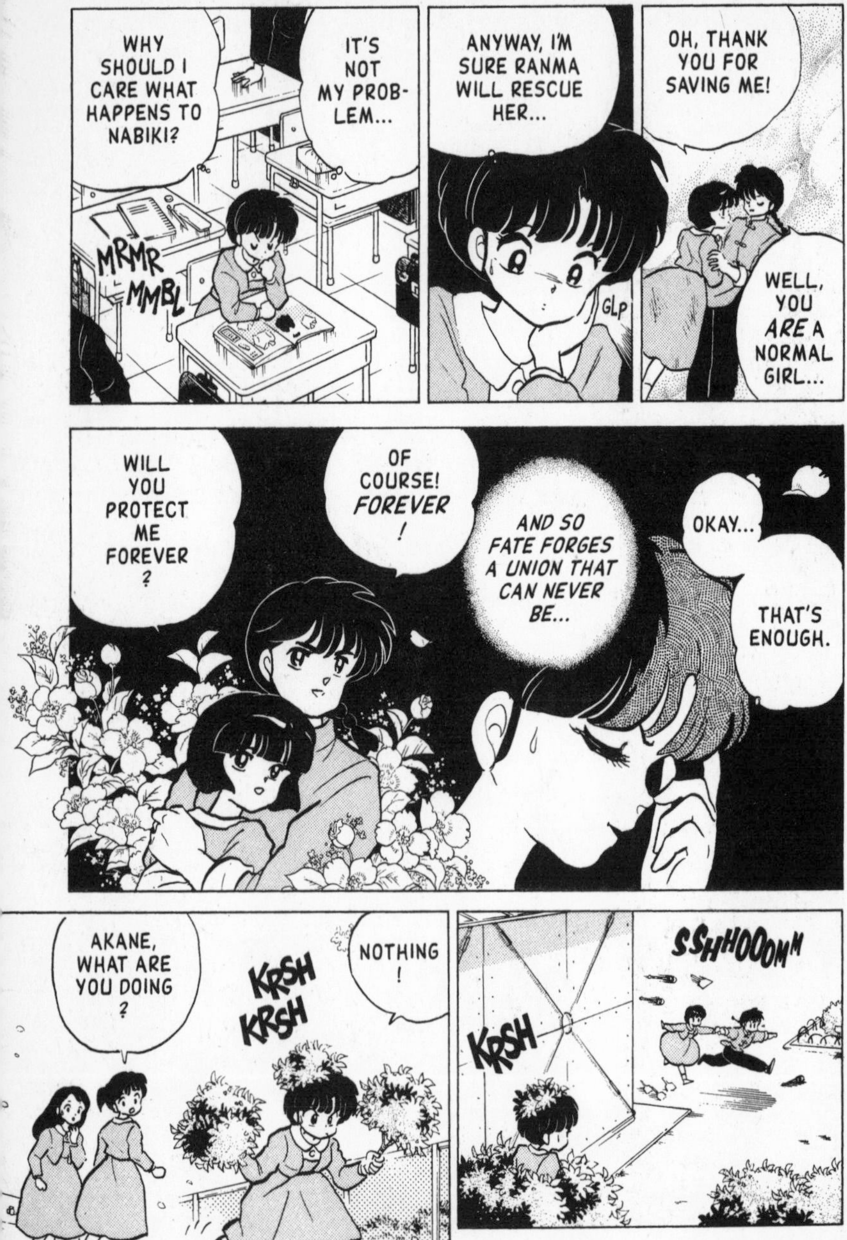
WHY SHOULD I CARE WHAT HAPPENS TO NABIKI?
IT'S NOT MY PROB-LEM...
MRMR MMBL
ANYWAY, I'M SURE RANMA WILL RESCUE HER...
GLP
OH, THANK YOU FOR SAVING ME!
WELL, YOU *ARE* A NORMAL GIRL...
WILL YOU PROTECT ME FOREVER?
OF COURSE! *FOREVER*!
AND SO FATE FORGES A UNION THAT CAN NEVER BE...
OKAY...
THAT'S ENOUGH.
AKANE, WHAT ARE YOU DOING?
KRSH KRSH
NOTHING!
KRSH
SSHHOOOMM

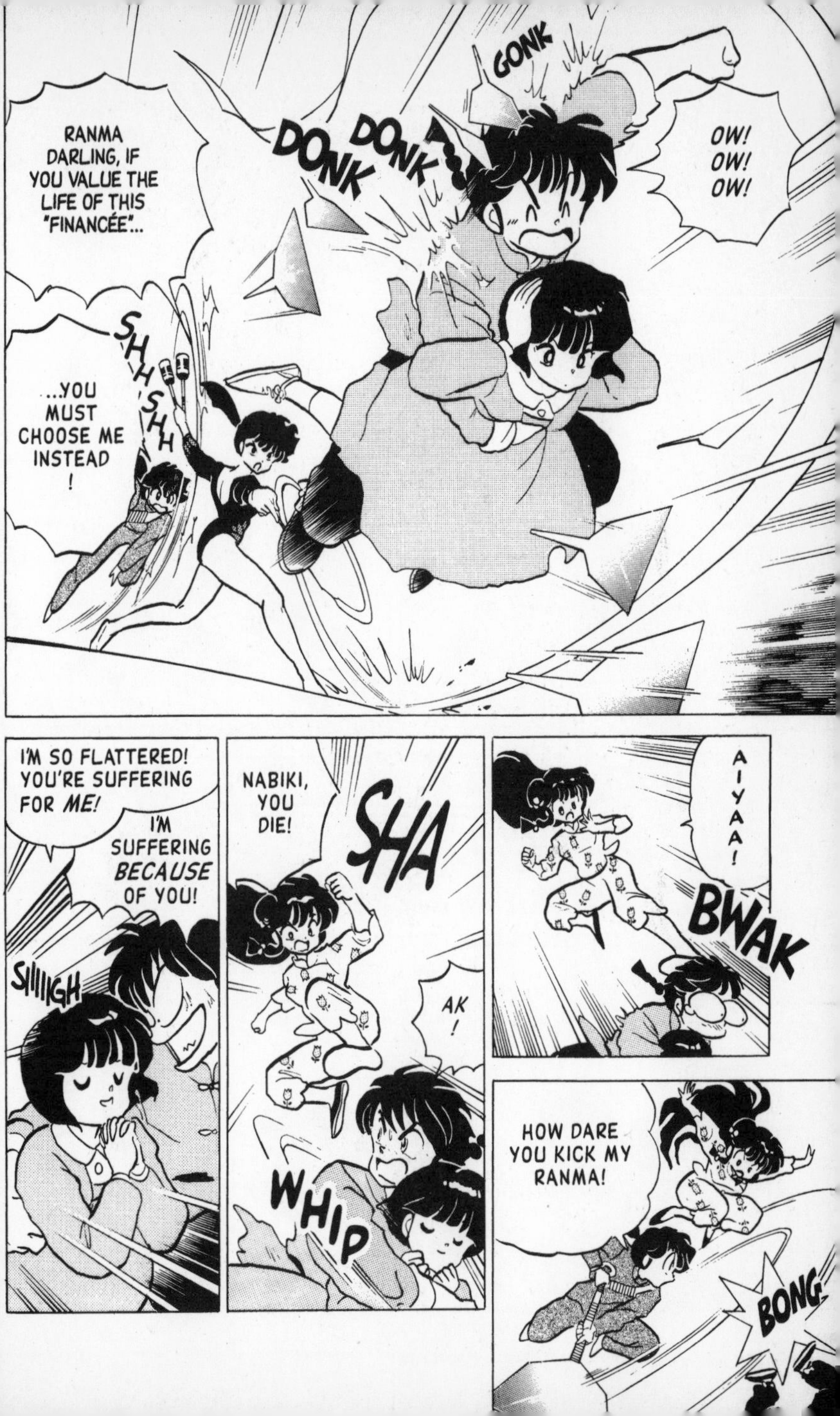
RANMA DARLING, IF YOU VALUE THE LIFE OF THIS "FINANCÉE"...
DONK
DONK
GONK
OW! OW! OW!
SHHHSHH
...YOU MUST CHOOSE ME INSTEAD!
I'M SO FLATTERED! YOU'RE SUFFERING FOR *ME!*
I'M SUFFERING *BECAUSE* OF YOU!
SIIIIGH
NABIKI, YOU DIE!
SHA
AK!
WHIP
AIYAA!
BWAK
HOW DARE YOU KICK MY RANMA!
BONG

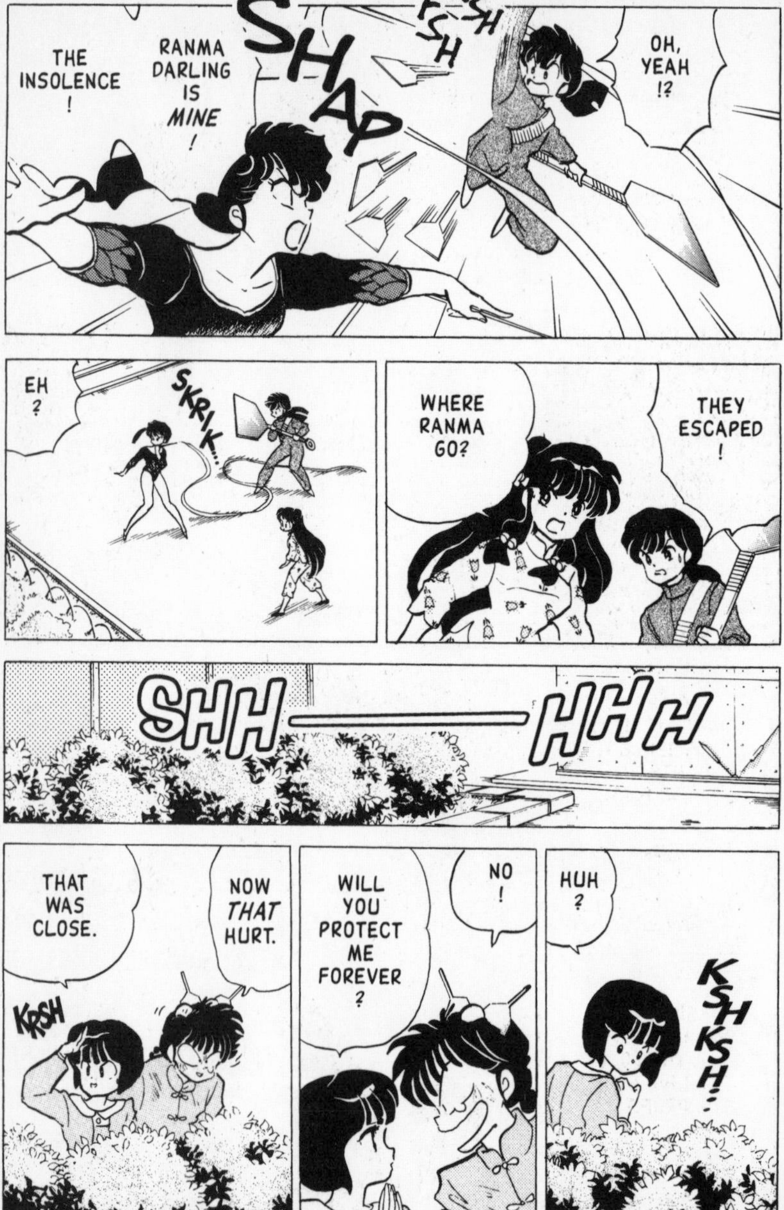
THE INSOLENCE !
RANMA DARLING IS MINE !
SHAP
FSH FSH
OH, YEAH !?
EH ?
SKRIK...
WHERE RANMA GO?
THEY ESCAPED !
SHH——HHH
THAT WAS CLOSE.
NOW THAT HURT.
KRSH
WILL YOU PROTECT ME FOREVER ?
NO !
HUH ?
KSHKSH!!

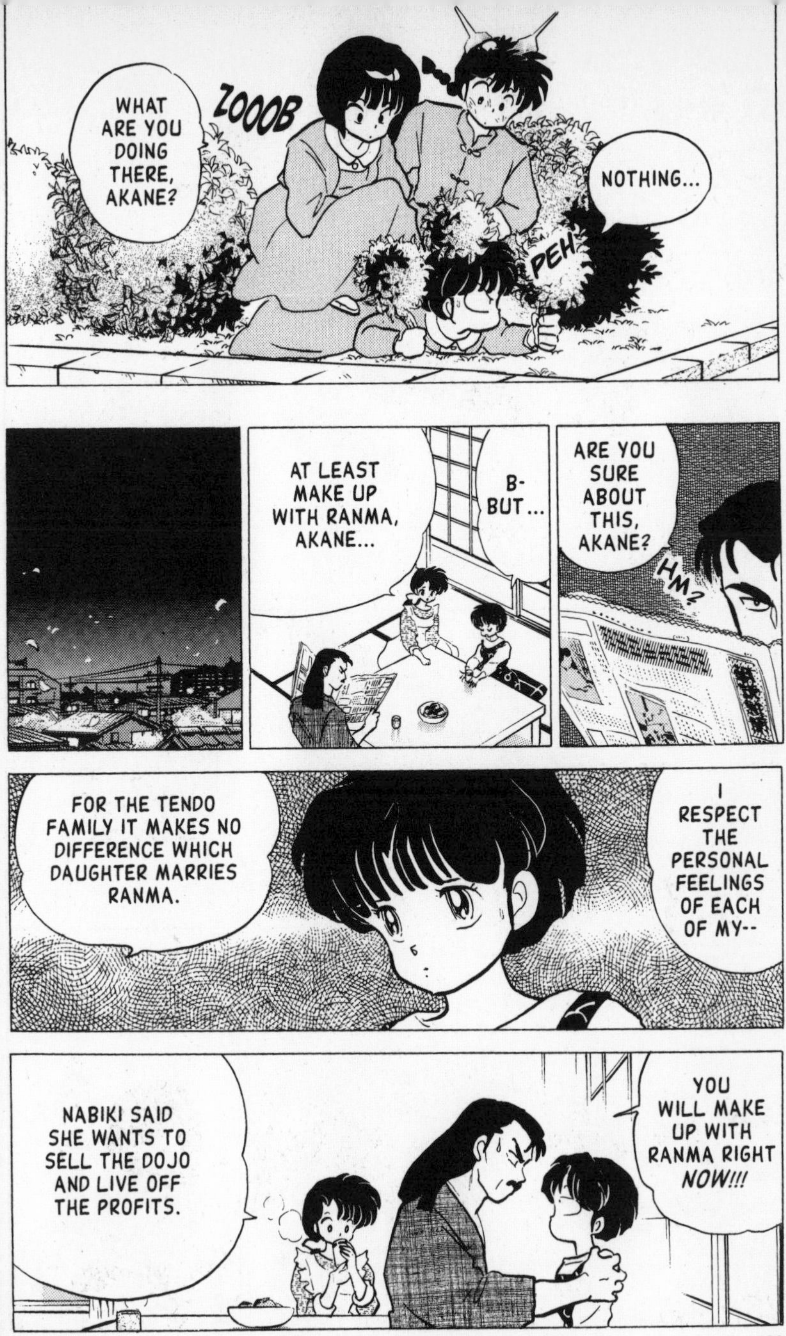
WHAT ARE YOU DOING THERE, AKANE?
ZOOOB
NOTHING...
PEH
AT LEAST MAKE UP WITH RANMA, AKANE...
B-BUT...
ARE YOU SURE ABOUT THIS, AKANE?
HM?
FOR THE TENDO FAMILY IT MAKES NO DIFFERENCE WHICH DAUGHTER MARRIES RANMA.
I RESPECT THE PERSONAL FEELINGS OF EACH OF MY--
NABIKI SAID SHE WANTS TO SELL THE DOJO AND LIVE OFF THE PROFITS.
YOU WILL MAKE UP WITH RANMA RIGHT *NOW!!!*

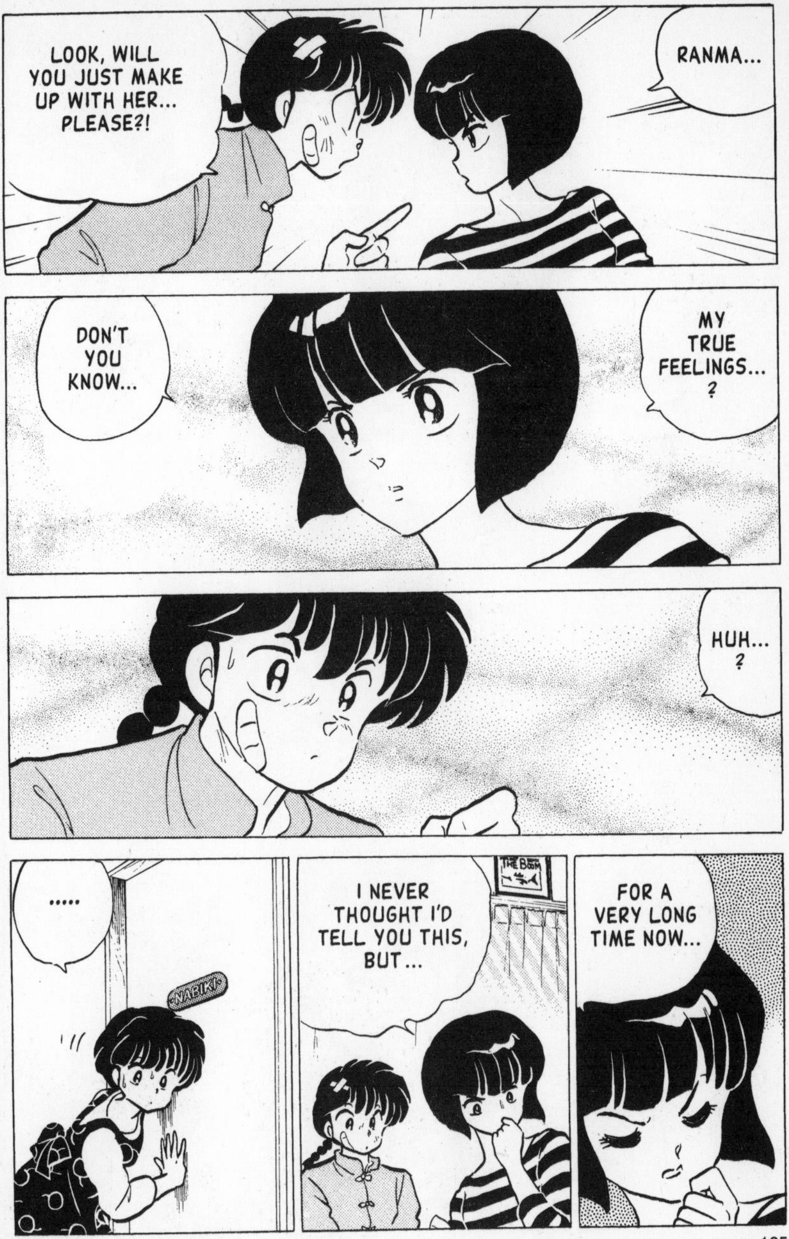
LOOK, WILL YOU JUST MAKE UP WITH HER... PLEASE?!
RANMA...
DON'T YOU KNOW...
MY TRUE FEELINGS...?
HUH...?
.....
NABIKI
I NEVER THOUGHT I'D TELL YOU THIS, BUT...
FOR A VERY LONG TIME NOW...

Part 11
NABIKI'S FEELINGS

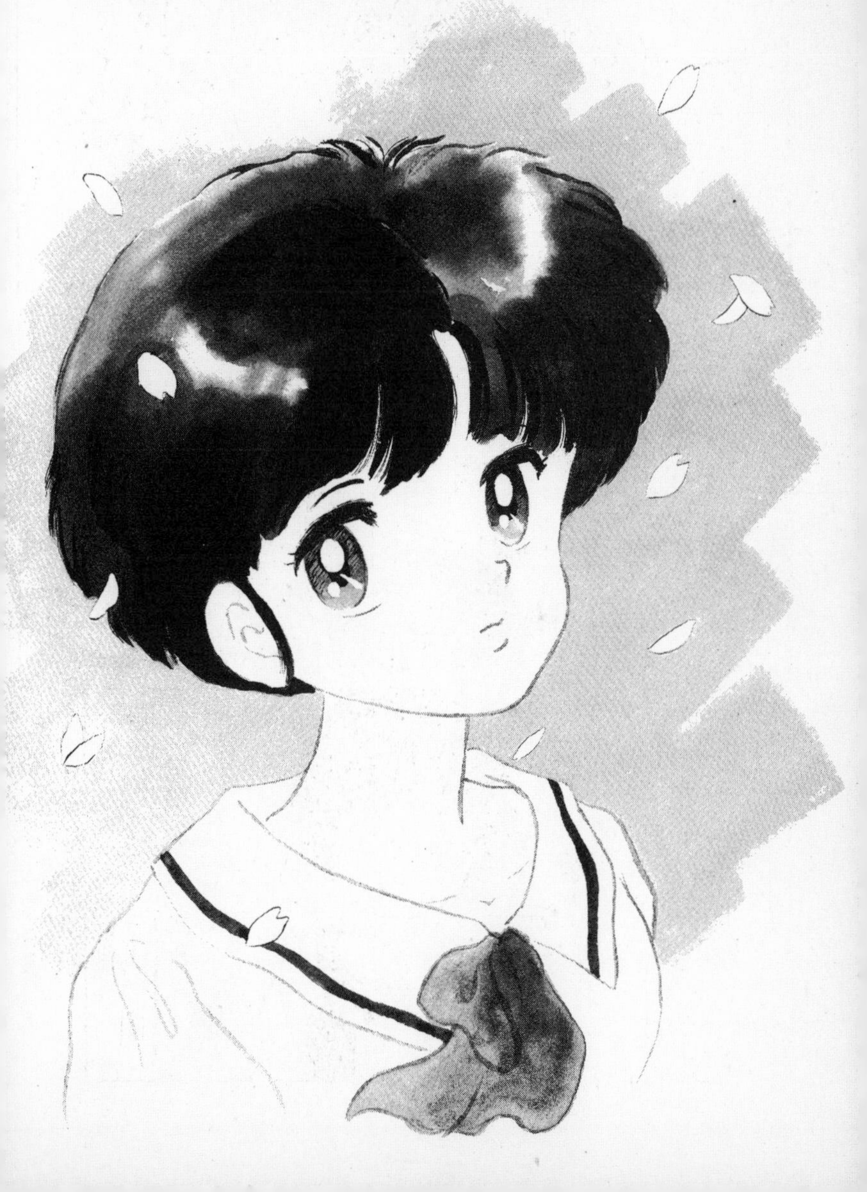

168

169

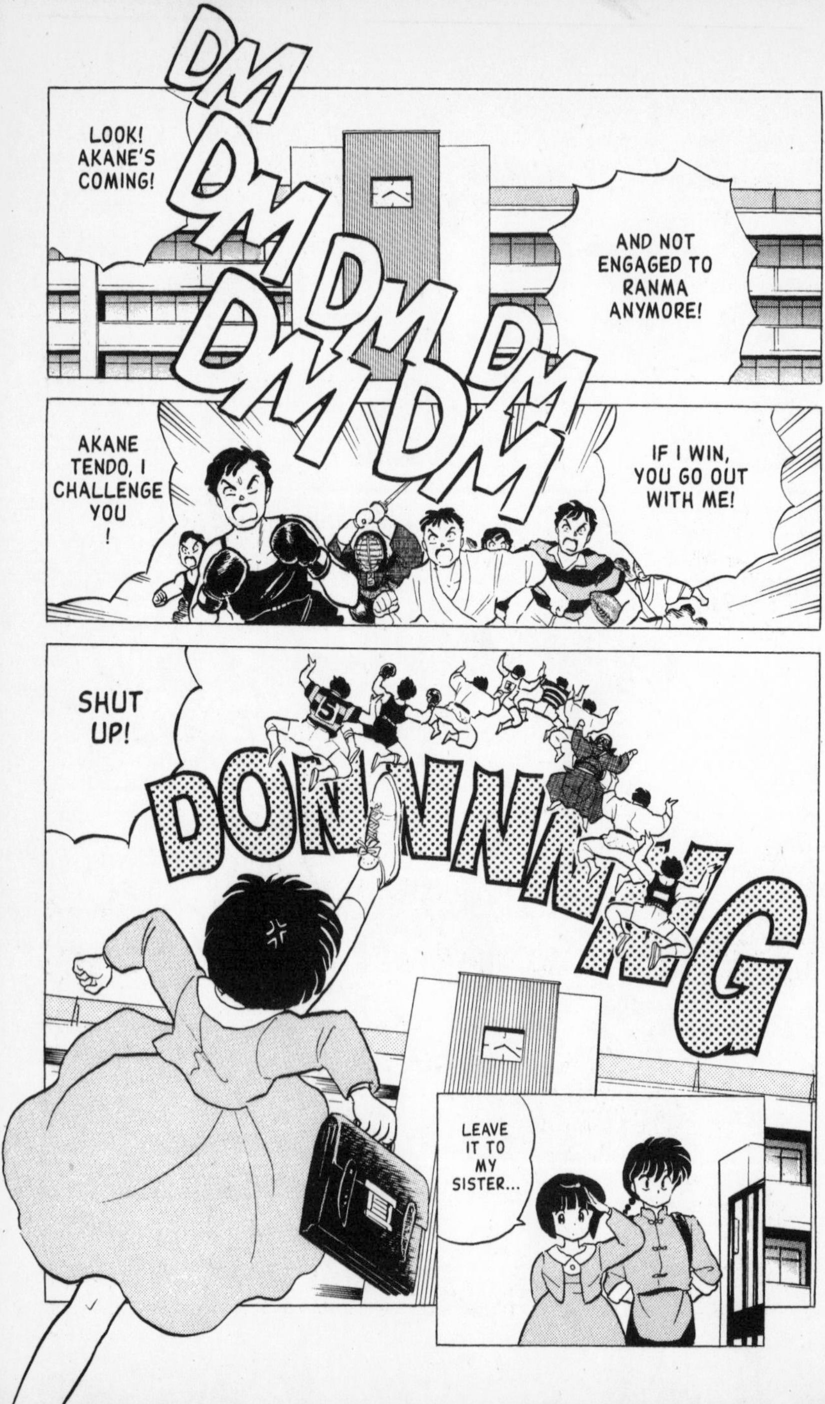
LOOK! AKANE'S COMING!
AND NOT ENGAGED TO RANMA ANYMORE!
DM DM DM DM DM DM DM DM
AKANE TENDO, I CHALLENGE YOU!
IF I WIN, YOU GO OUT WITH ME!
SHUT UP!
DONNNNNG
LEAVE IT TO MY SISTER...

178

179

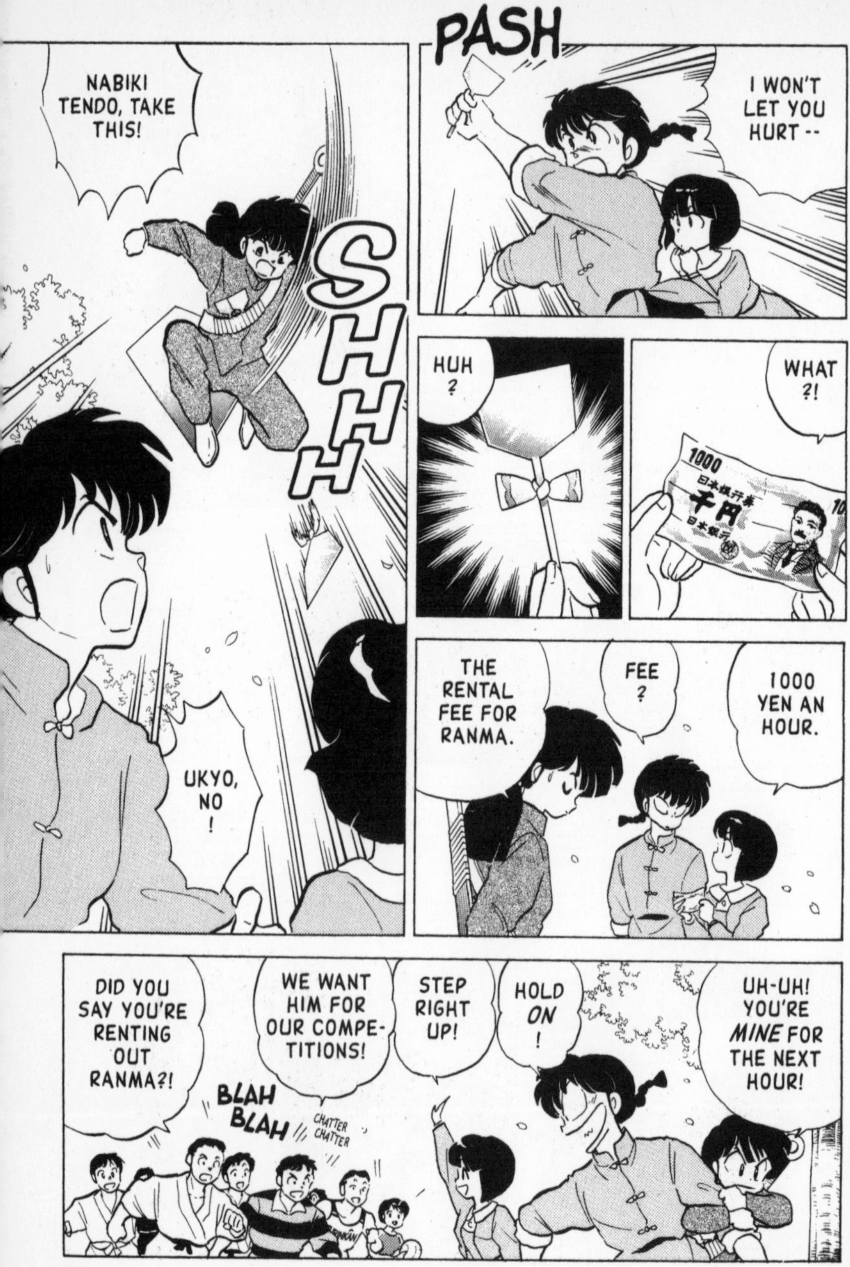

NABIKI TENDO, TAKE THIS!
SHHHH
UKYO, NO !
PASH
I WON'T LET YOU HURT --
HUH ?
WHAT ?!
THE RENTAL FEE FOR RANMA.
FEE ?
1000 YEN AN HOUR.
DID YOU SAY YOU'RE RENTING OUT RANMA?!
BLAH BLAH
CHATTER CHATTER
WE WANT HIM FOR OUR COMPETITIONS!
STEP RIGHT UP!
HOLD ON !
UH-UH! YOU'RE MINE FOR THE NEXT HOUR!

182

Part 12
I'M THE VICTIM HERE!

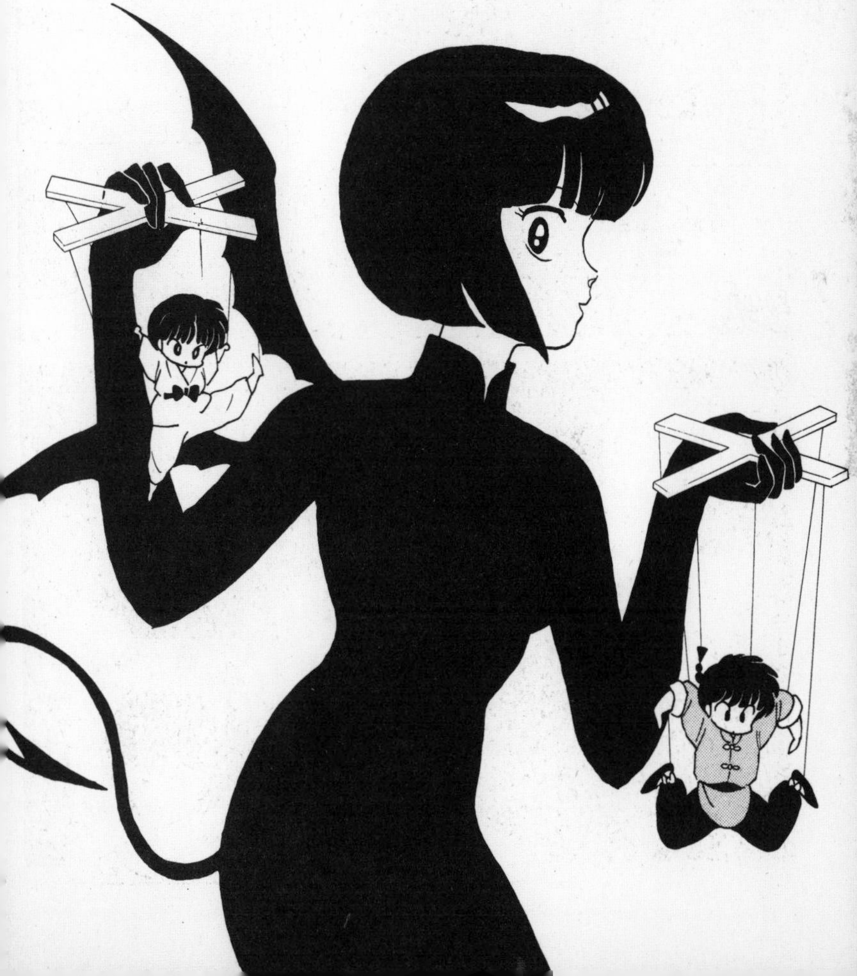

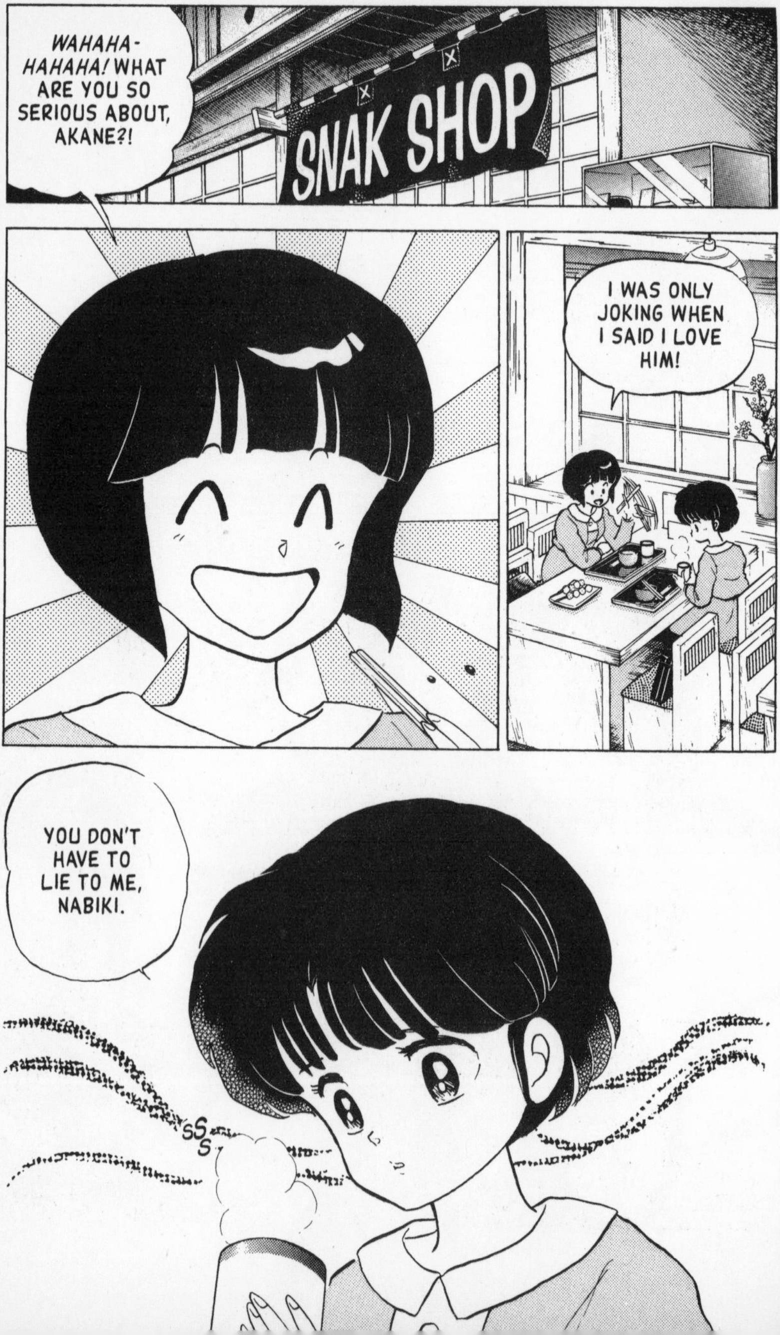
WAHAHA-HAHAHA! WHAT ARE YOU SO SERIOUS ABOUT, AKANE?!
SNAK SHOP
I WAS ONLY JOKING WHEN I SAID I LOVE HIM!
YOU DON'T HAVE TO LIE TO ME, NABIKI.
SSS

185

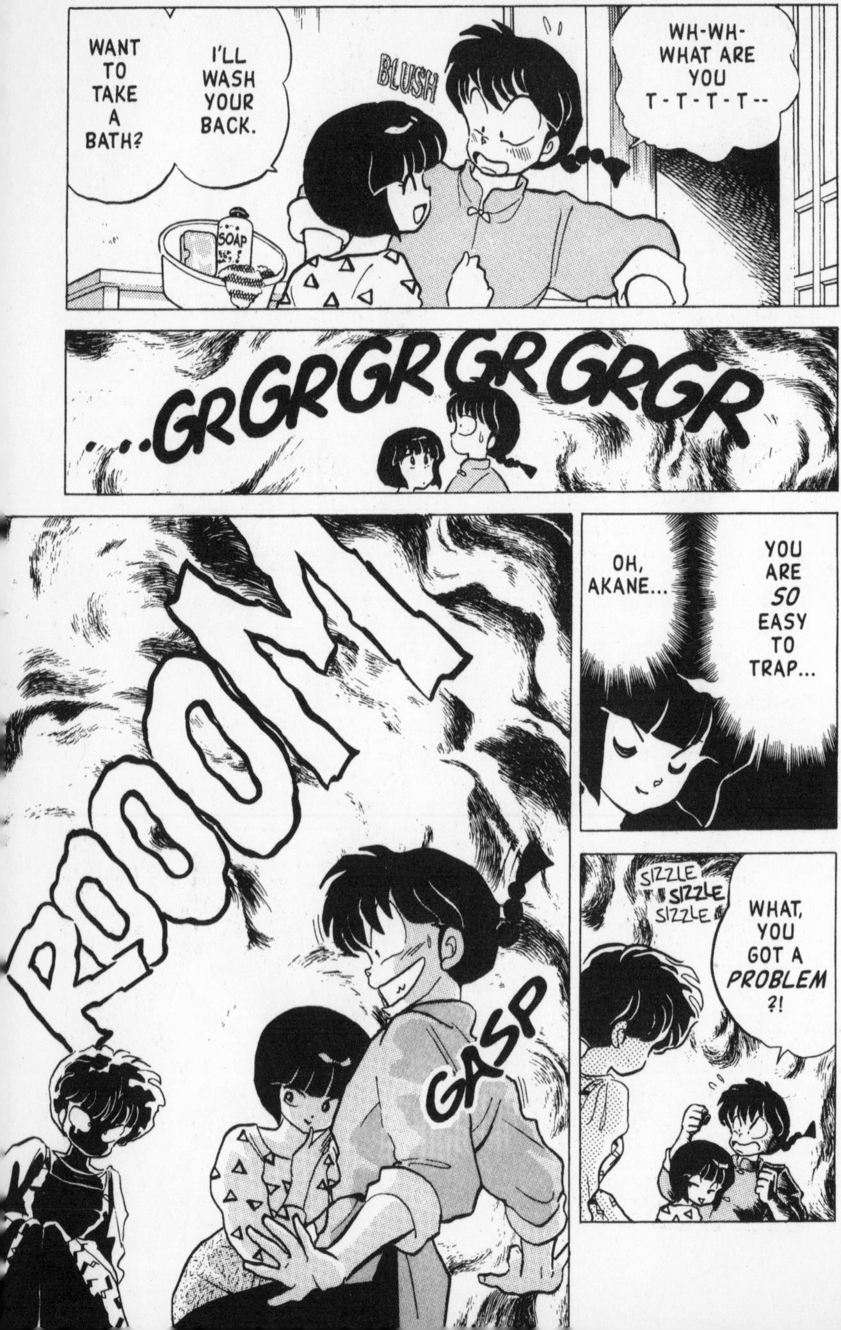
WANT TO TAKE A BATH?
I'LL WASH YOUR BACK.
BLUSH
WH-WH-WHAT ARE YOU T-T-T-T--
...GRGRGRGRGRGRGR
ROOOM!
GASP
OH, AKANE...
YOU ARE SO EASY TO TRAP...
SIZZLE SIZZLE SIZZLE
WHAT, YOU GOT A PROBLEM ?!

189

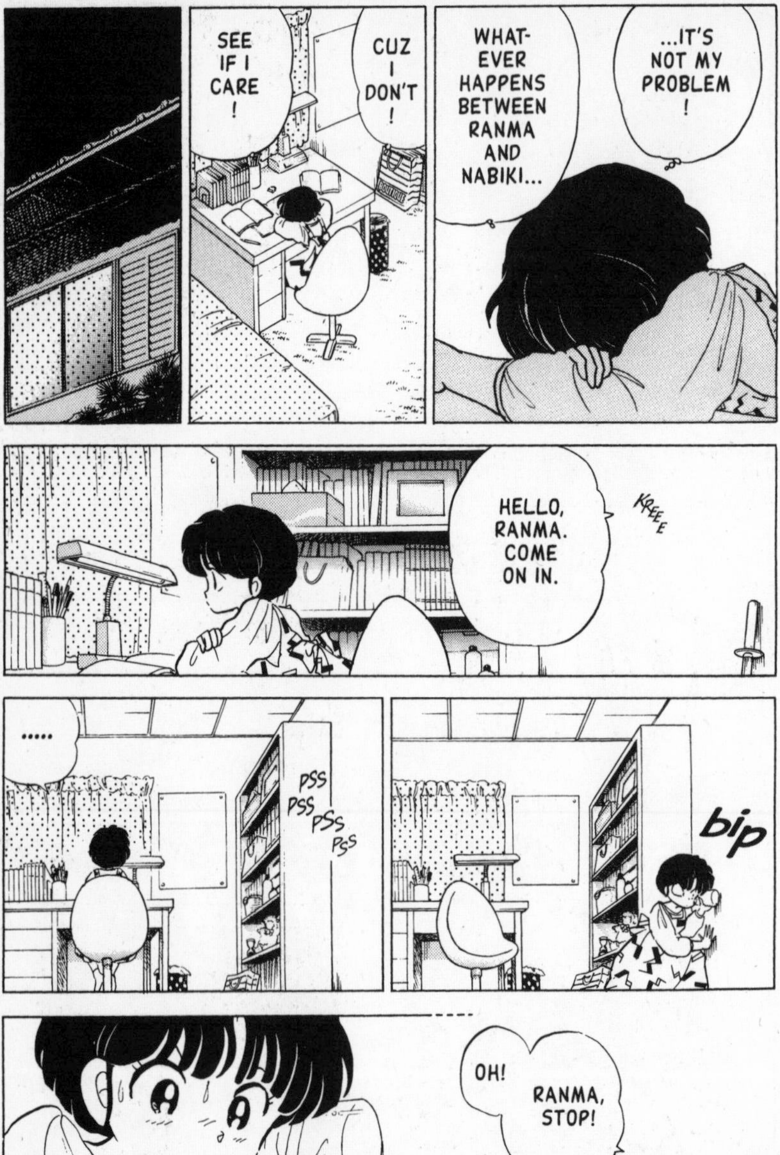
SEE IF I CARE!
CUZ I DON'T!
WHATEVER HAPPENS BETWEEN RANMA AND NABIKI...
...IT'S NOT MY PROBLEM!
HELLO, RANMA. COME ON IN.
KREEE
......
PSS PSS PSS PSS
bip
OH!
RANMA, STOP!

194

195

196

Part 13
I'M SORRY, AKANE

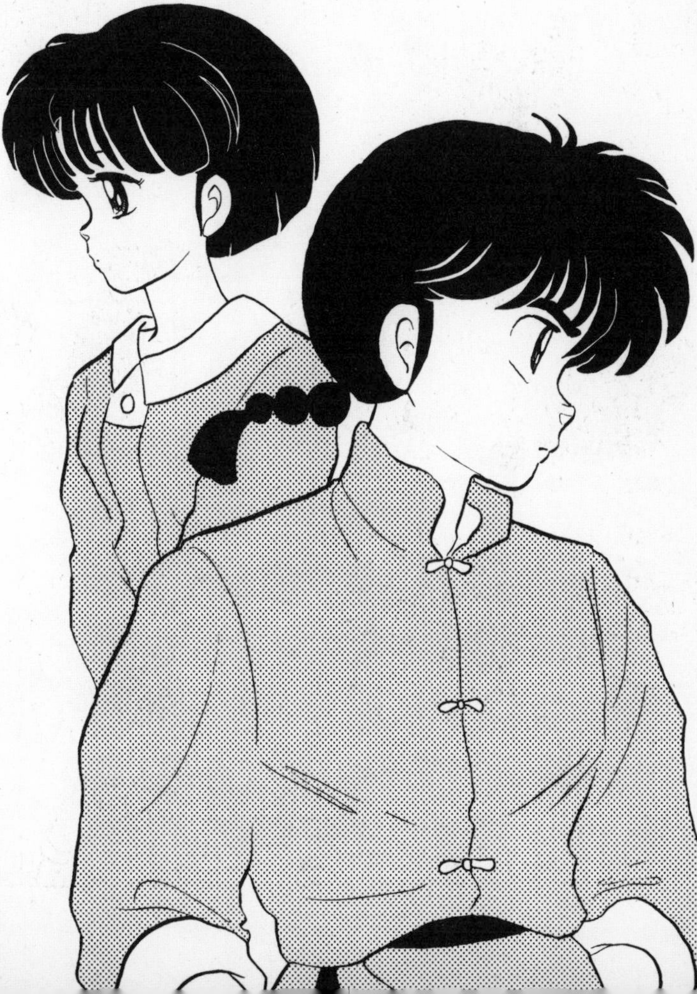

204

206

Part 14
MAZE OF LOVE

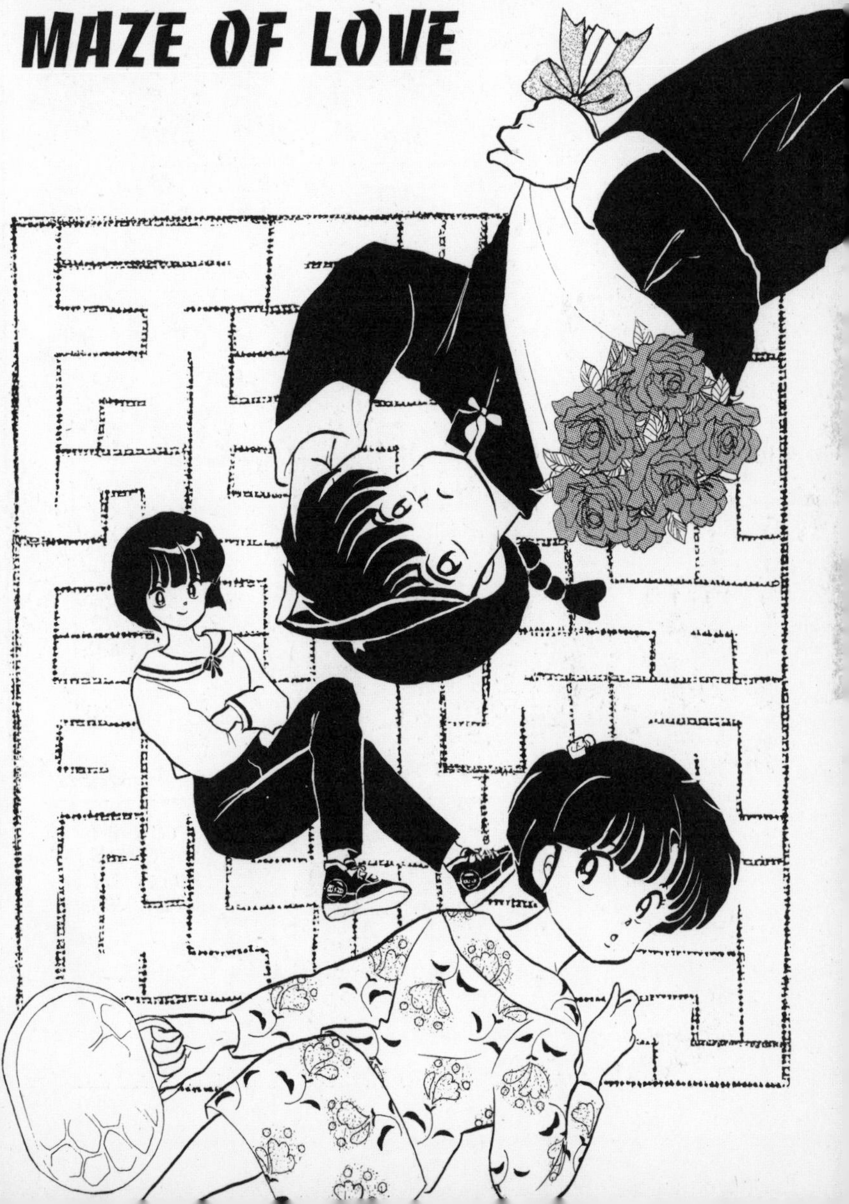

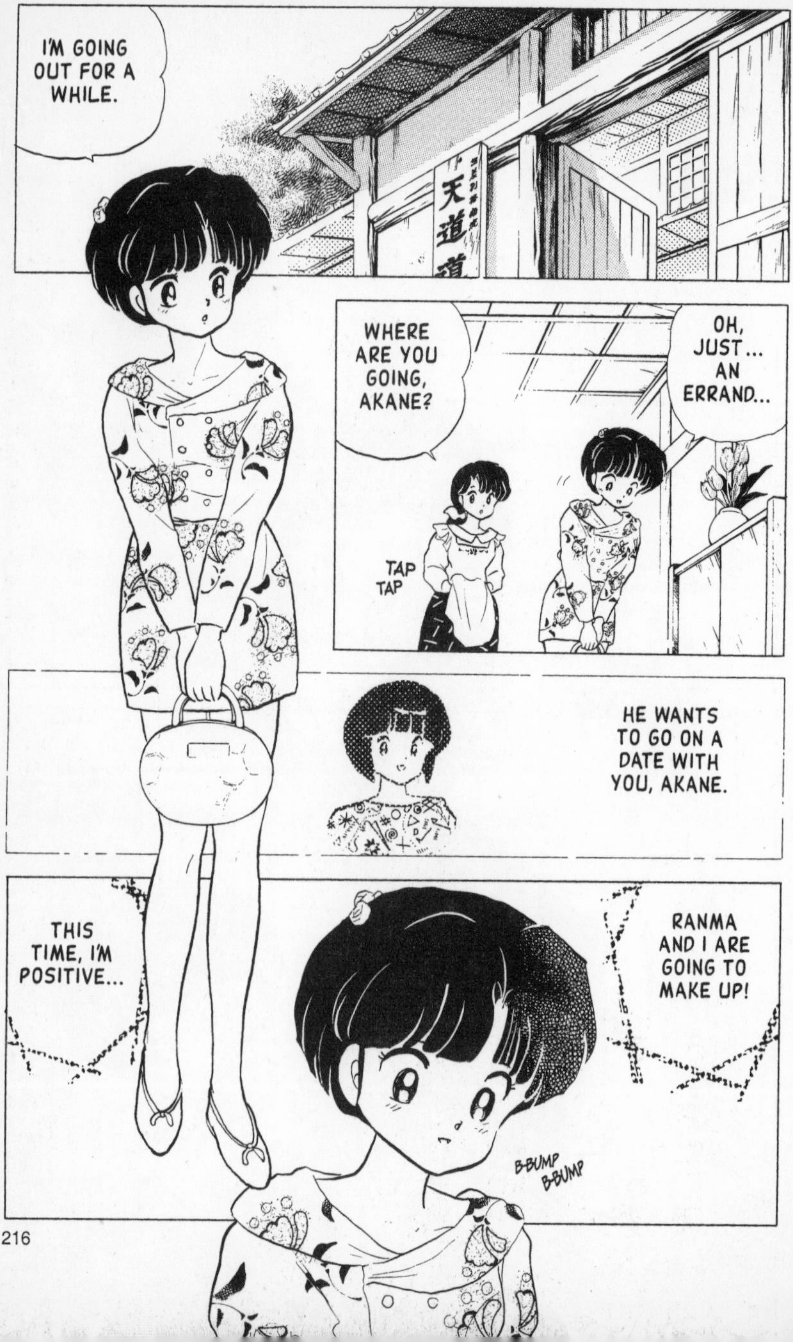
I'M GOING OUT FOR A WHILE.
WHERE ARE YOU GOING, AKANE?
OH, JUST... AN ERRAND...
TAP TAP
HE WANTS TO GO ON A DATE WITH YOU, AKANE.
THIS TIME, I'M POSITIVE...
RANMA AND I ARE GOING TO MAKE UP!
B-BUMP B-BUMP

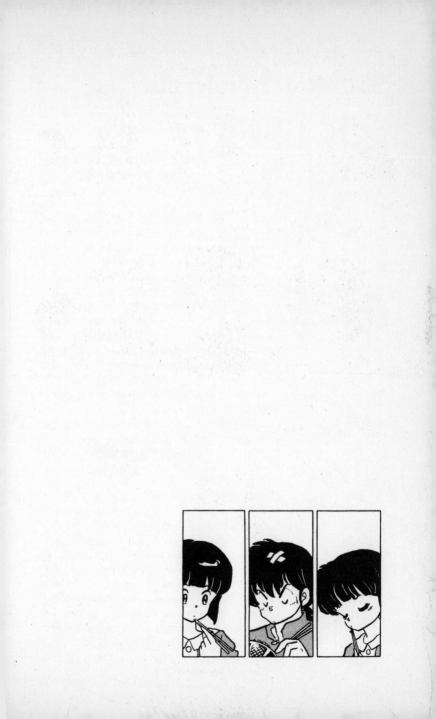

About Rumiko Takahashi

Born in 1957 in Niigata, Japan, Rumiko Takahashi attended women's college in Tokyo, where she began studying comics with Kazuo Koike, author of CRYING FREEMAN. She later became an assistant to horror-manga artist Kazuo Umezu (OROCHI). In 1978, she won a prize in Shogakukan's annual "New Comic Artist Contest," and in that same year her boy-meets-alien comedy series URUSEI YATSURA began appearing in the weekly manga magazine SHÔNEN SUNDAY. This phenomenally successful series ran for nine years and sold over 22 million copies. Takahashi's later RANMA 1/2 series enjoyed even greater popularity.

Takahashi is considered by many to be one of the world's most popular manga artists. With the publication of Volume 34 of her RANMA 1/2 series in Japan, Takahashi's total sales passed one hundred million copies of her compiled works.

Takahashi's serial titles include URUSEI YATSURA, RANMA 1/2, ONE-POUND GOSPEL, MAISON IKKOKU and INUYASHA. Additionally, Takahashi has drawn many short stories which have been published in America under the title "Rumic Theater," and several installments of a saga known as her "Mermaid" series. Most of Takahashi's major stories have also been animated, and are widely available in translation worldwide. INUYASHA is her most recent serial story, first published in SHÔNEN SUNDAY in 1996.

EDITOR'S RECOMMENDATIONS

If you enjoyed this volume of Ranma 1/2, then here is some more manga you might be interested in:

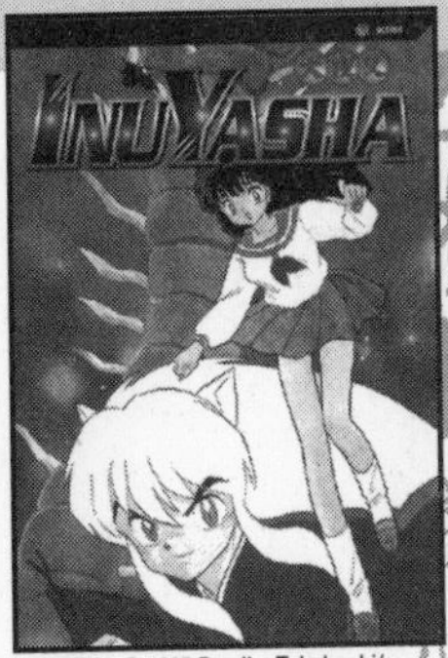
INUYASHA

INUYASHA

Feudal-days adventure and fairytale monsters combine in this wildly popular fantasy series—now also animated, airing on Cartoon Network's "Adult Swim"!

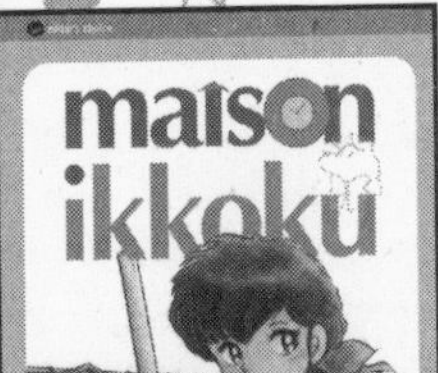
maison
ikkoku
Rumiko Takahashi 1

MAISON IKKOKU

A little more "retro" in its art style, and more "serious" than either Ranma 1/2 or Inuyasha, Maison Ikkoku nonetheless features all the charm, comedy and romance that's made Takahashi a household name in manga worldwide.

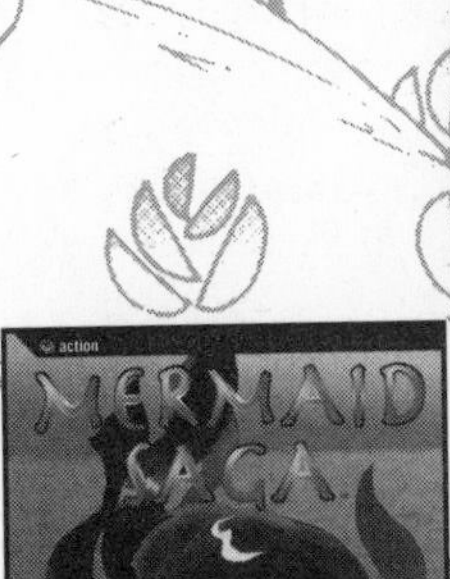
MERMAID
SAGA
Rumiko Takahashi

"MERMAID" SERIES

Conceived in part as interrelated shorts, Takahashi's "Mermaid" Series blends pre-Inuyasha fantasy and horror with her trademark—feisty heroines and earnest, honest male leads.

Half Human, Half

When Kagome discovers a well that transports her to feudal era Japan, she unwittingly frees a half-demon, Inuyasha, and shatters the sacred Jewel of Four Souls. Now they must work together to restore the jewel before it falls into the wrong hands...

INUYASHA

The manga that inspired a phenomenon!

Only $9.95!

FULL COLOR adaptation of the TV series!

Only $11.95!

action

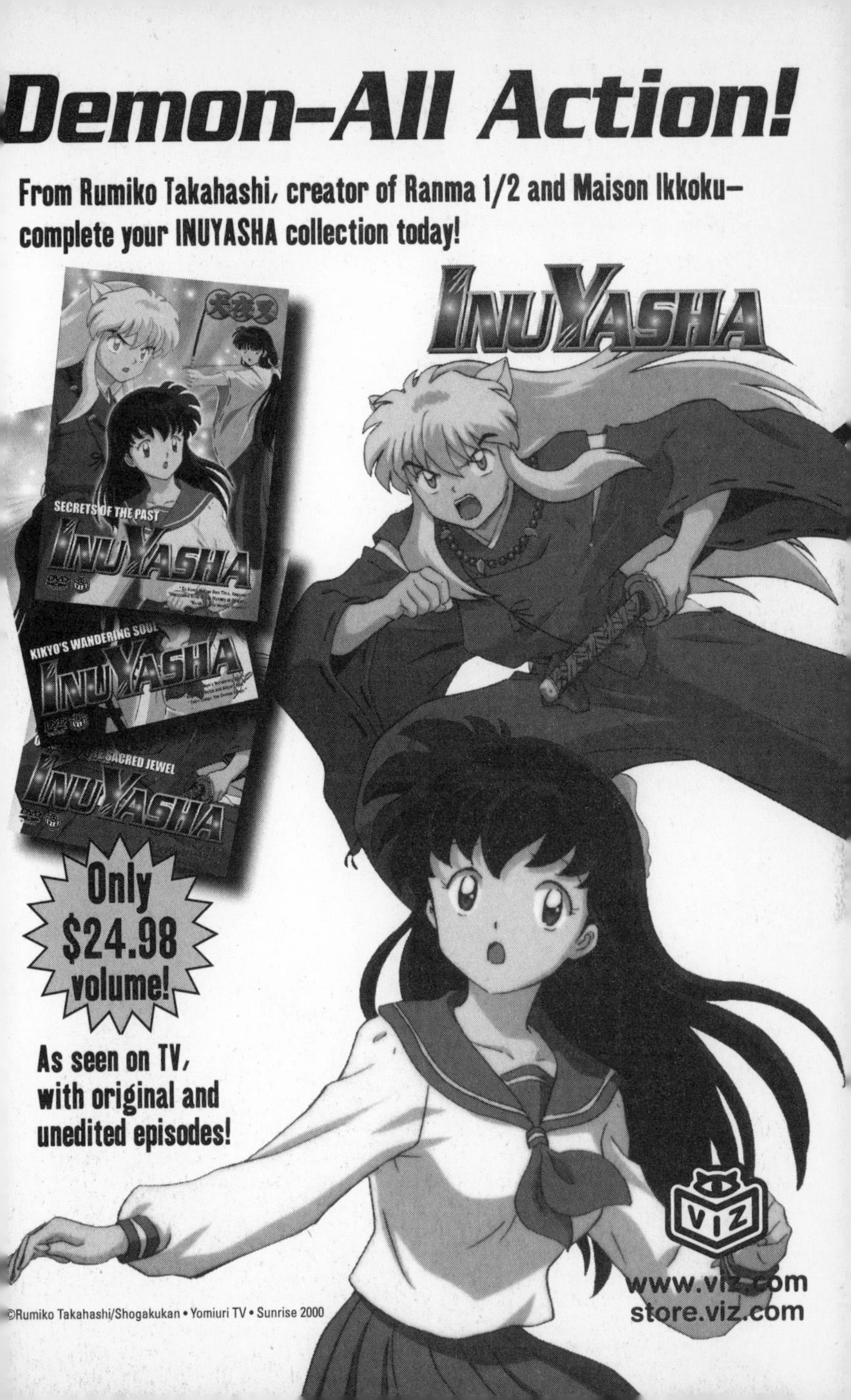

Demon-All Action!
From Rumiko Takahashi, creator of Ranma 1/2 and Maison Ikkoku—complete your INUYASHA collection today!
INUYASHA
SECRETS OF THE PAST
INUYASHA
KIKYO'S WANDERING SOUL
INUYASHA
SACRED JEWEL
INUYASHA
Only $24.98 volume!
As seen on TV, with original and unedited episodes!
VIZ
www.viz.com
store.viz.com
©Rumiko Takahashi/Shogakukan • Yomiuri TV • Sunrise 2000

COMPLETE OUR SURVEY AND LET US KNOW WHAT YOU THINK!

☐ Please do NOT send me information about VIZ products, news and events, special offers, or other information.

☐ Please do NOT send me information from VIZ's trusted business partners.

Name: _____

Address: _____

City: _____ **State:** _____ **Zip:** _____

E-mail: _____

☐ Male ☐ Female **Date of Birth** (mm/dd/yyyy): ___/___/_____ (Under 13? Parental consent required)

What race/ethnicity do you consider yourself? (please check one)

☐ Asian/Pacific Islander ☐ Black/African American ☐ Hispanic/Latino

☐ Native American/Alaskan Native ☐ White/Caucasian ☐ Other: _____

What VIZ product did you purchase? (check all that apply and indicate title purchased)

☐ DVD/VHS _____

☐ Graphic Novel _____

☐ Magazines _____

☐ Merchandise _____

Reason for purchase: (check all that apply)

☐ Special offer ☐ Favorite title ☐ Gift

☐ Recommendation ☐ Other _____

Where did you make your purchase? (please check one)

☐ Comic store ☐ Bookstore ☐ Mass/Grocery Store

☐ Newsstand ☐ Video/Video Game Store ☐ Other: _____

☐ Online (site: _____)

What other VIZ properties have you purchased/own? _____

_____

How many anime and/or manga titles have you purchased in the last year? How many were VIZ titles? (please check one from each column)

ANIME	MANGA	VIZ
☐ None	☐ None	☐ None
☐ 1-4	☐ 1-4	☐ 1-4
☐ 5-10	☐ 5-10	☐ 5-10
☐ 11+	☐ 11+	☐ 11+

I find the pricing of VIZ products to be: (please check one)

☐ Cheap ☐ Reasonable ☐ Expensive

What genre of manga and anime would you like to see from VIZ? (please check two)

☐ Adventure ☐ Comic Strip ☐ Science Fiction ☐ Fighting

☐ Horror ☐ Romance ☐ Fantasy ☐ Sports

What do you think of VIZ's new look?

☐ Love It ☐ It's OK ☐ Hate It ☐ Didn't Notice ☐ No Opinion

Which do you prefer? (please check one)

☐ Reading right-to-left

☐ Reading left-to-right

Which do you prefer? (please check one)

☐ Sound effects in English

☐ Sound effects in Japanese with English captions

☐ Sound effects in Japanese only with a glossary at the back

THANK YOU! Please send the completed form to:

NJW Research
42 Catharine St.
Poughkeepsie, NY 12601

01/6

All information provided will be used for internal purposes only. We promise not to sell or otherwise divulge your information.